BLOOD and BANQUETS

A Berlin Diary 1930–38

Bella Fromm

Foreword by Judith Rossner

A TOUCHSTONE BOOK
Published by Simon & Schuster
New York   London   Toronto   Sydney   Tokyo   Singapore

To My Mother
Whose Memory I Cherish Across the Vale of Years

TOUCHSTONE
Simon & Schuster Building
Rockefeller Center
1230 Avenue of the Americas
New York, New York 10020

Copyright © 1990 by Carol Publishing Group

1   3   5   7   9   10   8   6   4   2

Library of Congress Cataloging in Publication Data is available

ISBN 0-671-75139-5

Publishing History: *Blood and Banquets* was first published in Great Britain by Geoffrey Bles, 36 Essex Street, London, in 1943. The same year an excerpt from the book appeared in *Harper's Magazine*. An edition was published in New York by Garden City Publishing Company, Inc., in 1944. Bella Fromm's daughter survives. At her request, she does not receive telephone calls or answer letters. Only the Chief Archivist of the Bella Fromm Archives at Boston University knows her name. A royalty is being accrued from the sale of copies of *Blood and Banquets* by Carol Publishing Group.

Queries regarding rights and permissions should be addressed to Carol Publishing Group, 600 Madison Avenue, New York, N.Y. 10022.

Foreword

Most of us who are at least occasionally introspective have wondered about the qualities that identify us, about how we came to possess those qualities and who we might have been under other circumstances. If we are traditionally observant Jews, we find reinforcement of our identities in the rituals of home and synagogue. Those of us lacking in Jewish custom and ceremony, but having no doubt that we are Jews, cope with that fact of our existence in a variety of ways dependent upon who we are, how we feel about who we are, and the nature of our resources. If we are New York Jews who reached wordly consciousness during or after the forties, the chances are that we have not suffered as adults from being Jewish, except perhaps in being deprived of an occasional tennis game at some suburban club. This is not to say that if we grew up in a lower-class neighborhood in, say, Brooklyn or the Bronx, we've never been called a dirty Jew. But we have had the luxury of belonging to a dominant group and it has been easy to separate ourselves from any distorted image held by others.

I was born in the Bronx in 1935 to educated first-generation American parents. We observed the major holidays, usually, at the homes of my father's more religious relatives, the lesser ones not at all. There was neither joy nor learning attached to the holidays, in my memory, with one exception—the year my father built a beautiful little arbor in our back yard for Sukkoth, which I think we must have celebrated happily that year. I was a rebellious child and I think it is safe to say that even had my parents found wisdom or solace in religious ritual, I would have been unwilling or unable to share it.

Bella Fromm was born in 1900 in Nuremberg to a family that had come to Germany from Spain in the early seventeenth century and produced Fromm-Sichel wines. She appears to have adored her mother, had little to do with her father, who is never mentioned, and, if later friendships provide any measure, gotten along beautifully with her peers. If religious practice was an important part of her life, there is no indication of that fact in these journals. While in her early teens she had a brief marriage that produced a daughter. When inflation took her fortune, she became a gossip columnist for *Vossische Zeitung*, the most liberal of the papers owned by the powerful Ullsteins, who were family friends.

Bella appears to have been an attractive and stylish woman of substantial intelligence, wit and charm. Doubtless there were other Jewish women possessed of these virtues. What made Fromm unique was that she helped endangered Jews by obtaining visas, money and whatever else they needed to survive, while moving in social circles that included high Nazi officials without ever denying her own Jewishness. She even managed to write about these parties entertainingly in her column.

In other words, Bella Fromm had the desire and the ability to distinguish between right and wrong and act accordingly. She behaved as I would have wanted to behave had I lived in Nazi Germany, right down to the moment when, advised by her childhood friend and lover Rolf, a Nazi party official who was a constant help to her and other Jews, that her arrest was imminent and she could do nothing further to help others, she packed what goods she could and came to the States.

The following are brief excerpts from the journal you are about to read, chosen because of my sense that they are particularly appropriate to our time and place.

November 12, 1930 . . . The American contralto, Marian Anderson, was charming and inspiring. A remarkable voice. Everybody present was enraptured.

It is interesting to note the hostile reaction in the National Socialist press: "Clamor About a Negress."

August 15, 1936 . . . Olympic games . . . The lack of sportsmanship of Germany's First Man is disgusting and at the same time fascinating. He behaved like a madman, jumping from his seat and roaring when the swastika was hoisted, or when the Japs or Finns won a victory. Other champions left him cold and personally offended at their victories over their Nordic contestants.

The manner in which Hitler applauds German winners in an orgiastic frenzy of shrieks, clappings, and contortions, is painful proof that the whole idea of the Olympic games is far too broad for his single-track mind. This is *his* show, and *his* Germans are supermen. That the whole world must admit. He has said some remarkable things.

"The American Negroes are not entitled to compete," he said, for example. "It was unfair of the United States to send these flat-footed specimens to compete with the noble products of Germany. I am going to vote against Negro participation in the future. . . . ."

He means it, too. Although it is his policy to bid every winner to his box, to congratulate him and shake hands, he has repeatedly snubbed and ignored the colored American representatives. Whenever one of the tall, graceful, perfectly built dark-skinned athletes scored a triumph, Hitler left his seat hurriedly and returned only when the signal for the next event was sounded.

January 26, 1934 . . . I have seen Bormann. He is one of those blond Nordic types that Nazis like, with a slit of a mouth, cruel eyes, and an overbearing manner. His hobby is persecuting churches, and he reads stories of Christian martyrs with relish.

What interests me most about these excerpts, as well as many other portions of this book, is that they were written by a Jew in Nazi Germany whose sense of immediate danger and grave injustice to her own group did not prevent her from registering and regretting bigotry and hatred toward others. I have no doubt that, had the occasion arisen, she would have helped Anderson or any other human guilty only of belonging to the wrong identifiable segment of humanity.

The need to find villains, scapegoats and inferiors in one group or another seems to stretch across all time and space, and most people want to believe that their prejudices originate in reality rather than in their own neuroses and uncertainties. But prejudice by its very definition does not begin with experience. Bella Fromm appears always to have known this, and always, when possible, to have done what was required to spare herself and others its ghastly consequences.

JUDITH ROSSNER

NEW YORK
July, 1990

Contents

Author's Note

In preparing this book, I made excerpts from the original entries in my diary insofar as I considered the subject matter to be of general interest. In making the selections it was my object to help clarify the great historical enigma: How was it possible for the culture-loving nation of Goethe, Schiller, and Kant, of Mozart, Beethoven, Bach, and Brahms, to succumb at last to the new barbarism of Adolf Hitler?

The parts of my diary which are contained in this book stand just as they were originally written except in two particulars. I made my entries, of course, in German, and I, myself, helped to translate them into English. From time to time the names of people occur who were well known to me in Germany and who may, in some instances, not be well known to the American public. I, therefore, took the liberty, as I prepared the book, of inserting occasional background information so that the reader could better understand what I had written in my diary.

BELLA FROMM

New York City
August, 1942

Introduction

At a diplomatic luncheon in the spring of 1932, on one of my earlier visits to Berlin to study the changing scene in the fast-dying German republic, I found myself seated beside a charming woman whose name and identity had been lost, so far as I was concerned, in the jumble of many varied introductions but who was evidently intimately known to everybody else.

Conversation quickly revealed that my luncheon companion was conversant not only with the German political situation and what was going on behind the scenes but with the international repercussions aroused by the current developments and especially by the phenomenal growth of the new Nazi party which it was my mission in Berlin at that time to study closely. She knew everybody and gauged accurately what each personage counted for in the developing setup. Among other things, she seemed to know all about myself and my mission—an advantage which I did not at first share so far as she was concerned, for she was extremely discreet. She preferred to ask questions rather than answer them and to listen rather than to talk. I quickly sensed a journalistic colleague and it presently developed that the lady was Frau Bella Fromm, diplomatic columnist of the *Vossische Zeitung* with whose daily writings I was already familiar.

At many other diplomatic gatherings in the succeeding few years, I encountered "Frau Bella," as everyone in her intimate circle called her, and I came to have great respect both for her knowledge of what was going on behind the facades of Republicanism and Hitlerism and her keen intuition as to whither all this was leading. It was always worthwhile to read her daily column in the staid *Vossische* ("Aunty Voss" to sophisticated Berliners) concerning the doings in diplomatic Berlin, not because it directly revealed dark secrets but because to anyone knowing the personalities discussed, it contained valuable hints which could be interpreted with profit to general understanding.

Others also seemed to find it so. I noted at the luncheons, the teas and the dinners which it was part of our joint duty to attend that the *Vossische* writer was almost invariably a participant in whispered confidences, from the women especially. Later, when I had the privilege of closer acquaintance with her, I was frequently astonished to see how much she knew and how much more she divined, yet how little of it appeared in her column. I, myself, when Mrs. Fromm came to know me better, was from time to time the beneficiary of some of this information and it helped me materially in correctly appraising the trend of events.

It was common knowledge, for instance, after the blood purge of June 30, 1934, in the little circle surrounding "Frau Bella," that she had anticipated some violent outbreak by the extremists of the new Nazi regime and had warned General von Schleicher, ex-Chancellor and their bitter foe, that he was in danger. The General had laughed at her fears.

"They won't dare to touch me, Bellachen," he had told her.

But five days after the intimate little dinner she had arranged at her house to convey the warning, the General was dead—assassinated in the wide roundup of Hitler's opponents, and his wife with him.

The Nazi shadow over distraught and bedeviled Germany deepened as the months rolled by. Things happened in its twilight that no censorship could conceal. Preparations for the war which was to put Nazism in domination over the whole world, if the Nazi plans only came to fulfillment, became more open and avowed. No one was safe who did not echo the Nazi propaganda and devote all energies to furthering Nazi intentions. Foreign correspondents who risked criticism were expelled. The few who remained were constantly being cautioned.

To be Jewish in Germany meant being the special butt of Nazi spoliation and persecution. Mrs. Fromm had devoted friends in the highest circles but they saw their influence waning, and from all sides she was importuned to get out while there was still time. Her column under her name disappeared from the *Vossische*. Then that newspaper monument of all that had been solid and respectable in Germany gave up the ghost too. The great House of Ullstein, which published it, was "Aryanized" and taken over by the Nazis. Its ownership, long afterward, was revealed as resting with the publishers of Hitler's *Mein Kampf*, with little doubt that the profits went to the Fuehrer himself. No wonder that he could forego his salary as Chancellor.

Germany was fast reverting to the Dark Ages. When I returned to Berlin from other sections of my continental beat in the late autumn of 1938, it was to a city of short rations and straitened friendships. Many of the old acquaintances upon whom I had relied for factual infomation had vanished, among them "Frau Bella," whom at our last meeting I had implored to leave while there was still time. I was told that she had taken my advice and gone to America, but I had no direct word from her.

A year later and the war was on, involving half of western Europe and constantly spreading. I myself, in turn, had to move across the ocean, for my continental beat could be traveled no longer. I spent the next year in Canada but my health compelled me to return again to New York.

In my office at *The New York Times*, late in 1940, I was told that a "foreign lady" was asking to see me. It was Mrs. Fromm and I heard from her the story of her initial struggles to make a place for herself in the new environment. She had "risen" by that time to the humble post of typist in a relief agency. I learned also, for the first time—the lady keeps her secrets well—of the existence of her secret Berlin diary. The confidences bestowed upon her during the years that saw the rise of Hitlerism had not been wasted; they had been preserved in loose-leaf papers which by devious ways she had marvelously managed to smuggle out of the Reich in advance of her own exit.

She read me extracts, and I saw at once that she had valuable material for a book. Anyway, it was desirable that mechanical typing should give way to some occupation more in consonance with the lady's mental ability and past environment. The aspiration has been duly fulfilled, and now the book has been written.

Those who, like myself, spent the crucial years before the outbreak of this war in the country in which the war was planned and brought to pass, will appreciate at full value this record of the development of Nazism and the steps by which it attained a stranglehold over the German people. There are, however, thousands of others who will find in it the explanation of the thing that has puzzled them—how a monstrosity like Hitler could attain the power he did in a country we accounted civilized. Mrs. Fromm calls many of the entries in her diary a record of trivia. They are far more than that, because for the first time they tell the story of the slow strangulation of the German republic and the dawning German democracy. No one not a German by birth and upbringing and no one not admitted to the inner circle of Berlin social life could have compiled that record. To understand what has happened and why, perusal of it is essential.

It is with sincere pleasure that I write this introduction presenting Frau Bella Fromm to the American book public with the hope that she may become in time as familiar and welcome a figure in that circle as she was for long years in the journalistic world of Berlin. She has one characteristic which should commend her because it has become also an outstanding feature of the attitude of good Americans: She hates Hitlerism, its practices and proponents with a fervor that can scarcely be matched even in this land of the free in an era when we are all pledged to the smashing of the evils it typifies.

FREDERICK T. BIRCHALL
Chief European Correspondent of
The New York Times from 1932 to 1939

Blood and Banquets

My Life in Germany Before Hitler

Here in America they call me an enemy alien, but it is a peaceful, pleasant thing to be, after what I have lived through in what used to be my own country. I am anything but an enemy, and hope I shall not always be an alien.

I have not been here long, but already I feel at home. It is not easy to pull up your roots. But sometimes your roots are pulled up for you and there's nothing you can do about it. You accept it as an immutable fact of living, and you go on, if they let you.

I loved the way of life in old Germany, its culture, its country-side. I was born in Nuremberg. Soon after my birth, however, my parents returned to one of our family estates in the Main Valley. There I spent most of my childhood. The Main River always delighted my heart, with its lovely curves and its calm green waters. The little lakes and the woods answered an old need of my deeper self, the self that had become a part of the land. For seven generations, my family had lived on the same beloved place in Bavaria. I was the first of the family to go north, to Germany's capital. I loved Berlin, too. I loved its concerts and theaters, its museums, its university, and its sport clubs. These things were Germany. They were my country. I was rooted deeply in its soil and in its history and in its language.

The language has been almost the hardest to give up, the mother tongue that expressed thoughts, the language in which I wrote. Then the Nazis started to violate that language. They did with it what they have done with culture, the rights of man, the privileges of human beings. They used words in a strange, brutal fashion. They used slogans that were made up of German words, slogans that had no place in the mind of anyone who was accustomed to the words of Goethe and Heine. The language sounded German. But in its use by the Nazis, it became practically

3

foreign, because they gave words whatever new meanings they wished. And these new meanings were based on injustice, on lack of reason, on violence and force.

The Germany I left was very different from the Germany that I had lived in most of my life. The same skies were overhead, the same sun and stars were in the sky, the same winds blew, but they all seemed touched with an inhuman, impersonal coldness, as though they had nothing in common with what went on under them.

I was an only child, brought up simply and modestly. The remembrance of my happy childhood has helped me often since. It is curious, and probably significant, that I can never recall a rainy day when thinking of my childhood home. I always see our big garden, its old trees and narrow, twisting little paths, in the bright sunlight. I see myself, always in a white dress, rushing to that little place under the old walnut tree where I knew I would find Mutti, my mother. I see flowers around that place, which later became intertwined with the childhood of my own little daughter, Gonny.

My parents died young. I inherited the old house and garden, and everything else. It was peaceful, pleasant, and rather wonderful there, near the Main River. When life became too heavy for me to bear, I generally fled to the old place with Gonny and hid there until the strength seeped back into my soul. When marriage became unbearable, I found the peace I needed at home.

When I was a child, the Bavarian princes would come to visit us. Friendly visits, without etiquette, without formality. Prince Ludwig of Bavaria, afterward the last king, would call and wander over our old vineyards and through our ancient cellars. This was long before an obscure Austrian became Chancellor of Germany. Prince Ludwig would come without bodyguards, without detectives.

I can see him now. A modest and amiable old man, with baggy trousers. Around his neck he wore what we used to call an "iron" necktie; that is, it was permanently made up in its knots and convolutions and was bound round the neck with a rubber band.

When I was ten, I started to write in my diary. At the start, it was something in the nature of an intimate letter to my mother, whom I worshiped and to whom I confided all my thoughts. Her reaction was important to me. Her influence guided me in those years of my life and still does.

I had no thought of publication for this diary, no thought that any eye other than my mother's would ever see it. After she died, I kept up the habit. I did not do it with the idea of setting down anything of historic value. It was only that I felt the need of talking to someone about what was happening to Germany and to me. I lived in the midst of politics. My friends referred casually to things that afterward became front-page news. The diplomats with whom I mingled later on talked at the "white table" of what was happening around the "green table." I could not escape it.

Shortly before the start of the First World War, I was married, and later on, Gonny, my child, was born. During the war, I worked with the Red Cross and received their medal. I was also decorated with the cross created by our late King Ludwig. My parents died, and after that, a divorce released me from an unhappy marriage. When the inflation came along, I lost most of the money I had inherited and was faced with the necessity of earning a living for my child and myself. Since I was in constant touch with people who were making history, or who were destined to make it, it was natural that when it became necessary for me to get work, I turned my contacts and my milieu to account and entered newspaper life. I secured a connection with the Ullstein papers.

It was not long before I began to see things through the eyes of my international friends. I saw, long before they came to pass, the shadow of things that were to darken the civilized world. And it was always a matter of despair to me that others, who saw this shadow just as clearly, or more so, should show such little concern about the state of things. I saw hope and treachery, intrigue and sordid triumph. I saw the breaking down of all that we had lived with and loved.

Many Germans saw those things. But many Germans belong to the type that toadies to its superiors and tramples upon its inferiors. For the first time, I began to understand the terrible word "Boche," as I watched the development of Hitler's Germany. I began to understand the truth about the Germans: They had developed as a people more cruel, more sadistic than it had hitherto been believed possible for a civilized people to be. And I was compelled to come to the conclusion that civilization, as we know it, was very little more than a thin veneer over the average German, ready to be brushed off when the right call came from the right pagan deity. The words "right," "wrong," "human," "inhuman," have no meaning except the meaning one chooses to give them, and these words soon came to have new meanings imposed by men of ill will.

I saw what was happening, and through my friends in the diplomatic corps, I was aware of the reactions of the outside world. Through my position as friend and as columnist to the diplomats, I saw and heard more than most. There was nobody to stop it, nobody important who dared to speak out. I spoke out, of course, as did some others, but our words, thin and weak against the gathering brown hurricane, were hurled back into our faces.

I recognized early that this would not stop in Germany, that the poison would permeate the whole world. There are men everywhere who would sell out humanity for their own personal profit. There are stupid and emotional masses everywhere who can be found to follow them, given a few slogans and some nice uniforms. I saw the start of it, the thin trickle of a dangerous poison that gathered strength and became a flood, first engulfing Germany, and then threatening the world.

Even now there are those who say it cannot happen here in America. But it can. It *can* happen here! It can happen anywhere, unless you do something about it ruthlessly. The secret of these so-called supermen is bluff; their potent formula is to weaken through fear. Their courage is the courage of the stronger who overrun the weaker. Call their bluff, stand up against them before it is too late, and it will all melt away. They are only men, cruel men, power-greedy men; and they can be disposed of the way any band of criminals is disposed of.

The time has passed when we can do anything about Germany. Even after the final victory, it will take generations of re-education to free the minds of the German people. But there is still time for the rest of the world. We who have lived through this in Germany perhaps feel it all more keenly than you do. Yet there was a time when we were as you, when the gangsters had not yet made us prisoners, when the bullies had not yet cowed us. That would have been the time to stop them there. And now is the time to stop them here.

* * *

The leaves of my diary go back a long way into the years, and much of it would have no general interest. I will quote, therefore, only from those entries which I feel illuminate the time and the society in which I lived, the society in which Nazism was cradled.

These early entries, made long before the world had ever heard of Hitler, are necessary to obtain a picture of the malignant growth of the Nazi monster.

These are personal experiences. Teas, dinners, balls, conversations, trivia at the time, and perhaps trivia today, in retrospect. But they were my experiences, and they foreshadow the coming of the terrible dictator and his reign of fear. It is possible that, from an account of the daily events in the life of one journalist, the reader may become aware of the shadow that crept over and finally blotted out the light of civilization and culture in Germany and now hangs horribly over the rest of the world.

I have always had a premonition of coming events. I cannot explain this. It just happens to me. Most people do not believe statements of that kind, yet I know it for a fact in my own case. In 1917, there were many people who believed in the probability of a victory for Germany. I wrote in my diary:

August 18, 1917:

I am at home nursing Mutti, who is very ill. Had word from Rolf. He is with General von Mackensen's staff at the Bulgarian front. "We are all sick and tired of the whole game," he writes me.

I wrote him in answer: "We will have to be as hard as steel to face our fate squarely, and to be ready to bear it. We all hope for a speedy end to this terrible war, although it will not end in victory for Germany, but it may give the world a new start. I don't see too much hope for the future of civilization and culture in general. As to the Jews, I dread an era of medieval darkness."

I don't know why I wrote him this, but I felt the urge to do so. I knew the war was lost.

* * *

Rolf was the dearest friend of my childhood and has remained my friend all my life. He is three years older than I. Tall, blond— what the Nazis call a perfect Aryan. He is a member of one of the noblest families in Bavaria. Rolf is not his name. I cannot name him, because, though far from a convinced Nazi, he is high in the councils of the party. He has been of invaluable aid to me, and to many others, through his connections and position.

* * *

October 6, 1918:

Mutti has gone. She suffered a great deal and had long known that she was doomed. She lived only forty-eight years. Now I am all alone with my child.

She had arranged everything and insisted that I should not wear mourning, "as so many of our youngest and best are dying every day." She asked that the child be sent away; that Gonny be not permitted to see the coffin. "Such things mark a young and tender heart forever," she said.

November 9, 1918:

Revolution! When the news came it was not unexpected, but it was shocking nonetheless: Revolution. The Navy mutinies. Workers' and soldiers' councils set up. The Emperor flees.

I drove out to Mother's tomb. A heavy fog was spread over the country. Despair was written in the faces of people. They looked hungry, scared and weary. I went by horse because of the gasoline shortage.

On the way home, I passed groups of people in the village streets. I stopped to inquire. "Berlin gives in. General strike. The Jaeger regiment is on the march. They want the Emperor to abdicate. He brought about the disaster. He is going to be brought to Berlin before a court-martial."

"Where is King Ludwig?" I asked. Nobody knew.

I am sorry for the Emperor, but, after all, the "Prussians" are an arrogant lot. Our king, a man of the people, is not a sword-rattler. He is warm-hearted and kind.

* * *

So the Weimar Republic came into being. Friedrich Ebert, the first President of Germany, was a man of the people. A man without pomp, simple and forthright, who wore about his shoulders, as though it were a mantle, the dignity of mankind. He was esteemed by everyone. Naturally kind and good, he could always find the right word to say, the simple but effective word. An atmosphere of honesty and frankness radiated from him in all his dealings with the important internationalists he had to bargain with to find a better way of life for his country.

He did not like to take vacations, feeling that he owed it to his people to stay on the job. A little lodge was built for him at the Schorfheide. Not a palace, like the one Goering now owns at the same place. Sometimes I met him and his Minister of War, Otto Gessler, riding in the Grunewald forest. He never rode a horse into town, however.

"These are times when men are starving," he said, "and I do not wish to ride on horseback among them."

I met him once at the fair at Leipzig. He liked the theater passionately, and he said that sometimes, when he sees the great amount of work on his desk, he hardly dares attend a play. "And then I go anyway," he told me. "But it makes me feel so guilty that I go back and work the rest of the night. After all, I am only a human being."

He lighted a great black cigar and then suddenly remembered that I hated cigars. He started to throw it away. I put out my hand. "Please," I said. He put the cigar back in his mouth with a contented sigh.

Louise Ebert, his wife, was as simple, modest, and likable as her husband. They were perfect hosts and gave even the great state receptions with modesty. I never saw a glass of champagne at their table. The First Lady of Germany always set the table herself. Even the most formal dinners ended in one hour.

The Danish Minister, Herluf Zahle, who has been in Germany almost longer than any other diplomat, once said to me: "How nice and comfortable we used to feel at Ebert's. When I think of that, and compare those dinners with the pretentious and world-shaking fetes that the new gang put us through..." His voice trailed off regretfully into a reminiscent silence.

Once a nobleman remarked that the home and entertainments of the President should display a bit more luxury.

"No," said the First Lady. "We lost the war. They would not think well of us if we went on as though nothing had happened."

And then came the Kapp *Putsch*.

* * *

March 13, 1920:

I was riding my horse, Strolch, through the Uhlandstrasse toward the Tiergarten. We ran into an almost solid hail of bullets at the railroad bridge, with marksmen shooting from above the tracks and from down below in the little park. Strolch, whom I had bought from an officer, paid no attention whatever to the whizzing bullets. He trotted on without so much as pricking up his ears. My friend, Oswald von Breitenbach, son of the former Minister of Railway Traffic, had a harder time of it with my other horse, Totila, who dashed off in a panic and couldn't be stopped until he had put two miles between himself and the firing.

Oswald returned with exciting news. The *Landschaft-Direktor*, Wolfgang von Kapp, had joined forces with the Nationalist general, Walter von Luttwitz, in an attempt to stage a *coup d'état*. This, they thought, was their moment to crush Ebert and his government. Von Breitenbach was excited, and I got the impression that the affair had his secret approval.

March 14, 1920:

Dinner party at George Wertheim's, whose store is known as the Berlin "Macy's." Oscar Haac, the genius of the business, gave an amusing description:

"Yesterday, at six o'clock in the morning, the *Reichswehr* occupied the store. When I appeared at seven, the entire ground floor had been 'conquered.' Their rifles piled in pyramids, the soldiers awaited orders. I took charge of the negotiations and started to parley with the major in command.

" 'What is your reason for moving in here, Herr von Platen?'

" 'I haven't the faintest idea, myself,' was the amazing reply.

" 'On whose order did you come here?'

" 'I am not permitted to talk about it.'

"I finally managed to convince the major that he had taken his men to the wrong side of the Vossstrasse. 'Your soldiers were probably sent out to protect Wilhelmstrasse from the Chancellery to the Presidential Palace. The buildings on that side also belong to us. I'll see that they are opened for your troops right away.'

"This proved a brilliant idea. The soldiers took their new positions. The store opened at nine o'clock—business as usual."

March 20, 1920:

Dinner at the Hotel Kaiserhof with Von Breitenbach, Dr. Max Glaser of the Krupp Works, and Admiral von Karpf, one of the tutors of the imperial princes. They regretted that the Kapp *Putsch* "had not been well enough prepared."

"Haven't you people had enough fighting for a while?" I said with a touch of disgust. "Why don't you leave Germany in peace now?"

I knew the answer, of course. Dr. Glaser was of the opinion that

Germany was showing too great a Leftist tendency and that something should be done about it. The others agreed.

"It seems to me that anti-Semitism is assuming such proportions that it's quite frightening," I said.

Dr. Glaser smiled. "Don't worry, Bella. I'll protect you if we have any pogroms."

"Thanks, Doctor," I said. "It would be much better if we stopped the tendency before it got that far."

There is tension and foreboding all over Germany. There have been armed clashes for months; the Right against the Left, the Right and the Left together against the Ebert government. A great number of "fighters' legions," all of them with patriotic and chauvinistic names, have sprung into being. They agitate against the government, against religion, against capital, against anything, so long as it gets them followers and notoriety. Many of these are backed by the Reich's army. Bavaria is worse than northern Germany. Adolf Hitler, a former World War corporal, is the chief troublemaker there. He and his followers are continuously in the news.

Here in Prussia they don't pay too much attention to such movements. Germany is receptive to new politial ideas, however—to anything that will remove from people the constant reminder that they have lost a war, that they are a defeated nation.

February 24, 1922:

Had a rather amusing evening with my friend, Paula B. Paula was brought up like a nun. Suddenly, she started to behave in quite unnunlike fashion. Her father threw her out of his respectable house. An entirely new set of values is springing up. Values—or perhaps the lack of them—that the older people know little about.

Tonight, Dr. Johannes Werthauer came. He is a wealthy lawyer, a divorce specialist. When he brought me my divorce decree some time ago, he proposed to make me his wife. We had let that drop, compromising on the promise of friendship and a substantially lower fee.

Werthauer owns a gorgeous little castle in the west of Berlin, the fashionable quarter. His predictions were interesting.

"The dollar will climb to a million marks," he had told me a year ago. He also said that in ten years the anti-Semites would rule Germany.

Werthauer is a great friend and collaborator of Paul Boncour, the French statesman, and a guiding spirit in the League of Human Rights.

June 22, 1922:

Went to Bad Brueckenau with Gonny and the governess for a couple of weeks. The night before our departure from Berlin a week ago, I went to an informal dinner party at Walther Rathenau's. He is now Minister of Foreign Affairs. He is the same warm friend as ever. A balanced personality, brilliant and cultured.

It seems to me that the situation is critical, and Rathenau seemed to feel the same way. He was very serious. He was worried about the radicals who pop up in so many groups, "Free Corps," "*Stahlhelm,*" "National Socialists," "Corps Escherich," "Brigade Ehrhardt" and whatnot.

"When the war was over, these people could not find their way back to a normal state of life. Now they do not even want to get back into regular activities. The lust to kill and rob is in them," he said.

We parted very cordially. I had a foreboding that we might never see each other again.

* * *

And so it happened. He was murdered on June 24.

* * *

One year later came a day when I had my first personal experience with the "New Germans." That was ten years before Hitler seized power.

* * *

May 20, 1923—Kitzingen:

Back again at the dear old home where I spent the happiest days of my life.

There are "radical" disturbances everywhere. Young people with whom I went to school no longer greet me. One of them thought his name not Aryan enough. He changed "Frobenius" into the more Teutonic "Froben."

Today was wash day. Johann and Lisbeth took the laundry to the bleaching ground. My plot adjoins that of Mrs. Enners, my old

Latin teacher's wife. He was a grumbler. But he had always treated me decently in school.

When Mrs. Enners saw my servants, she set up an outcry. "I won't have my things bleached next to that Jewish stuff."

The watchman at the bleaching ground told Lisbeth: "That hag 'Misery' has bewitched them all."

He referred to a woman named Elend* from Wuerzberg, twenty miles from my home. She has been addressing crowds here, speaking for the New Paganism and anti-Semitism. It is sickening. My people have lived here for generations. They have always been good Germans and have proved their loyalty and their patriotism over and over again.

A strange wind blows from Munich and Nuremberg. *National-Sozialistische-Deutsche-Arbeiter-Partei* is one of the new parties that has been stirring up plenty of trouble in Munich. It is led by Adolf Hitler. They say he has almost hypnotic power.

The most important rival group is in Nuremberg. It is called *Deutsche-Soziale-Arbeiter-Partei*. Their leader is one Julius Streicher, schoolteacher by profession and Jew-baiter by conviction. He is the publisher of a pornographic paper that has attained a considerable circulation.

* * *

November 15, 1923—Berlin:

Unfortunate Germany! In constant turmoil, in constant unrest. A series of attempted *Putsche* has once more thrown the country into a state of excitement. In Munich, the National Socialists, with Adolf Hitler and General von Ludendorff, tried a *coup d'état*. On November 9, there were sudden revolts staged by Leftist elements in Saxony, Hamburg, and Thuringia.

The value of the mark continues to drop to unbelievable figures, astronomical figures. When you go shopping, you have to carry your banknotes in suitcases. Savings accounts have been absolutely wiped out. In order to mail a letter inside Germany, I had to pay several million marks for a stamp. Germany's money is worth less than a scrap of paper. Foreigners can buy anything in Germany for a microscopic sum of their gold-backed currency.

---

*Elend means misery. This Elend woman later on became a Nazi woman leader in South Franconia.

Before I left Kitzingen, I called on one of Mother's old friends, an old lady who had been one of the wealthiest women in that part of the country. I found the huge house stone-cold. All the rooms were practically empty. I found the old lady, shivering in blankets, by the fireplace in the only heated room in the house.

"For heaven's sake, Aunt Paula!" I exclaimed. "Where are your rugs, your pictures, your furniture?"

"All gone, child," she said. "All gone to an antique shop in Munich, piece by piece. I used to have an income. That is no longer worth anything, and my furniture and pictures have gone for bread, week by week. When the last of it goes..." She shrugged her shoulders hopelessly.

February 28, 1925:

The first President of the German republic is dead. We watched the funeral procession, deeply moved. Many of us held divergent political views, but all of us, in our party, loved Ebert. He is gone, but our Germany remains, and one wonders in which direction our country will turn—toward democracy or reaction? Either is possible.

March 3, 1925:

I went to call on Mrs. Ebert yesterday. Her grief has great dignity.

"I was moved by the state funeral procession of my poor husband. But I know he would not have wanted so much pomp."

She is right. He never introduced any government ceremonial, nor did he desire personal honors. I shall never forget how tactlessly he was treated when he appeared at the *Staats* opera during the first constitutional celebration on August 11, 1921. He had his seat in the small first-tier box where Emperor William II used to sit during command performances. When Ebert's sturdy little figure appeared, bowing politely toward the "elite" in the orchestra seats, nobody even bothered to get up and show respect for the President of the German republic.

March 5, 1925:

Otto Gessler, Minister of War, is the first presidential candidate. Others are Fritz Thaelmann for the Communist party, and General von Ludendorff running on the National Socialist ticket. Field Marshal von Hindenburg, who now resides in Hanover, wrote a tersely significant note to Ludendorff asking him not to run under these auspices, saying that it was a disgrace for a general of his standing to link himself with this rabble.

* * *

Four weeks later, Hindenburg himself was a candidate.

March 25, 1925:

Far into the night we listened to the campaign results. Long after midnight came the news: Hindenburg was elected.

I do venerate the great soldier. But is he the man Germany needs right now? Isn't he too old? Too weak? Too easily influenced? When I think of how William II, after his escape on November 9, 1918, managed to induce Hindenburg to plead full responsibility for the Emperor's flight from Spa to Holland in order to rehabilitate the Emperor in the eyes of the world...well, then I start to wonder.

The German people fought for democracy. Now, after six years the republic has elected a hundred percent monarchist and soldier, a man with no political training!

August 25, 1925:

Met an old acquaintance, Bruno Loerzer, a flier during the World War. He is very chummy with a number of those involved in the National Socialist movement, Captain Paul Koerner, Erhard Milch, Captain Herman Goering—all former World War fliers.

Loerzer said: "This man Adolf Hitler is out of jail. You never can tell what's going to happen. He wrote a book, *Mein Kampf*, with Rudolf Hess, while they were imprisoned in Landsberg. You ought to read *Mein Kampf*. If there's anything in it, we're going to have another war. Will you nurse me again, Frau Bella?"

I shrugged my shoulders. "That depends on which side you're on, I guess."

"What do you mean by that?"

"I've read extracts from the book," I answered.

January 15, 1926:

I went to the first winter soiree of the Netherlands' Minister and his wife, Baron and Baroness de Gevers. Mammi von Carnap introduced me. I could not have found a better *Chef de protocole.*

Mammi, who is very ambitious and likes to meet new people and go everywhere, usually takes me with her. She had an important place in imperial circles before the war. Her husband, Moritz, was Chamberlain to Wilhelm II. They are received in all circles.

The de Gevers impressed me with their ability to separate their guests tactfully. Many of the international visitors are not too well received by some of our "old elite," who are still fighting the war.

The end of the war brought many social changes. Since 1919 things have rather centered around the diplomatic corps. Before 1914, the corps was only more or less a part of the general elite of the court. Not all of the courtiers used to reside in Berlin. But during the winter season, the *Junkers*, the owners of huge estates, always flocked to the capital in large numbers for a round of gay social life.

With the coming of Hindenburg, some of the former nobility began to return to Berlin during the season. They had not done this for some time, having retired to their estates in a huff after the revolution and taken up residence in smaller towns like Darmstadt, Dresden, Meiningen, or Hanover, where there was still the flavor of a miniature court and some sort of princely household to give them a whiff of the royal atmosphere they had always enjoyed so much. Now, during the social season, they are returning to Berlin and flocking in tremendous numbers to the horse shows, theaters, restaurants and social events.

The "elite," of course, is different today. The old crowd with plenty of money has partly vanished. Their places are taken by new people with new fortunes. They strive very hard to be "accepted," and do inveigle a stray diplomat into attending an occasional lavish party. Many jokes are made about the social efforts of these *nouveaux riches.*

"I am not ashamed that I made my money during the war," a Berlin manufacturer told me once, "but I am ashamed that my dear wife tries to lead people to believe that we were born in our villa at Wannsee. She wants the place to be socially important. I know, of course, that we function simply as a place for people to obtain a free meal. If the lobster and the turkey ever give out, the guests will disappear permanently. Poverty has its compensations," he said bitterly.

At the de Gevers, it was really funny to see the host and hostess divide their guests like the sexes at a Quaker meeting. Diplomats were steered to the right of the ballroom, German guests were guided to the left. When Pierre de Margerie, French Ambassador, arrived, Mammi hissed in my ear, "There's that nasty Frenchman again."

It's going to be difficult to restore amicable international relations again, with our old aristocracy refusing to play the game.

February 10, 1926:

Mammi took me to a tea at Margarete von Hindenburg's, the Field Marshal's daughter-in-law. She is the President's hostess. The young Hindenburgs are both most unattractive. They are ungracious and haughty. Margarete von Hindenburg lacks elegance, dresses in bad taste, is awkward and self-conscious. A young French attaché called her the "Prussian petty officer in petticoats." Oskar von Hindenburg gives an impression of morose gloom.

The Old Gentleman, as he is respectfully called by his intimates, dropped in for half an hour. There was a deep hush when he entered. It was the first time I had met him, and I found him overwhelming. Six foot five, with short-cropped hair. He moved about somewhat painstakingly. In the chivalrous manner of the old school, he kissed the ladies' hands.

When he returned to his quarters, I was allowed to accompany him. Passing through the anteroom, we turned to the left, into the President's sitting room, which leads into his cabinet. A truly Prussian atmosphere reigns here! War pictures along the walls: "Schwerin's death at Prague," a portrait of the Iron Chancellor, one of Frederick II. Heavy, dark tapestries; heavy, dark furniture. Deep armchairs and a round table in one corner. The light radiates moodily from a Flemish chandelier.

There, by the window, is the bulky desk which I have seen in so many photographs. I can imagine him sitting there, drawing the famous vertical stroke with his oversized pencil—the margin stroke which marks his approval. My eyes are attracted by some faded paper, under glass, in a simple wooden frame. *Ora et Labora*, is written on it. Hindenburg noticed that the handwriting aroused my curiosity.

"My father wrote it for me when I entered the cadets' corps," boomed his deep voice in back of me. He has the deepest voice I've ever heard in a human being.

Looking through the window, one has a lovely view of the garden, the well-kept lawn, flower beds, old trees and gravel paths. Here the Old Gentleman takes his morning walk between 7:30 and 8:00 A.M., with his sheep dog, Rolf. Before he returns for breakfast, he goes to fetch a parcel of foreign newspapers at the back door, from an old vendor. "I ordered them because the chief of the Government Press Department, Zechlin, tells me only what he wants me to know," Hindenburg confided once.

October 2, 1927:

Hindenburg's eightieth anniversary. After celebration mass in the tiny *Dreifaltigkeits Kirche*, a long line of officials went to offer their congratulations at the Presidential Palace.

As I was entering my name in the register, the Papal Nuncio, Monsignore Eugenio Pacelli, went by. International and diplomatic society is filled with stimulating and interesting personalities, and the Ambassador of the Vatican is one of the most outstanding of these. When his tall figure appears, in his reception robe of scarlet and purple damask, he quickly becomes a focal point for all eyes. His face is ascetic, his features are cut in the lines of an old cameo, and it is seldom that the shadow of a smile crosses them.

As he went by, his calm poise delighted me. He talked to me for a while, and I was happy to see him. I kissed his ring with real pleasure.

* * *

October 1, 1928:

I'm going to have to start a new life. Things never run smoothly for me too long. Some blow, political or personal, has always occurred to shove me into a new turmoil of problems and worries. The inflation has practically wiped out my inheritance. Up to now, I have spent a great deal of my time in voluntary welfare work. My mother had done it all her life, and I felt that I ought to continue where she had left off. I hope to be able, still, to look after those needy ones.

I'm going to enter journalism. My international and social contacts may stand me in good stead. The Ullstein papers offered me a connection.

When I took my first copy to the paper, Dr. Misch, the editor, said: "That's charming, Bella, very charming, indeed, but much too flippant. There's a great deal you will have to learn about social reporting. A social reporter does not write realistically. Just remember this: Every ambassadress is a beauty. Every minister is an excellent politician—the best in the world, in fact. Every newcomer in the diplomatic corps is always the shining star of the homeland's Foreign Office. If you remember these things you can never go far wrong."

Well, that isn't going to be too pleasant. I have rather a penchant for plain speaking. From now on I'll have to write with a double pen—the column for public consumption, and my diary for things as I actually see and hear them.

* * *

That's how I became a newspaperwoman. Usually, when you get a job through your connections, it doesn't work out. But this time it did. The Ullsteins took me on. This is a large house, the largest in Germany. I wrote a social column for the *Vossiche Zeitung*, a rather highbrow democratic paper with two issues a day, and another for the midday paper, *B.Z.* There was much more to the House of Ullstein, of course. The *Morgenpost*, with 600,000 daily copies, had the widest circulation. The *Tempo* was the problem child. "Neither father nor mother," as they say in Berlin. Too late for noon consumption, too early for the evening news. It was, nevertheless, an amusing and interesting paper.

In addition, our house published magazines and books of every description. A very large business, employing many thousands of people. I felt glad and elated to be admitted to the staff.

Dr. Misch was very cooperative and helpful. "Let's have society reports in the American manner," I suggested. "Lively, with plenty of pictures." He agreed that it might be worth trying.

No other Berlin paper had ever done anything of the kind. My columns immediately became popular. It was a quick success. But there was really a lifetime of preparation behind it. My classmates had always considered me something of a bluestocking. Their attitude was not unmixed with a trace of contempt. Learning was frowned upon in our set. But my mother had been wise beyond most mothers. She saw to it that I accumulated a decent and civilized background. I am grateful to her. I have passed this on to my little Gonny, for I early realized that one cannot depend on an inherited income. She studied photography and became assistant to a famous photographer in Berlin. Then I managed to get her as my assistant, and she accompanied me with her camera to the parties.

I loved every minute of my work and became exceedingly busy, sometimes laboring fourteen to sixteen hours a day. I covered many things: society, fashions, food, ice hockey. Best of all I liked to do politicial interviews. I also arranged welfare parties and fashion shows.

The amount of work was terrific, necessitating two secretaries. When I discovered that my first secretary, Tilla Kraus, could spell correctly, it lifted a great weight from my mind, as spelling was never a notable accomplishment of mine. She was very fond of me, and the work was enlivened by the small jealousies between her and my stout and warmhearted Gertrud Meyer, the other secretary.

I wrote for out-of-town papers under the name of Isa von Franken, as the Ullstein house reserved the right to the use of my name in their papers. The connections of my youth and the good name of my family proved invaluable. I was received everywhere, getting stories that were denied to many others.

It was lots of fun, until that Austrian psychopath came too close. And now let my diary speak for itself.

* * *

July 16, 1929:

Scorching hot at the Davis Cup tennis match in the Grunewald. William Tilden, the matchless American champion, was present, and he appeared pleased when Daniel Prenn, the German champion, beat the light Englishman, Bunny Austin. As a matter of fact, "Big Bill" beamed, for Danny had gained his victory with a racket Tilden had brought him as a present from America.

I sat in the honorary box, next to the French Ambassador, De Margerie, proud and happy about the German victory. A remark by Count von der Schulenberg, member of the Tennis Guild, startled me.

"Of course, always those Jews!" he said.

"What do you mean?" I threw at him angrily.

He had the grace to blush. "The Jew would win, of course."

"He won for Germany," I said. "Would you have preferred to have the Englishman win?"

October 4, 1929—Paris:

Dinner with Briand. Yesterday our Minister of Foreign Affairs died.

"Gustav Stresemann signed his own death warrant at the Hague Conference in August," said Briand, "when he undertook the strain of a journey to Geneva immediately afterward. His work had some result. He worked to liberate Germany, and to a certain extent he had success. He managed to improve the peace terms and to restore international relations. The loss of this dear friend means much to me, but to Germany it means more."

Briand was irritated at the lack of gratitude "yonder, across the Rhine." He was particularly vehement against Hugenberg, the leader of the Nationalist party, who, he declared, has weakened Germany to her very marrow. "He is responsible for stirring up the people's protest against the Young Plan. His agitation must be considered a personal affront by all of us who are striving for a policy of mutual agreement."

From 1914 to 1918, Alfred Hugenberg was on the board of directors of the Krupp Works. In 1916, he bought the Scherl publishing house and built it up into a tremendous organ of Nationalist propaganda. He is the great disseminator of National Socialist ideas to an entire nation through newspapers, books, magazines and films.

November 7, 1929:

The Russian Ambassador, Nikolai Krestinsky, and his wife received, to celebrate the anniversary of the Revolution.

We are courting the Russians. All the ministers, the foreign diplomats and quite a few high military officials were present. It seems as if Bismarck's old dream of a Russian alliance was still haunting the mind of the people around General von Seeckt, the creator of the *Reichswehr*.

The Russian Embassy is one of the oldest and best-known buildings of the capital. Tsar Nikolai I was the first foreign potentate to establish his own embassy in Berlin. The hall, with its huge logs burning in the fireplace, reminds the visitor of "Little Mother Russia." The white marble staircase, covered with the softest carpets from Smyrna, glowing in a deep warm red against the white of the steps, leads to the reception rooms.

The Russians entertain on a great scale. Caviar is flown from Moscow, heavy wines from the Crimea. The hosts and their staff shower the guests with their attentions. The Russian Embassy employs Russian servants exclusively. Only on the occasion of these receptions is German help hired to assist the house person-

nel. Strange how the Russians withhold themselves personally
from the abundant food and rich drinks, which seem there for the
guests only. Does their abstinence emphasize the Spartan doctrine
of modern Russia?

At dinner parties, eighty guests are usually seated at two long
tables in the rococo room with the marble walls and the heavy gold
decorations. Precious damask, covering the table, stresses the
deep glow of red roses, the hostess' favorite flower. The heavy
wine is poured in costly crystal cups, all relics of the former
Imperial Ambassador's household. The only modern objects are
the multicolored plates and dishes, a product of present Russia. A
strange discrepancy between the dignified asceticism of the hosts
and the almost crushing pomp of the palace.

December 3, 1929:

Saw a friend of my childhood today. He lived through the war
and has remained active as a *Reichswehr* officer. He's on his way
through to Russia. "This is confidential," he said. "The *Reichswehr*
has assigned me to a four years' job in Russia, to supervise the
construction of airplanes. Owing to the Versailles Treaty, we
cannot do much of that sort of thing here. The treaty said nothing
about not building them in Russia. What we are going to do there
is of the most extreme importance."

It must be, because his salary is magnificent.

He is a protégé of the "geopolitician" General Oskar von
Niedermeyer, although a close friend of Hitler's accomplice,
General von Haushofer, is anti-Hitler. Both of them, however, are
responsible for the *Drang nach dem Osten* and *Lebensraum* ideas that
the National Socialists use so freely. Haushofer was the teacher of
Rudolf Hess and frequently visited him and Hitler during their
stay in the Fortress of Landsberg.

1930

Contemporary Events

March	*13*	Hindenburg accepts the Young Plan.
March	*28*	Social Democratic *Reichskanzler*, Hermann Mueller-Franken, resigns.
March	*30*	Dr. Heinrich Bruening, leader of the Catholic Center party, is appointed Chancellor of Germany.
April	*22*	Signing of the London Naval Reduction Treaty.
June	*30*	The Rhineland is freed from allied occupational army.
July	*18*	The German *Reichstag* is dissolved.
September 14		The *Reichstag* election brings 107 seats for Hitler's National Socialist Workers party.
September 19		The Nazi party members arrived at the first session of the newly elected *Reichstag* wearing brown shirts and shouting *Deutschland erwache! Juda verrecke!* (Germany awake! Judea perish!).

February 1, 1930:

Ball at the English Embassy, at 70 Wilhelmstrasse, right next to the President's house. The building has much dignity, with its four strong columns framing the entrance. When the speculator Straussberg went bankrupt, the English government bought the house from him. It is now a perfect masterpiece of British taste.

23

To reach the ballrooms one has to pass through a magnificent two-story marble hall in which fountains splash with refreshing coolness.

Both Sir Horace Rumbold and Lady Ethel, née Fane, speak fluent German. Lady Ethel is known for her quiet charity. Sir Horace was born into diplomacy. His father represented Great Britain in Vienna.

I heard the "Bavarian intrigues" openly discussed. The host said to De Margerie, the French Ambassador, "I have given an extensive report to London. I don't approve of this illegal army, in spite of the temporary ban on uniforms."

I am under great obligation to Sir Horace. Several months ago he said, "I wonder why German society circles give so little consideration to international diplomats in the press. America and England, in this regard, are far ahead of you." We decided to do something about it. He kept his word, pulling the right wires. As a result, I now enjoy the privilege of accompanying the Chief of Protocol whenever a newcomer is expected at a railway station or airfield. This enables me to get a quick interview from arriving diplomats. I can have a short profile in the *B.Z.*, and a more detailed interview in the evening edition of the *Vossische Zeitung*.

February 2, 1930:

Went to the station to meet the new American Ambassador, Frederic M. Sackett. A gentle-looking man with, obviously, very good background. Mrs. Sackett is an attractive woman of great distinction.

February 12, 1930:

Silver wedding at house of important banker. Snobbish and elaborate affair. Many celebrities who had been induced to come by the promise that other celebrities would be there. *Reichsbank* president, Hjalmar Schacht, and his wife present. I understand she adorns, or rather amplifies, her bosom with an expensive swastika in rubies and diamonds whenever the occasion appears suitable politically or socially. Although Schacht was helped to his present eminent position by sponsors like Professor George Bernhard, editor of the *Vossische Zeitung*, the banker Jacob Gold-schmidt, and other non-Aryans, he is not above using the swastika as his insignia whenever he thinks it will suit his purpose. Tonight he said to me, "Why not give the National Socialists a break? They seem pretty smart to me."

Schacht belonged to the liberal party. He was a devoted Republican who turned conservative. Is National Socialism to be his next step?

March 27, 1930:

Tea at Yvonne Wilhelm's, wife of the French Embassy's Commercial Attaché. As always, some fourteen or sixteen painters hanging around, all of whom, at one time or another, have painted the portrait of their beautiful hostess. Her receptions are quite outstanding. Omer Wilhelm himself never appears. An atmosphere of intrigue and secrecy always overhangs these affairs.

On my way home, I ran into Dr. Erich Josef Gustav Klausener, Prussian Ministerial Director, head of the police force at the home office, chief of the Roman Catholic Action. He said: "We expect Dr. Heinrich Bruening, leader of the Center faction at the *Reichstag*, to be the coming number one man. Kurt von Schleicher at the War Ministry, together with his comrade-in-arms, Oskar von Hindenburg and the intrigue-loving Secretary of State, Otto Meissner, have softened up the Old Gentleman and convinced him of the urgent need for some drastic changes in personnel."

March 29, 1930:

The cabinet of Hermann Mueller-Franken, Socialist leader, has resigned. Is this to be the end of democracy as we have had it here? That would be the only reason to consider the change important, for neither socially nor politically has Mueller been successful.

Mueller, who does not like entertaining, is colorless and seemingly insignificant in his rare social appearances. Mrs. Mueller, on the contrary, enjoys being seen everywhere, dragging along with her a stout and noisy daughter and an attenuated, chain-smoking niece. Mrs. Mueller gave me more than one headache during the first weeks of her social activity, as I keep mistaking her for Mrs. Loebe, wife of the *Reichstag* president. Both of them are completely average and devoid of distinction of any kind.

April 1, 1930:

Tea at Lady Rumbold's. The appointment of Dr. Bruening as Chancellor—a change from Social Democrat to Centrist—is the big gossip.

Bruening, a sincere and unpretentious man, is not going to move into the Chancellery. He will continue to reside in his two-room apartment at the "Hedwig's Home." He has worked out a household budget for his own needs, running into only a few hundred marks a month.

Hindenburg has charged Bruening, as his confidant, to rule without the *Reichstag.* A presidential government, in other words. This is going to be a change in policies, a withdrawal from parliamentarianism.

May 6, 1930:

Luncheon at the French Embassy, the attraction being André Maurois and his wife. She is *très grande dame.* She wore black, with a touch of white trimming. Looked expensive and original.

Madam Helène de Portes also there. A really striking personality. She has quite a salon in Paris. Her relations with Paul Reynaud have been commented on, in whispers, behind plenty of closed doors.

May 27, 1930:

Garden party at the Presidential Palace. I felt my knees wobbling when the Old Gentleman, leaning heavily on a cane, bent to kiss my hand. Haven't seen him for some time. Shocked to notice how aged he looks. Suggests a bronze cast—something for eternity.

May 28, 1930:

"Hindenburg Day" at the racetrack. I've staged so many fashion shows at the Union Club tracks that I generally find myself acting as hostess at all affairs of the exclusive racing club. Together with the board of directors, I welcomed President von Hindenburg. Later, seated at the tea table, with most of the diplomats and their ladies attending, I asked:

"Herr General Field Marshal, may I pour you some tea?"

He grumbled, genuinely irritated: "Mercy, no, little lady, I can't stand that fashionable brew. I stick to my good old cup of coffee."

August 15, 1930—Paris:

I'm here to cover the fashion shows. The truth is they bore me. I think it would be more practical to have men cover them. Men would have much more enthusiasm for the slim models, the good-looking faces, the champagne served on such occasions at smart Paris fashion shows.

Luncheon with my old friend Aristide Briand in the Bois de Boulogne made up for the agonies I had suffered in the light-flooded showrooms. He seemed tired and worried.

"The reactionary streak in south and middle Germay bothers me more than you might imagine. Did you ever notice the similarity between the National Socialists and the Communists? Just listen to their speeches. The arguments are so alike that you have to wait until the end to see whether the raised hand is open or clenched."

October 14, 1930:

At the new elections in September, one hundred and seven National Socialists obtained seats in the *Reichstag*. There's a touch of panic in certain quarters. Should one leave Germany and wait outside to see what will happen? Surprising how many people feel that it might be the prudent thing to do.

A handful of noisy roughnecks! They made their appearance in the chamber clad in brown, giving the Hitler salute. They shouted in chorus: "Germany, awake!" On their way to the *Reichstag*, they celebrated their victory by an attack on several department stores. Twenty of the delegates chose bright daylight to assault the windows of stores in *Leipzigerstrasse*. No one saw them. No one caught any of them.

The projectiles, casually aimed, hit only non-Aryan targets, by some odd chance. The street became a mass of splintered glass.

"The Awakening Germany," they call it. The party bosses gave a confused explanation, hardly an apology, that had to do with "Communistic provocation" which aroused "spontaneous outbursts of rage." This attitude is shameless enough, but what dismays me more is the exceedingly cautious reaction of conservative papers who were themselves the first to toss the discreet hint about the "provocation" to the brown ruffians.

November 12, 1930:

"Tea with Spirituals," at Madame Cahier's, the famous singer and pupil of Gustav Mahler. The American contralto, Marian Anderson, was charming and inspiring. A remarkable voice. Everybody present was enraptured.

It is interesting to note the hostile reaction in the National Socialist press: "Clamor About a Negress."

November 17, 1930:

The American Ambassador and his wife are showing people here what "entertaining" means in the States. Even the international diplomats are stunned. The Sacketts serve lobster at tea, an unheard-of luxury in Berlin!

The Ambassador has rented a small but aristocratic palace in the most fashionable quarter of Berlin. A gigantic and aged butler commands a small army of footmen in discreet blue livery. Mrs. Olive Sackett-Speed is the astonishing possessor of a social secretary, an extravagant novelty here. She is a perfect hostess and gathers as many members of the prewar courtiers in her house as possible.

Although there are quite a few of the old Potsdam set who still refuse to frequent the French Embassy, they decided, after a meeting of the *Adelsgenossenschaft* ("Union of Aristocrats"), to drop their calling cards at the Sacketts' as soon as the ambassador had taken his credentials to Hindenburg.

I met the Sacketts for the first time after their arrival, at a party in honor of Masaryk's eightieth birthday, at the Czech Legation. It was a great social event—dinner and a recital by Jarmila Novotna, who had just been engaged by the *Staatsoper*. I sat next to Mr. Sackett. "I like Berlin. It is inspiring," he said. "We are anxious in America to help Europe get out of the present crisis. We'd like to settle national controversies at the green table instead of on the battlefield." He is an observant and humorous person, and he kept up a running fire of light banter.

November 20, 1930:

I met Chancellor Bruening at one of the dinners. What a grand person! So much composure, such poise, such delicate features, such a beautiful speaking voice—and such disgusting huge cigars!

December 25, 1930:

A circular inquiry of the conservative *Deutsche Allgemeine Zeitung*, in its Christmas issue, met with general disapproval in diplomatic circles. The inquiry read: "How do you feel about Hitler's possible inclusion in the government?"

People who know what is going on behind the scenes will interpret this as the symptom of some very grave disease. One of the owners of the *Deutsche Allgemeine* is Von Stuelpnagel. He is the brother of General von Stuelpnagel, one of the most active figures in the *Junker* clique of *Herrenklub* intriguers. Besides, he is closely connected with the *camarilla* that clusters so closely around Hindenburg as to obstruct his view.

Some of the answers to the question were illuminating. Hindenburg's best friend, Count Oldenburg-Januschau, formulated his reply laconically and eloquently: "Rather Frick than Wirth." Schacht answered: "It is impossible to govern against the extreme right wing." Schacht is president of the *Reichsbank*, and an incurable turncoat. But why on earth a man like General von Seeckt should advocate Hitler's cause is beyond my understanding. "Not only do I deem Hitler's inclusion in the government desirable, I think it is a necessity!" A man of the old era, an upright officer, could not possibly fraternize with that gang!

1931

Contemporary Events

April	*14*	King Alfonso flees from Madrid, and Spain is proclaimed a republic.
June	*20*	President Hoover proposes a one-year moratorium on international debts.
July	*?*	Various big German banking institutions close.
September	*21*	Great Britain suspends the gold standard.
September	*22*	New French Ambassador, André François-Poncet, arrives in Berlin.
September	*28*	French Premier Pierre Laval and Foreign Minister Aristide Briand visit Berlin.
		Laval's first meeting with Dr. Joseph Goebbels, propagandist of the Nazi party.
October	*19*	Italian Foreign Minister Grandi visits Germany. Italy all-out for better relations with Germany.

February 10, 1931:

Attended *Reichstag* session with Yvonne Wilhelm. We wanted to hear Doctor Joseph Goebbels. He is a Nazi party deputy, and very greedy for power.

"The Doctor," as they call him, almost a dwarf, hobbled to the speaker's desk. But before he did so, the Communists had indulged in a veritable flood of invective. Apparently that was just what he needed to start him right. You have to be impressed by the way he uses the German language, whether you like him or not. A kind of combination of Mephisto and Savonarola, sinister and frantic, intriguing and fanatically obsessed. He uses his hands violently enough for Yvonne to remark, "Funny way of speaking for a full-blooded Aryan." But his voice is soft enough, and he knows how to make the most effective use of it. He's apparently not stupid. He has managed to snatch the wealthy industrialist Guenther Quandt's beautiful wife right out from under the husband's nose.

He was outright rude to the Chancellor of the Reich, blaming him for everything. I admired Dr. Bruening's control. He listened with complete calm. Another man might have hit the raging dwarf right across his big mouth. But the Chancellor maintained an aloof superiority, as though he would not contaminate himself by any possible contact with such a dirty creature.

April 14, 1931:

The Spanish Ambassador has been recalled. The King has left Spain, and the country has become a republic. At the first tea at the embassy of the Spanish republic, I noticed two huge rectangular spots on the wall of the dining room. The pictures had obviously been removed in a hurry. That's how living kings are buried.

May 22, 1931:

Dinner at the house of Hassan Nachat Pasha, the Egyptian Minister. Hassan Nachat Pasha, the young and vivacious favorite of King Fuad I, is particularly fond of Berlin prewar society. He likes to adorn his elaborate dinner table, usually covered with priceless lace and choice delicacies, with the presence of a certain slender lady, the widow of a German prince. Nachat is a brilliant host, combining oriental lavishness with the urban perfection of Western civilization.

It was a glittering affair, attended by Abdel Fattah Yehia Pasha, Egyptian Minister of Foreign Affairs. Quite a crowd was there. Among them was the new Minister of Afghanistan, Ghulam

Siddiq Khan, European-minded and schooled. He is King Aman Ullah's brother-in-law.

As soon as dinner was over, Nachat's Egyptian wife retired. Her illustrious husband, the pasha, in spite of his progressive views in general, seems to cling to good old oriental principles where women are concerned. Ghulam Siddiq Khan, too, seemed to believe that "he who loves his wife leaves her at home." With the lady retired and dinner finished, the oriental gentlemen turned their attention to the beauties of Western civilization.

June 17, 1931:

Interesting match at my tennis club, the *Rot-Weiss*. I played doubles with my trainer, Roman Najuch, against Lord Cholmondeley and his wife, who was born a Sassoon. Crown Prince Wilhelm came in and looked on. When the match was over and the Cholmondeleys had gone, he invited me to have tea with him in the clubhouse. Knowing what happens to the reputation of any woman seen with the Crown Prince, I was compelled to refuse. I told him why. He smiled and was a pretty good sport about it.

"This is the second rebuff I have received in your set. I asked Lilly to come with me for a motor ride along the Avus. She shook her head."

"'It might be too embarrassing,' she said, 'if an accident occurred and our bodies became unrecognizable. I might sleep eternally in the Hohenzollern tomb at the Charlottenburg Mausoleum, and I think you might be rather uneasy, throughout eternity, in the Jewish cemetery at Weissensee.'"

July 4, 1931:

Fourth of July celebration at the American Embassy. The Sacketts awaited their numerous callers on their flag- and flower-adorned terrace. The afternoon reception was in the beautifully kept garden, with lovely American women balancing their teacups in well-groomed hands and chatting merrily with the younger set of the diplomatic corps.

The evening reception was also an enjoyable and successful affair. Mr. Sackett, although looking tired and overworked, was in good form and seemed pretty confident as to the success of his recent trip to the States. He had had endless talks and negotiations in Washington in his attempt to arrange help for Germany. His close friendship with President Hoover stood him in good stead. Mrs. Sackett complained a little that she had not seen much of her husband lately.

September 22, 1931:

At the Friedrichstrasse Station, 8:37 A.M. A gentleman in gray alighted from the North Express. Gray from spats to car, which had been shipped along with him on the same train. A little crowd of gentlemen in black received the gentleman in gray. The black group gathered on the platform were: Chief of Protocol von Tattenbach, his complete staff, and the members of the French Embassy. The gentleman in gray was De Margerie's successor, Professor André François-Poncet.

François-Poncet is a man of the *Comité des Forges*, the French heavy industry. He represents the two hundred ruling families of France. Last year, he was Secretary of State for National Economy. Malicious tongues said it was an observation post.

He is a friend of Tardieu. For many years Tardieu has been leader of the conservative opposition in France. François-Poncet is also the pet of radical leader Herriot. He is said to be sponsored by Pierre Laval, backed by Paul Reynaud, and sent to promote Franco-German mutual understanding. Anyway, judging from the very first impression, there seems little chance of François-Poncet's laying his cards upon the table.

He is well-groomed, elegant, in his middle forties. His gray attire is elaborately calculated and perfectly touched off with well-balanced notes of black in his tie and where the shoe appears under the gray of the doeskin spat. Clever brushing of the hair covers his little bald spot. The hair, of course, is gray around the temples, matching the hue of the gray pearl adorning his tie. An imposing forehead. Vivacious dark blue eyes. Nose and chin forceful and prominent. Judging from his old pictures, he has changed from upward-pointed mustaches to the fashionable elegance of a tiny Menjou-brush. Altogether an impressive-looking man, although he gives the effect of planned dapperness.

Within an hour of his arrival, he had presented his credentials to Hindenburg. This was not the composure I had known to be

French. This seemed the Prussian timing—Prussian speed. It seemed quite new, too, in Berlin diplomacy.

Young De Margerie remained as personal secretary to the new man, as he had been to his father. He was kind enough to obtain a special reception for me, scheduled for two o'clock.

At two o'clock sharp, the door was flung open. "We have already met. I have to thank you—the only lady who welcomed me. That must be a good omen," the ambassador said politely.

Again he reminded me of Adolphe Menjou. Or rather, of the smooth, distinguished, well-paid headwaiter at the Hotel Meurice in Paris. He spoke German fluently, almost without any accent.

Economic affairs, he hinted, were going to be his main preoccupation. Something like a French-German industrial alliance. He repeatedly used the word "cooperation," not "mutual understanding." Collaboration between the economically well-equipped, capital-lacking Germany and the economically and technically inferior but financially prosperous France. His diction was unfaltering, precise as steel. A mixture of pointed intelligence, ambition, and purposeful strength. Embarrassing questions were avoided with smooth dexterity: "Ask me that some time later. I have to find out first. I have to get started. I am quite sure that my work here is going to be extrrremely interrresting." He rolled his "r's" like thunder peals.

So that's what the modern French politician looks like! And I had always been convinced that my friend Aristide Briand was typical of the French statesman: slightly careless in appearance, easygoing. Whatever had been crumpled or creased about Briand was extremely sleek and impeccable in François-Poncet. Briand looked to me like the personification of the French soil and the French population. François-Poncet was not so easily classified. With all his good intentions for collaboration and exchange, this was more the representative of unyielding power as compared to Briand's warmhearted friendship for Germany. Briand appealed to the heart; François-Poncet to the head—that's where the difference lay.

At three o'clock, the official reception followed. François-Poncet delivered a neat little speech in German. When the press left, everybody was presented with a copy of the address in French. Then François-Poncet had his picture taken.

I felt like tapping his shoulder when I left and warning him: "Take it easy!"

September 24, 1931:

Quite a few "Potsdamers" at Sackett's. The prewar aristocratic elite did not try very hard to get friendly with the French diplomats.

However, the press reports concerning the unusual setup at the new French Ambassador's, the great scale of his entertainment program, have caused quite a stir in the old elite. Two more important French statesmen are expected, Briand and Laval. Elaborate preparations are being made for their welcome. There seemed no alternative: Calling cards had to be dropped at the French Embassy.

Who is going to be invited? As long as the wind had blown anti-French, nobody had been interested. Now, since the Wilhelmstrasse has changed tactics, they all flock back. Not to lose touch. To help court the French, if in the long run it would mean helping their own position.

Mammi von Carnap seemed very agitated when she learned that I had already been introduced and had sipped my tea at the French Ambassador's. She pestered me insistently for an introduction to Briand and Laval. I remembered how she, the perfect example of the *ancien régime*, used to object to the "nasty French."

September 29, 1931:

What a rush and struggle to obtain interviews and invitations! I felt a little ashamed. Councilor Guerlet and Secretary de Margerie took care of me. I attended everything, even the big dinner at the embassy.

Two tables were elaborately decorated with yellow roses. Foreign Minister Briand was seated next to Dr. Curtius, his German colleague, Berthelot, French Undersecretary of State, and the German Cabinet Ministers von Guerard, Dietrich and Treviranus were at the same table with the Secretaries of State Schaeffer, Meissner, and Trendelenburg.

The Italian Ambassador Orsini Baroni was at François-Poncet's table with Pierre Laval, Sir Horace Rumbold, Minister Joseph Wirth, Chancellor Dr. Bruening, Lord Mayor of Berlin Dr. Sahm, German Ambassador to Paris Hoesch, Secretaries of State von Buelow and Puender.

I took an immediate dislike to Laval. He showed off as soon as he felt anybody's attention on him. He pretended blasé indifference. When he thought himself unobserved, his face showed natural brutality.

François-Poncet drank to the President of the German Reich and the President of the French republic. The movie truck with sound equipment had arrived at the Pariser Platz entrance of the embassy. The Frenchmen looked into the drizzling rain and stepped out on the balcony with Bruening. From below cheers: "*Vive la paix! Hoch* Briand! *Hoch* Bruening!"

When Briand left to return to the Hotel Adlon, he took my arm and invited me for a little chat. He outlined his idea to me: "If only I could succeed in working it out! It's an old dream of mine and of the French to unite Europe in one great alliance of countries, like the United States. That would exclude the danger of another European war. Europe's civilization is at stake, if we can't live in peace. If we could, without the use of force, create a union, I would die happy. I visited the tomb of my dear departed friend, Gustav Stresemann, this morning," he said. "I promised him to try to take care of the peace in Europe. I hope God will help me and give me the strength to keep this promise."

He seemed so excited that I was deeply moved.

Well, Laval did not look to me as if he shared Briand's ideals. Briand had introduced me, and he asked me afterward: "Why didn't you talk to him a little bit?" "Because I did not like him, Your Excellency," I said. "He looks sly. He looks like a gypsy."

Laval's teeth, yellow from too much nicotine, remind one of a wild animal's. His legendary white tie, twisted into a bow as for formal occasions, emphasizes his black hair and his yellow complexion. Although Briand, too, is a passionate smoker, the cigarette dangling from his mouth has nothing revolting about it. When Laval does the same thing, it looks disgusting. Briand is charming, lovable in his kindness; Laval is like a stock market gambler, scheming and efficient.

I did not want to hurt Briand's feelings by judging his disciple too severely. He felt, anyway, that I disliked Laval and said: "One shouldn't judge by looks only, my child."

He gave me his autograph. "Do you want Laval's, too?" I shook my head. "I don't want to deal with people who have secret meetings with that Dr. Goebbels," I said, remembering what Mammi had confided to me tonight. Briand's face suddenly looked twenty years older. He may have felt the truth, and for several minutes he seemed to have forgotten everything around him.

November 8, 1931:

It was thrilling to attend the fourteenth anniversary of the Soviet Republic. The new Soviet Ambassador, Leo Chintchuk, and his wife, Maris, were receiving. There was a most sophisticated, elegant, charming, and attractive young woman, dressed in Paris' latest and adorned with the world's most exquisite jewels! I learned that this delightful creature was Natalia Alexandrovna, wife of the Commissar for Culture, Anatol Lunatcharski. She is a well-known actress and *the* leading lady of the Soviet society. One of the secretaries of the embassy told me she is one of the few Soviet ladies who entertain in Moscow.

November 10, 1931:

Visit of Paul Painlevé, formerly French Prime Minister, Minister of the Air Force, and a mathematician.

Had a very hard time getting hold of him. Finally, I asked the French Commercial Attaché, Omer Wilhelm, to obtain an interview for me. At length I got the invitation, for an unusual hour. Breakfast at the Hotel Adlon at 10:30 A.M.

Omer came with me. We had to wait for a full thirty minutes until the vivacious little gentleman asked us in. What a mess the room looked, with papers, periodicals, and books covering chairs, tables, and floor. Painlevé pushed aside enough to give each of us a seat and apologized: "I had to work, to jot down impressions, to read the papers. It was very late when I retired last night, and that's why I overslept this morning."

I busied myself taking shorthand notes of his impressions and views. He told us about a luncheon at the French Embassy the previous day:

> We had an excellent luncheon. But I am afraid Albert Einstein and I were too deep in talk and thought to pay sufficient homage to the food. We talked and argued and talked right through the fruit and cheese. Simultaneously, we helped ourselves to a delicious looking pear each. Returning to our topic, we started peeling—well, when we had solved our problem we found ourselves sitting there, pears peeled to the stems with all the delicious fruit in a silly mess on our plates.

November 12, 1931:

Jimmy Walker, the Mayor of New York, is in Berlin. A busy program of sight-seeing, taking the fashionable night clubs in his stride. He donated a prize cup for the riding tournament.

At the tournament tonight, I saw him sitting in the box with all the "big shots." He walked around with the Lord Mayor of Berlin, Dr. Sahm, whom we call the Long Codfish, because of his tiny head on an enormously tall body.

All the women seemed fascinated by Jimmy Walker.

Police Commander Heimannsberg was present. He told me a peculiar story:

> When Hitler held his recent Sports-Palast speech, Vice-Police President Bernhard Weiss and I had the meeting watched and controlled by a troop of especially reliable and trustworthy policemen. The next day, a police officer came to report at my headquarters. A man of whose integrity and Republican convictions I was almost a hundred percent sure. He had been posted by the entrance gate when Hitler arrived. When Hitler alighted from his car, he evidently mistook the Republican giant for one of the bodyguards assigned to his personal protection. He strutted up to him and grabbed his hand. While holding it in his famous, straightforward, he-man grip, he gazed into the police officer's eye with that fatal hypnotizing and irresistible glare which swept the poor officer right off his feet. Clicking to attention, he confessed to me this morning: "Since last night I am a National Socialist. *Heil* Hitler!"

November 16, 1931:

The press is taboo at Hindenburg's annual formal reception in honor of the diplomatic corps. They are not allowed to come in even after dinner, as is the custom in many diplomatic houses.

I decided to try to get a first-hand story if possible. In masculine disguise, I drove to the Kaiserhof, parked my car, and loitered around the Wilhelmstrasse neighborhood. I was sufficiently inconspicuous to be able to get close enough to observe everyone who drove up; and, with my knowledge of the diplomatic auto plates, I was able to reconstruct all I needed about those inside to produce a rather accurate and vivid column for the next day's issue, much to the irritation of the other writers.

December 1, 1931:

Foreign Press Ball. Wilhelmstrasse etiquette has invented something new. It is felt that, in view of the depression, public officials should not be seen eating and drinking—with obvious enjoyment. From now on, cameramen will be allowed to take only post-digestive pictures. The table is usually pretty messy, and it cannot be said that the act of digestion improves the appearance of a diplomat. It seems rather silly to me, as I think the masses would not approve of their betters living in the same Spartan fashion that they, themselves, must, perforce, do. No one believes it, anyway.

December 12, 1931:

Everyone is glad to be invited to the home of the Secretary of the American Embassy, Clarence Hewes, whose wife is the daughter of Guggenheim. Mrs. Hewes' excellent taste, her wealth and connections, make her an exemplary hostess; her guests never have a dull minute.

For tea at the Hewes', where I met the Japanese Councilor of Embassy, Shigenori Togo. His German-born wife has already mastered her husband's language well enough to translate plays from German into Japanese. Slyly persistent in working for her husband's advancement, she has seen to it that she has "friends" everywhere. Her character is deeply hidden, and her first marriage is just never mentioned. It is known, however, that she was left in undisturbed possession of a daughter by the German predecessor of Shigenori Togo.

The wife of the new French Ambassador also attended. Mme. François-Poncet arrived only after the embassy was renovated. She does not think everything perfect yet. She wants to change and improve a lot, to bring paintings and tapestries from Paris. She has already become one of the chic hostesses of Berlin and is perfectly cast for the role. Her talking is animated and her manner amiable. She is a charming personality, absolutely *grande dame* and most attractive with her titian hair, slightly twinkling blue eyes, and lovely skin. She dresses extremely well, preferring soft light colors that match her own tints and make her appearance a most delicate one. I am very fond of her and feel that she likes me very much.

1932

Contemporary Events

January 9-10   Chancellor Bruening discusses the extension of Hindenburg's presidential term to avoid a too-heated election. Hitler, as leader of the second largest party, opposes Hindenburg.

January 27   Hitler speaks before the big industrialists on the invitation of Thyssen, in Dusseldorf-Rhineland.

February 26   Adolf Hitler, in order to become a naturalized German citizen, is sworn in as *Regierungsrat* at the Brunswick Legation in Berlin.

March 13   Hindenburg obtains relative majority in election. Hitler runs second. New election is announced.

April 10   Hindenburg elected a second time as President of the Reich with 19,350,240 votes.

April 14   Hitler's private armies, the S.A. and the S.S., disbanded by emergency decree of Hindenburg.

May 6   Hindenburg's second presidential term starts.

May 30   Chancellor Bruening and his cabinet resign.

June 1   Hindenburg nominates Franz von Papen Chancellor, as "the man of his confidence." Germany is governed with *Notverordnungen* ("emergency decrees").

June 4   The *Reichstag* is dissolved.

June	15	Hindenburg lifts ban on S.A. and S.S. formations.
July	9	Lausanne Treaty is signed. Germany is freed from reparation payments.
July	20	Papen dismisses high police and government officials and appoints himself head of these offices.
July	31	Another election for the *Reichstag*. Hitler shows a gain but cannot secure a majority.
August	13	Hitler sees Hindenburg. Asks to be appointed Chancellor. Hindenburg refuses the demand.
August	28	Hitler's follower, Hermann Goering, is elected President of the *Reichstag*.
November	6	Another election in Germany. Hitler loses votes.
November	16	Papen's cabinet resigns.
November	21	Hindenburg asks Hitler for his cooperation in a coalition cabinet. Hitler turns down Hindenburg's suggestions.
November	23	Hitler opens new campaign. Thyssen provides new funds.
December	2	Kurt von Schleicher, Minister of War, is appointed Chancellor of Germany.

January 15, 1932:

Louis P. Lochner of the Associated Press spoke to me this afternoon at the Sacketts' about the considerable extent of National Socialist preparations. He seemed seriously disturbed by the steady spread of their power and their growing number of followers. In his opinion, Bruening could put an end to it if he proceeded rigorously enough. Miles Bouton of the Baltimore *Sun*, who overheard our conversation, had information about Schleicher's intention to make Bruening negotiate with the National Socialists. No one can be completely informed about what is happening here without consulting the foreign correspondents. There are rumors that Bruening may resign. Bouton had heard that Hitler might be given a seat in the government merely to avoid a new presidential election. Hitler, however, had flatly refused.

January 29, 1932:

Society slowly gets accustomed to the originally plebeian National Socialist movement. People from the upper crust are turning to Hitler. They close their ears to his constant blasts against the aristocrats and the privileged classes, the *feine Leute.* My grandfather had a simple description of that type of turncoat: "You spit in his eye and he asks if it rains."

Conrad von Frankenberg, my companion at the races, had been in Dusseldorf where Hitler delivered a speech to the industrial leaders. Thyssen had made the arrangements for the Rhineland meeting. What induced him to choose January 27, ex-Kaiser Wilhelm's birthday, for the spectacle, God knows.

"Thyssen, in an address, pleaded for support of the Hitler party. The fervent Catholic Thyssen apparently had not read the Hitler bible very carefully."

Gonny had talked to numerous people in the Rhineland. They had all seemed enthusiastic. Old Kirdorf, president of the coal syndicate, had been in a virtual state of ecstasy, and so had General Litzman, victor of the Battle of Brecziny.

Dr. Gustav Krupp von Bohlen-Halbach, Director Kloeckner, and the big men of I.G. Farben made considerable donations on the spot. General von Ludendorff, who could not afford to part with any important sum, had pledged to take payment for interviews with foreign, especially American, reporters—and he will give the money to the National Socialist party. There was a rumor that the ore and coal potentates even suggested legislation for a ten percent tribute of their incomes to the good cause.

"Also, there have been arrangements for special openings to place important National Socialists within the industrial concerns: Jobs which would be effective on the payroll only—and very much so!—but which, would require neither skill nor knowledge, nor even the presence of the respective jobholders behind their desks."

He saw Franz von Papen and the head of the National party, Alfred Hugenberg, in Essen: "Papen has always played ball with the winning side. Now the political playboy deserts the black camp and joins the brown. It is there that he expects his bread to be buttered."

Gonny also mentioned the rumor concerning Bruening's suggested resignation in favor of Hitler. He said Bruening was advised to undertake this step by Schleicher and Oskar von Hindenburg.

The Crown Prince was willing to figure as a presidential candidate. He had, however, hinted a threat that should this prove impossible, he'd rather follow Hitler, since to a Hohenzollern, Hindenburg did not seem very trustworthy.

February 1, 1932:

A dreary Press Ball. Everybody gloomy and depressed. Unemployment increasing and the National Socialists causing trouble everywhere. When Otto Meissner tried to shock me by the statement that Lammers is a National Socialist, I answered with a blunt "And you?" Meissner preferred to drop the matter. As if I did not know that he had talked with Hitler for half an hour at the Kaiserhof recently.

February 12, 1932;

Got reserved seats for the celebration of the anniversary of the papal coronation at St. Hedwigskirche. On leaving, I had a little talk with Chancellor Bruening. Afterwards, I went to pay my annual visit to the Nuncio, Cesare Orsenigo. Saw the table was already set for the twenty-four illustrious dinner guests. Hindenburg was to be among them, and Bruening, whom the Nuncio holds in very high esteem. How gorgeous the vessels looked. A gift of Hindenburg to Eugenio Pacelli, the predecessor of Orsenigo. A lavish display of white and yellow tulips embellished the table.

My visits at Orsenigo's house have always been such a comfort to me. I told him: "I would be indescribably happy if only I could share in the mysticism with which your church so mercifully surrounds its adherents." Orsenigo held out his hand for me to kiss his ring and said: "I do understand your feelings, my child, as I do respect your scruples and that you have to be firm and remain faithful to the religion of your forefathers in times like these. But let me tell you that you will find our arms open to you if ever you wish to join us…"

The Catholic church has had this fascination for me ever since I was a child. During the years of public school and high school, I daily spent many hours with the nuns at a nearby convent.

February 23, 1932:

Thirteen American organizations sent out invitations for the celebration of Washington's two-hundredth birthday. I was Ambassador Sackett's personal guest among the five hundred people seated at small tables, but was not pleased to have Alois Westrick as neighbor. He is Dr. Albert's associate. During the war, Albert played a dubious role in the United States as an assistant to Von Papen. He holds this job on the board of directors of the German Ford plants, I suppose, rather because of his American wife than because of personal popularity in the United States.

Ambassador Sackett and the representative of Columbia University, Dr. Woodbridge, enthralled us by their speeches. Charles Kullmann, from the Metropolitan, sang.

I was glad when dinner was over and I could rise, for Westrick had been wisecracking in a nasty way all through dinner, tearing the American celebration to pieces.

February 25, 1932:

Luncheon at the Sacketts'. Frederick T. Birchall was there. He had recently arrived in Berlin from Geneva, where he covered the Disarmament Conference as the newly appointed director of the European Service of *The New York Times*.

He is very much liked by everybody and is on particularly good terms with Ambassador Sackett. English-born, and in appearance and manner he is the typical gentleman of the old school: elegant and chivalrous. His goatee has become more silvery since our last meeting during his visit in Berlin in 1929 when he was Managing Editor of *The New York Times*.

He is sharply critical of the National Socialists:

"I saw Hitler and his cohorts for the first time in 1929. Today, it seems to me, they already typify Germany. You meet them everywhere," he said angrily. "They are unavoidable, constantly parading and acting as if Germany was already theirs."

February 27, 1932:

Luncheon given by the Councilor of the French Embassy, Pierre Arnal, and his wife. All rather incensed about the peculiar goings-on at the Brunswick Legation. Hitler, in order to acquire German citizenship, arranged to have himself attached to the Brunswick Legation in Berlin, as *Regierungsrat.*

His aged Excellency, poor Dr. Boden, Minister of Brunswick, never knew what hit him. One day in advance of the ceremony, the legation was invaded by a horde of Hitler bodyguards. They occupied the entire building, turned it upside down in their search for possible hidden bombs, and made a general nuisance of themselves.

The English don't think it funny, as Hanover and Brunswick are the soft spots of all history-loving Britishers, and to have the Austrian housepainter naturalized by the Brunswick government seemed a personal affront to every wearer of the old school tie.

Breen, one of the English diplomats, said: "Why you naturalize that agitator instead of kicking him out of the country once and for all, along with his whole mob, is incomprehensible!"

You do not have to be an Englishman to feel that way about it.

March 6, 1932:

I have the feeling that the brown plague is becoming more and more contagious! One can't get away from their distasteful presence anywhere these days. Today, I had luncheon at the Kaiserhof with Baron Eduard von der Heydt, manager of the *Thyssenbank*, private banker and adviser to Emperor Wilhelm II. Eduard is the owner of a castle near the exiled Emperor's place in Holland. He has a priceless collection of East Asian art and some exceptionally valuable pictures.

The Kaiserhof grill was a nice picture of Nazi chiefs, relaxing in comfortable chairs. Some even showed up in their ugly brown uniforms. Quite a selection of them: Ritter von Epp, Munich group leader; Prince "Auwi," the fourth son of Wilhelm II; his friend, Count Wolff Helldorff, and Captain Ernst Roehm. Roehm had been in Bolivia reorganizing the army, and now Hitler, as a measure of precaution, has recalled him.

When Julius Streicher, publisher of the pornographic Nuremburg weekly, went by, the Brown party tendered him a unanimously cold shoulder. "There's a Nazi whom even the Nazis can't stand," said Heydt.

"I can't stand any of them," I retorted.

Heydt protested: "Do you think I can?"

"You'd better have a eye on your friend Fritz Thyssen, if that is so," I said. "He backs the whole gang financially."

Heydt said he couldn't do anything about it. He was well aware of the enormous danger.

"I took the precaution of placing quite a few of my valuable paintings with foreign museums, as a loan," he added, thoughtfully.

That is typical. They think of National Socialism in terms of the danger to a few canvases, their own wealth, themselves. They'll regret it, one fine day.

March 9, 1932:

In these days of internationl journalism, it is very fashionable to cover Russia. My American colleague, Knickerbocker, came through Berlin. His lectures on "Red Commerce" were extremely interesting and very well attended.

March 10, 1932:

Schulze-Pfaelzer, the "miniature National Socialist" in our office, had a proclamation on his desk this morning from the party press bureau:

"10 Lenzing,* 1932.

"We National Socialists are rising to power! Just when, is a question of time only. Please think about it. *Today* is the day to lend us your support. Don't appeal to the National Socialists once they are recognized as fit to govern, if you have denied them support in the days of their decisive struggle!"

It takes a strong stomach to stand this sort of thing. Empty, illiterate, ominous!

I hear Hitler absolutely declines to have his speeches recorded on sound films. A member of the foreign press asked Brueckner, his adjutant, for the reason. He shrugged his shoulders. "You can't alter a sound film," he said.

March 11, 1932:

Assigned to take pictures of the Old Gentleman, as the papers of the House of Ullstein are supporting him. I had an idea I wanted to snap him by his palace back door, where he sneaks out mornings to get his foreign papers. He was as docile as a child, or

---

*Lenzing in Teutonic means March.

rather, as an obedient soldier. We got shots in the garden, in his study, behind his desk. One I liked especially showed the *Ora et labora* device. We worked fast, not to bother the Old Gentleman too long.

When I was ready to leave, Hindenburg said, "You should try to be more punctual."

"I've never been late in my life," I said with astonishment.

"That's just it," he laughed. "You were three minutes ahead of time."

A strange man! Kindly and grumbling, stingy and generous. Holding fast to the most rigid observation of etiquette. On the other hand, begrudging himself the expense of a new hat. His old one is in such a state of dilapidation that his valet, who experiences a feeling of shame, has urged him repeatedly to get a new one. "This is good enough in these times of depression," he said.

March 12, 1932:

Chancellor Bruening spoke for Hindenburg's reelection at the Sports-Palast. The diplomatic corps attended. He spoke brilliantly. The public was enthusiastic. I sat next to Zivojin Balugdzic, Minister of Yugoslavia. The wonderful old man with the wise eyes and the white goatee sighed: "Hindenburg must win. The fate of the whole of Europe depends on it."

"And what if Hitler wins?" I asked.

He shrugged his shoulders and his eyes went dark.

Hugenberg, head of the German Nationals and spokesman for a united front of his party with the National Socialists, raises millions every year for the backing of the National Socialist party.

Both Mr. and Mrs. Hugenberg dance attendance on the Hitler crew. I think they may live to regret it. For if—God forbid!—Hitler comes through, he will probably have no use for the Hugenbergs and their kind.

March 13, 1932:

This is approximately how the people of the German Reich voted for President: Hindenburg: 18 million; Hitler: 11 million; Thaelmann: 4 million. Hindenburg's votes came to 49.6 percent of the total.

Since no candidate had the necessary 51 percent, the election must be held again.

March 15, 1932:

Tea at the home of Countess von der Groeben. Some talk about the "Painting Squads." These are gangs of roughnecks who drive through Berlin every night, painting swastikas and "We want Hitler" signs on the streets and buildings. A more important weapon in radical propaganda than is generally thought. The police try to stop them, but do not seem to get very far. One wonders how earnestly they really try.

Baron von Brandenstein was there. I think the Chamberlain to the Duke of Mecklenburg, who has his finger in many pies, is not adverse to more than a casual touch of the National Socialist doctrine. I heard him say that Hitler would abolish intermarriage, and that he will put all aristocrats in jail who are married to non-Aryans or have Jewish blood.

"Thank God," said Conny von Frankenberg. "In that case, they will all be together at last in prison and have a really exclusive circle."

April 14, 1932:

S.S. and S.A. formations having been disbanded by emergency decree, today Hindenburg decreed the same ban for all organizations of a similar character, regardless of party. This general decree was a consequence of Hitler's bellowing protest to the earlier decree.

April 15, 1932:

My friend "Poulette"—Wera von Huhn—and I were invited to a lecture at the National Club. This club pretends that it is without political party aims, being a purely social fellowship of German men and women for the strengthening of "national thought" and the reconstruction of the old powerful Germany. It looks to me as though they would be nearer to the truth if they eliminated the word "thought" and made it read "socialist."

During my Berlin years, Wera has become one of my closest friends, although she is more than twenty years older than I. We are, as a rule, the only two newspaper reporters at the more intimate diplomatic receptions. She speaks many languages, has seen most of the world, and is on exceedingly friendly terms with the Hohenzollerns.

"Heavens, Poulette!" I said. "If your husband, who was such an intimate friend of Bismarck, had seen you and me in that company!" Arthur von Huhn had written the political editorials for the *Koelnische Zeitung*. Their home was frequented by most of the great of prewar Germany.

Poulette seemed to brood over my remark. No, she did not think her late husband would have liked her to attend lectures at the National Club. During the summer of 1921, Hitler delivered his first speech at this club.

April 24, 1932:

Dr. Walter Zechlin, chief of press of the Foreign Office, has been transferred to Mexico as German minister. This is a bad omen that Hindenburg should choose—voluntarily?—to separate himself from the man whose report was "something to look forward to every morning." Zechlin is regarded as an opponent of the National Socialists.

That puts three thousand miles of blue water between Hitler and another of his enemies. The strategy is transparent, but it seems to work. Perhaps because it is transparent.

May 3, 1932:

Rolf, my old childhood friend, is just back from a trip around the world. We lunched at the Hotel Bristol, sitting in the small dining room in order to thumb our noses at the social code which decrees the right people should sit in the big dining room.

Rolf will probably enter the Foreign Office. He is keenly interested in the National Socialist agitation, having heard much about it in England. In 1923, he had been an officer in one of the *Reichswehr* divisions sent from Berlin to subdue the roughnecks in Munich. Then he had left Germany.

Hans von Raumer, former Minister of Finance, stopped at our table for a moment. He told us about last night's elaborate bachelor dinner at the home of Otto Wolff, the iron magnate. Everyone was there. The place was full of very satisfactory gossip, including news of Fritz Thyssen, who talks of nothing nowadays but the "Red danger."

"Thyssen," said Von Raumer, "has never been a bright person. Just dumb enough to be afraid of Communism without inquiring whether the remedy might not be worse than the disease."

May 12, 1932:

Dinner at the Venezuelan Minister's, Dr. Eduardo de Dagnino-Penny. We decided that Chancellor Bruening was having a tough time of it, what with the Old Gentleman being influenced and guided by his son, Oskar, and his Secretary of State, Otto Meissner, a chameleon of prodigious color-changing dexterity.

Meissner has maneuvered himself into high place. I remember, years ago, when Hindenburg first became President of the Reich, Meissner was one of those who called to congratulate him. His real intent was to find where he stood in the new regime. Hindenburg, apparently aware of his visitor's uncertainty, told him a little parable:

"When a lieutenant is promoted, he keeps his old sergeant-major."

I imagine you could actually hear the weight tumbling off Meissner's troubled chest.

"Bruening is doing his best to avoid another inflation," said one of the guests. "He thinks it would be disastrous in the long run, though it might bring some present relief."

Kurt von Schleicher came in for his share of criticism about his attitude toward the Chancellor. Too bad. I really do not like to see Schleicher act that way.

May 21, 1932:

Went to the races with Conny von Frankenburg, who has just returned from Switzerland. He said: "I don't like to live in Germany any longer. I am disgusted by the dirty politics behind the scenes. As my crowd is involved in all that unpleasant business, I prefer to stay away. In Switzerland, you hear all kinds of rumors. They say Bruening is going to resign and a good-for-nothing will take his place. Schleicher will become Minister of War in place of Groener, who has dug his political grave by disbanding the Storm Troopers."

Conny spoke also about the ever-growing friction within the different party camps. Gregor Strasser was trying to collaborate with Bruening; Roehm was said to be working hand in glove with Schleicher.

Things are getting complicated here. I respect Bruening, and I am very fond of Schleicher, so it sickens me to learn that Schleicher is supposed to have brought about Groener's downfall and that he is trying to jeopardize Bruening's position.

May 30, 1932:

Bruening and his entire cabinet have resigned. Hindenburg did not move a finger for the man who did more for his election than anybody else. Hindenburg called Franz von Papen the "man of my choice," and charged him to form the new cabinet. If I remember right, he used to call Bruening "man of my choice" not too long ago. The Old Gentleman's tastes seem to be rather flexible. Also, subconsciously, he probably has a preference for nobility. Klaussner said that the only foreign diplomat in Berlin who liked the change in government was François-Poncet.

June 1, 1932:

Schleicher is Minister of War now. Major Marks is his newly appointed press chief. He has a vituperative tongue. Schleicher's adjutants are Commander Hans von Langsdorff and Captain Noeldechen. His Chief of Cabinet is Colonel Ferdinand von Bredow, a very efficient man and an old friend of mine.

I met Schleicher for the first time years ago, at a party given by the former Argentine President, Alvear, when he visited Berlin. Schleicher is one of the few men who possess almost irresistible charm. A courageous and farsighted man, he can be very sarcastic at times. His voice is well modulated and so is his laughter. The latter is a delight for the ear as well as for the eye. It reveals two rows of almost impudently white and healthy teeth. Being very vivacious, he gesticulates, exhibiting his delicate, well-kept hands. He scrutinizes newcomers with a rather furtive glance out of his great blue eyes. The following pressure of his hand is revealing. He will hardly touch the fingers of a person who arouses his dislike. His grip is firm and warm if he takes a spontaneous liking.

June 6, 1932:

Hindenburg was at the races today. We had all gathered in front of the *Kavaliershaus* and waited for the dark blue limousine with the high chassis and the license plate IA 2990. Just then Schleicher arrived. He took me by the arm, impatient for my congratulations, and asserted his immutable friendship for me.

"We are going to remain friends forever," he said. He asked me to come and see him whenever I wanted to. "You have been my faithful comrade all these years. My office has orders to admit you at any time without previous appointment."

As always, hostess duty at the Union Club. We all had afternoon tea with the Old Gentleman. He was charming and complimented me on the success of my recent racetrack fashion shows. Schleicher mentioned my column in the *Vossische Zeitung*.

Hindenburg became highly interested: "The *Vossische* is my

favorite paper. Mainly because it published the notice of my birth," he said.

June 8, 1932:

For forty years, an annual party for the benefit of children's recreation homesteads has been given in the old garden of the Foreign Office. The green plot beneath the old trees, in peaceful seclusion behind thick gray walls, held a gay crowd this lovely early summer afternoon.

Elizabeth von Schleicher, wife of the newly appointed Minister of War, blossomed forth under all the flattering attention that was showered upon her. I am very much devoted to Elizabeth. She is slim and graceful, amiable and sincere. Her flawless complexion and delicate coloring are the prerogatives of youth only. A strange contrast to Martha von Papen, four days ago advanced to the rank of hostess at the Chancellery. She came with her son. There was no flattering attention paid to her, but neither was there much to flatter. Frau von Papen, speedily working to establish connections with the press, invited me to tea in her house, on June 12.

A little later, I discovered the political author, Edgar von Schmidt-Pauly, with his Swedish wife. She is an intriguer, her husband an opportunist. He always presents me with his latest creation, inscribed to me. The one decent thing about him is his frankness.

"I approve of Papen's attempt to collaborate with the National Socialists, and I happen to know that he sees Hitler repeatedly," he said.

"And I happen to know that you, too, are a National Socialist," I remarked. Which he did not bother to deny.

He told me that he sees Von Papen quite often, lunching with him at the *Herrenklub.*

That club is my journalistic problem child, as I am extremely curious about what goes on there, and they do not admit ladies.

The general conception has been that it is just another social setup, where you can get excellent food and decent drinks. I am beginning to understand, however, that these culinary excellences are only secondary in importance to the political play that goes on there. It was established in 1919 by a descendant of Friedrich von Schiller, and drew on the old nobility and the exclusive con- servatives for its membership. A few newcomers have been admitted, but they have had to make up in hard cash for their deficiency in blue blood. There are three hundred and seventy-seven members: eight genuine princes; thirty-eight genuine counts; fifty-nine genuine barons; one hundred mere gentry; sixty-two landowners; thirty-four ministers.

The place is a hotbed of carefully camouflaged intrigue.

The National Socialist Frau General Manna von Winterfeld, née von Rotenhan, chaperoned Anneliese Henkell. Anneliese is now Frau von Ribbentrop. I had not seen her in years. She was never a very bright girl. The years have not made her any brighter nor have they improved her looks. Her husband is said to be closely linked with Hitler and his thugs. Ribbentrop works for his father-in-law's firm, taking frequent trips to England, where he trades in champagne and has managed to build up good connections in society. How the Henkells feel about his National Socialist inclinations would be hard to guess.

The Winterfelds have always been monarchists. Detleff von Winterfeld became a member of the conservative *Volkspartei* some years ago. They entertain a great deal. Lately you meet strange people in their house, people whom one would not have met there in the not too remote past. They are very correct in tuxedo, or even white tie, if the occasion calls for it. If you meet them in broad daylight in the street, you are very likely to behold them dressed in S.S. and S.A. uniforms. Which did not prevent Frau von Winterfeld the other day from executing her curtsy at the home of the Crown Princess, in a more courtly fashion than any of the other ladies present.

June 12, 1932:

Tea at the Papens. Frau von Papen is a born Boch von Galhau, connected with a great clan of French families. She is as homely as she is rich. She surpasses even Margarete von Hindenburg in lack of elegance. Her neck is squeezed into a corset of pearls. Her black dress is faded to a threadbare green and her mousy hair is done in a careless bun.

Von Papen appeared for a little chat with his wife's guests. I had met him before. His constant grin and his suave attitude have helped carry him a good distance.

I was mildly amused to see how much young Von Papen basks in his father's success. In fact, one would think he had a share in

Daddy's accomplishments. Present also were a couple of well-behaved, insipid daughters.

A family ill-favored enough to go far.

June 13, 1932:

Caught a terrific cold, with all the trimmings, including temperature. Too annoying just now, with the *Assaut d'Escrime*, a charity affair under the sponsorship of Hassan Nachat, which I am supposed to arrange. And a couple of days after that, the houseboat party Poulette and I are giving for the diplomatic corps is due.

June 20, 1932:

Mammi von Carnap came to see me today. As always, she was full of news: "Hindenburg seems in bad shape, aged, depressed. His supporters resent the breach of faith against Bruening. Papen has lifted the ban from the S.A. and dismissed the Prussian government. Papen seems always most lenient in his handling of the 'reconstruction-minded' part of the Right Wing. The so-called rebellious gang of the Left Wing, however, is treated most rigorously."

Well, this piece of Solomonic wisdom sounds like Pappi von Carnap to me. He is a proud, honest soul. His integrity has not been shaken by the republic. He asserts that no new form of government other than monarchistic will ever make him yield.

June 28, 1932—Bad Reichenhall:

The doctors decided I needed the cure. Have not been here for ages. I like the old places, where I played as a little girl, and am happy to be back in my beloved mountains.

Nature is perfect here, and only one jarring note is struck. Berchtesgaden is near, and it is there that Hitler lives, poisoning the pure mountain air. At the *Kur Promenade*, you see people who would not ordinarily be at Reichenhall for their health. What causes General Field Marshal von Mackensen to go stamping up and down the garden path? He seems to be uninterested in his surroundings, though the story is that he is present for relaxation. Strange, then, that he should make so many visits to Berchtesgaden to find his relaxation!

The Krupps, from the Rhineland, are here, too. They had tea with Hitler. A long way to go for a social call. People with simple minds might misunderstand, I should think.

Richard Tauber, who does not belong among the social visitors at the Berghof, is the center of attraction. He loves it. When he clears his throat, a whisper runs up and down the onlookers. When he opens his mouth, it is practically a news item.

July 13, 1932:

Went to Berchtesgaden yesterday. The S.A. had a monster parade. The word "monster" is fitting, I think. The brown monster rolled along the road from Reichenhall to Berchtesgaden. The pounding of their boots haunted my mind all night long. Will there be anybody who can stop the stamping of their feet all over Germany?

When I was small, I loved parades. I hate them now. The feet pound, pound, pound, and under their thunderous, insensitive impact lies my beautiful country.

Ran a temperature again. My ego's protest, I suppose.

August 12, 1932:

Back in Berlin, my mind still reeling from the effect of the Brown Shirt parade. I told Louis Ullstein about the dangerously hypnotic power of the movement. He waved aside my concern lightly.

"You're beginning to hear voices, Bella. You ought to do something about those nerves of yours." I wish it were only my nerves.

Mammi von Carnap told me over the phone that Hitler is going to be received by Hindenburg. Also that Papen had dismissed Braun and Severing, along with many other high officials, and appointed himself head of the police.

Mammi's report was on my mind the whole day, and tonight Rolf came in to welcome me home and bring me up to date on what has been happening.

"I was at police headquarters on July 20 when Papen's patrol of several young officers forced their way in, hand grenades in their leather belts. They presented a decree demanding the immediate resignation of President of Police Albert Grzesinski, Vice-President Bernhard Weiss, and Commander of Police Colonel Heimannsberg. A bullet or two might have changed the picture, but they could not well rebel against the orders of their superior. Besides, Prime Minister Otto Braun was ill and on leave of absence, but Home Office Minister Dr. Carl Severing had already meekly surrendered."

Hindenburg issued an emergency decree the next day, but we think it possible that he did not approve and was deliberately misinformed. Still, the fact that Hindenburg did not move a finger for a man like Grzesinski is almost criminal. After the desertion of the Kaiser in 1918, Grzesinski had lent the Field Marshal a helping hand, so that he could set up headquarters in Wilhelmshoehe, near Cassel.

This is his reward. Is it senility, or is it treachery?

August 13, 1932:

Mammi von Carnap was right. I saw Frau Meissner today, who told me confidentially: "Otto and the Major have persuaded Hindenburg to receive Hitler this afternoon. Papen is rehearsing Hitler for the audience this minute.

August 15, 1932:

Big tea at the Karl Schurz Society, where I met more than one character who might cause the founders of this liberal organization to revolve rapidly in their graves. There was the organization's secretary, Dr. Hans Draeger, who is beyond question a National Socialist. He helps make the place a hotbed of political intrigue.

He tried the old stupid trick of provocation, saying derogatory things about the National Socialists and noting well his victim's reaction.

On the way home, I met Commander Langsdorff of Schleicher's office. "What is the current Hindenburg reaction to our beautiful Adolf?" I asked.

He shook his head slowly, hesitating. "My Minister thinks we ought to include National Socialists in the government, but he's against Hitler. He's pulling for Gregor Strasser. That's all I know."

August 30, 1932:

The inevitable has happened! Hermann Goering, Adolf Hitler's intimate associate, has been appointed president of the *Reichstag*.

August 30, 1932:

"Kaiser Adolf" reviewed the parade of the members of his *Reichstag* faction. The great event took place at Hitler's Berlin residence, the Kaiserhof. I happened to have an appointment there with a friend, and we watched the show together. There was a crowd of onlookers, but there was nothing for them to look at.

Those who were willing to spend some money for the show sat in the lobby, sipping their tea and waiting for hours before anything happened.

A handful of National Socialists sat scattered throughout the lobby. They drowned their boredom in huge quantities of beer. Count Helldorff, the Berlin Storm Troop leader, was pacing the floor. He was the instigator of the Jew-baiting on *Kurfuerstendamm* in celebration of the Jewish New Year's Day, last year. Foreign correspondents dropped in. Familiar with Hitler's unpunctuality, they hung around for about an hour and then gave up.

Finally, at seven o'clock, the curtain rose. Side doors were flung open. The higher-up Brown Shirts poured in. The rather dreary looking lobby suddenly took on the gaudy aspect of a country fair. The monotony of the brown background was most successfully relieved by a colorful orgy of sky blues, bright reds, golden yellows, grass greens, and deep purples, distributed cleverly over a variety of badges, ornaments, cords, stripes and insignia. The Brown Shirts strutted around like peacocks, happily unaware of their absurdity. Their large brown trousers were of such widely exaggerated cut that they seemed to bear wings on either side. Although the brown shirts gave them an unkempt look, they seemed intoxicated by their own masquerade and lived up to their roles, walking through with a certain grimly juvenile belligerency.

When the faction had formed its ranks, a low murmur filled the lobby and, of a sudden, "Manitu," their Fuehrer, appeared. He crossed the lobby, his face bearing a seriously warlike expression. Hands flew up. *Heil* boomed in a multiple echo from the high ceiling.

Hitler knows his game. He is careful not to spoil his people with an overdose of his divine presence. He looked at no one. In a jiffy he had vanished through one of the side doors. I suppose he took his tea in splendid isolation. General von Epp, Minister of Thuringia, Frick, Gregor Strasser, and Dr. Goebbels stayed behind.

When the show was over, some people burst into laughter. Foreigners, of course. *They* have no reason to conceal their hilarity.

August 31, 1932:

I met Schmidt-Pauly at the lovely Frohnau Polo Grounds. I played dumb to make "vain Edgar" talkative. I asked, "What does a 'Government of National Concentration' really mean?"

"Well, just what Papen is trying to accomplish. He wants to rule in collaboration with the National Socialists. Hitler's audience with Hindenburg was not successful, but the Old Gentleman will be softened up. Papen has suggested that Hitler should send his confidential men to join the cabinet and that he should himself bide his time and keep in the background for the president. Papen is confident that Hindenburg will get used to the idea of a National Socialist form of government. There is no doubt that the leader of the strongest party must eventually become a member of the government."

Again and again I have heard this argument lately. Mostly from Nationalists and monarchists. First they deserted their Emperor. Now they desert the republic and turn to these gangsters. They think they can seize power, using the Brown mob as a tool. I suspect the tool will turn and ruthlessly sweep aside everybody who does not stand with them uncompromisingly.

September 11, 1932:

Whenever "Empress Hermine," Kaiser Wilhelm's second wife— the "Quotation Mark Empress," as Conny von Frankenberg calls her—comes to the capital, she attends one of the Countess von der Groeben's Sunday afternoon receptions.

This time the hostess, who is eighty-five years old, gave her "imperial" guest a slight inkling of what was in her mind. She said in her impeccably courteous and grand manner: "Your Majesty, I have been told that your sympathies are with the National Socialists. Is it true that His Majesty has made a donation to the National Socialists?"

Hermine stood there in embarrassed silence.

September 14, 1932:

Last Sunday, at the races, I was standing with Kurt von Schleicher, and Conny. "Isn't it funny that Papen had to dissolve his Reichstag before it had been in session," said Conny.

Talk of the wolf. Papen joined our group. Slick and smooth. First he kissed my hand. Next a smile: "Hello, Minister." Then: "How are you these days, Conny?" He was all exaggerated politeness—in public. "Frau Bella, wouldn't it be a good idea to take a group picture for your paper..."

I am sure he wants the photo published in my paper just to convince the world that he is on friendly terms with the Minister of War.

October 2, 1932:

Had tea at the Norbert von Baumbachs. He is a naval officer in the Ministry of War, and I've been suspicious of him for some time. Today's tea did much to confirm my suspicions. Pavel Skoropadski was the center of attention.

This Skoropadski is the same stooge who was Otto Meissner's friend when the latter was appointed temporary German Chargé d'Affaires to the Ukraine after the German occupation of the Ukraine in 1917, a "protectorate" which lasted until the Allies had won the war. General Hoffman, charged with restoring order in the Ukraine after the separation from Russia, had suggested that Germany appoint Skoropadski "hetman," or regent.

Since I saw Skoropadski sipping champagne at the Kaiserhof with Dr. Alfred Rosenberg, Baltic National Socialist and chief of the *Voelkischer Beobachter*, I have had no doubts concerning the hetman and the houses where he is generally to be found.

October 11, 1932:

The Egyptian Minister, Hassen Nachat Pasha, entertained about four hundred guests to celebrate his King's coronation day. There was a slim Egyptian dancer who gave a rather discreet approximation of her typical oriental dances. During this dance, I noticed that the apostolic Nuncio, Monsignore Orsenigo, whose crimson headgear stood out in the crowd, turned to the wall to scrutinize most intently an enormous portrait of King Fuad I, which is dazzlingly illuminated on festive occasions.

October 19, 1932:

They get in everywhere, these National Socialists. They are patient, they bore from within and from without. Especially do they court the diplomats. At a dinner the other night, they revealed their interest in the Far East by paying careful attention to Ghulam Sittiq Khan, Afghanistan Minister. The attending diplomats were practically surrounded by National Socialists. One of them was Viktoria von Dirksen; another, the former Secretary of State, Werner von Rheinbaben, her son-in-law.

Frau von Dirksen, relict of the *Geheimrat* Willibald von Dirksen, always a monarchist, has for years been an eager hostess of the National Socialists in her magnificent palace. Hitler, Goering, Goebbels, Helldorff, and the other accomplices have their weekly meetings at her home. When the Storm Troop organization was banned by Hindenburg, they used to arrive there in full uniform

concealed under long capes. She has acted as a mediator between
the National Socialists and the old courtiers. Her brother, Karl
August von Laffert, the "German Jules Verne," attends his sister's
receptions in the full splendor of his S.S. uniform. "Auwi," Prince
August Wilhelm, is generally to be found there in his brown
uniform, and both the hostess and her youngest daughter wear
the swatiska pinned conspicuously on their bosoms.

One of the lady's daughters is married to Werner von Rheinbaben. She is not a National Socialist, though the movement
fascinates her husband. Frau von Dirksen's stepson, Herbert, is
Ambassador in Moscow. I do not know if he is a Nazi. That may
come out later, when the occasion calls it forth.

October 20, 1932:

It really was a typical trick and well carried out. You've got to
give the National Socialists credit for that. They're masters at
turning other people's meetings to their own uses. There was to be
a meeting of the German National party. The subject to be
discussed was freedom of speech. They invited the National
Socialists to attend and join in the discussion, admission tickets to
be split fifty-fifty. That was their big mistake, because the National Socialists immediately had a few hundred extra tickets
printed—or rather, counterfeited—and handed out to party
members. Several hours before the scheduled meeting, every seat
was taken. By National Socialists. It left the hosts hanging around
outside the doors and in the lobbies and corridors.

November 10, 1932:

The Duce has sent a very pleasant man as successor to Orsini
Baroni. The new Ambassador is Vittorio Cerruti. Not to mention
Signora Elisabeth Cerruti, born Paulay. She is Hungarian by birth
and an extremely cultured and well-bred woman. She has been an
actress and is said to be Jewish. Marchese Antinori, the chief of
press of the embassy, introduced me before the official reception.
Mrs. Cerruti offered spontaneously to help me with my charity
work.

November 14, 1932:

At the wedding of Paula von Reznicek, born Heymann, to the
auto racing ace, Hans von Stuck. A gay wedding, glittering and
lively, like Paula herself. Ernst Udet, the flier, was best man. He is

working in a movie with Leni Riefenstahl, the film star, and Franz Sokal, the Hungarian motion picture producer.

Udet gave me a bit of a shock. He asked whether I knew Wilhelm Staar.

"Certainly. Poor devil. I helped get him a newspaper job."

"Exactly," said Udet. "As society columnist. Just made-to-order for him. He is a salon spy for the National Socialists."

I never suspected him. It seems there are traitors everywhere. Which reminds me that I bumped into Hjalmar Schacht this morning in the lobby of the Kaiserhof. The mob loitering there greeted him with raised arms and "*Heil* Hitler." I had caught him, wing collar, rather soiled vest, and all, on his way to the Fuehrer. He smiled wryly at me, a trifle embarrassed. Wonder what he's up to? Nothing that bodes good to any decent people, you can be certain.

November 16, 1932:

This week I was a guest at the Russian Embassy. Lots of the German *Lufthansa* people around. Talked to Director Martin Wronsky, who brought Erhard Milch with him. Milch is an intimate of Goering and has been working with him in the Bavarian motor plants.

Professor Ferdinand Sauerbruch, the famous surgeon and a gruff old bear, was deeply engrossed in a conversation with Albert Einstein. They stood there, unaware of the movement around them, regal in their intellectual aloofness. Einstein's head is beautiful to look at.

November 19, 1932:

Papen has had to go. Except for the German Nationals, the great mass of the people was against him, although he always assumed the right to speak in their name. Actually, he has never represented anyone but the small group of huge estate owners who thought that this might be the moment to seize power.

I think they underrate the radical movement. One of these fine mornings, they will awake to the fact that, in their search for willing tools, they have created a new master class.

November 29, 1932:

The National Socialists seem so certain of their eventual triumph that already they are allowing themselves the privilege of being selective. "Empress" Hermine's suggestion that some of the new people attend her charity bazaar was flatly turned down by the Brown heroes. They permitted it to be known that they wished to be left alone "by that Hohenzollern woman."

December 1, 1932:

Charity tea at Herman Gerson's department store. Sat with Edith Zarden, née Orenstein. Her husband is rather an important man in the Finance Ministry, and Schacht thinks highly of him.

"Bella, your Schleicher will be appointed Chancellor," she said in suppressed excitement. "I only hope my husband gets advanced, too. But please don't mention that in your column."

When Edith talks that way, it has already happened, in all probability. As though I need to be warned about what I write these days, when almost any word can come back and hit one squarely in the eye.

December 2, 1932:

The "Empress" had some one hundred thirty guests for tea today at her charity bazaar. Regret about the lost monarchy was frankly stated. Hermine had a rather superior smile on her lips, almost smug. For the Doorn household has no doubt that Hitler is going to smooth the path for the Hohenzollern restoration.

"Her Majesty" received in black velvet, lavishly trimmed with lace. It trickled down her back on a background of pink chiffon. I was careful to avoid the customary hand kiss when my turn came, as her white kid gloves looked by that time like an ordnance map in white and red from the lipstick of those who had kissed before.

December 8, 1932:

Dinner at Hassan Nachat Pasha's. Karl von Wiegand, Hearst representative, sat next to me at table. He has an uncanny flair for politics. Seeing him unexpectedly is always a sort of a shock to me. Dear Karl appears on the scene whenever a political melodrama is about to sweep the stage.

"When are the National Socialists going to seize the government?" I welcomed him. The dear old "alarm signal" seemed a bit taken aback. However, he did not guess that I was bluffing.

"It won't be long now," he said.

Wiegand has always reckoned on a National Socialists *coup d'état*. He has considered Hitler a man who really meant business ever since 1921, when he first interviewed him. I asked him whether he thought that the present setback of the radicals could not be used to bring them to a definite and permanent stop.

He gave no direct reply. "Hitler intends to abolish the treaty of Versailles. He wants to unite all Germans. He has no desire for the return of colonies if he finds a way for new *Lebensraum* within Central Europe, to install all the regained German subjects. One of Hitler's early associates, Professor Karl von Haushofer, has been studying the *Lebensraum* problem for years. He has persuaded Hitler that an expansion to the east, peaceful or by force, is an inevitable necessity."

December 10, 1932:

Colonel Theodor Duesterberg, Deputy Stahlhelm leader, is mad at my editors. "You are too Leftist. I will not have my name mentioned in your paper," he said to me during dinner at the home of the Hungarian minister, Koloman von Kanya. I bowed my head and let him thunder. "I hope the *Stahlhelm* comes to its senses before it is too late. They could stop that game. It is absurd to let a political party become a state within the state, with its own offices and international representatives. That can only end badly!"

The *Stahlhelm* is a politically active Rightist organization consisting of World War veterans. Duesterberg, one of the candidates in the last presidential election, is the real brains of the *Stahlhelm*. He has background, vitality, and courage—all of which Franz Seldte, the *Stahlhelm* chief, seems to lack.

Rolf said: "Duesterberg is a grand chap. I sometimes wonder whether his extraordinary intelligence is not, perhaps, due to a remote Jewish ancestor."

December 14, 1932:

Party for Ernst Lubitsch, a brilliant and witty motion picture man, given by Secretary of State Otto Meissner. I asked Lubitsch why he no longer worked here.

"That's finished," he said. "I'm going to the United States. Nothing good is going to happen here for a long time. The sun shines every day in Hollywood."

December 16, 1932:

Ball of the *Auslandsbund Deutscher Frauen*. This organization of German women abroad is becoming a sort of sounding board for radical propaganda. You hear a great deal of talk there about *Lebensraum*, and about the abolition of the treaty of Versailles.

A great many diplomats appeared at the ball last night. It surprises me that international circles attend these festivities at all, but I suppose it can be considered part of the job of being a diplomat.

The old Potsdam and Berlin elite were present in force, including Crown Prince Wilhelm and Crown Princess Cecilie.

Count Helldorff was asked why he did not wear formal tails. He announced in an exceedingly loud voice: "Because the S.A. uniform expresses my convictions. If the Hohenzollerns have any objections, let them kick me out of here." A thoroughly boorish character, an opportunist who has found that brutality pays good dividends.

It was rather disconcerting to discover how many new sympathizers for National Socialism are to be found in the ranks of the old-time nobility. The evening was studded with small annoyances. During dinner, Poulette and I had a dispute with Count Rex-Gieshubel.

"Times will improve for the landowners if Hitler comes to power," he informed us gratis. "And besides, Hitler will restore the monarchy." The old story. We tried to make him see how fatuous this idea was. That the National Socialists were simply using the "degenerate aristocrats" as very convenient stepping-stones. No use.

My irriation grew when I saw the emperor's fourth son, August Wilhelm, "Auwi," cross the dining room in the full splendor of a brown uniform.

Met Magda Goebbels there, the wife of Dr. Joseph Goebbels, Hitler's Berlin *Gauleiter*. She's had something of a career. I remember her as Mrs. Guenther Quandt.

When she left school, her foster parents found her a secretarial job. I don't know how good a secretary she was, but she was attractive enough to draw the notice of an exceedingly wealthy friend of her employer. She married him.

As Mrs. Guenther Quandt, she had everything she could wish for. Her husband adored her, and when she gave birth to a son, there seemed to be little left that a woman could want. She had been tossed around a bit by life, as her parents, named Rietschel, had separated soon after her birth. Mamma Rietschel had moved with her daughter from the Rhineland to Belgium, and when the

World War broke out and the German troops marched into Belgium, Mamma took herself and her daughter to Berlin. Magda was placed with a well-to-do Jewish family named Nachmann and was brought up with their daughter, who was about the same age.

Her mother married a Jewish waiter by the name of Friedlander.

With her marriage, Magda found herself in the exact center of a secure, luxurious, warm existence. But she could not take it. She became capricious and pretentious. Her husband, considerably older, dreaded her outbursts. She made his life miserable.

In November, 1926, a certain clubfooted Dr. Joseph Goebbels came to Berlin. He was welcomed by a handful of party comrades, but in the main, the population was totally unaware of his arrival. Hitler appointed the peculiar looking dwarf *Gauleiter* of Berlin and head of the National Socialist propaganda office. His job was "to conquer Red Berlin."

But business in Berlin was improving. Agitators could not reap much of a harvest on comparatively healthy economic grounds, so the Doctor advertised for an additional job. That's how Goebbels became tutor to little Harald Quandt.

Goebbels is a fascinating talker, and it was not long before Harald's mother became interested, despite the tutor's crippled foot. There was such fire, such verve, such absolute logic in the man. She went to meetings with him occasionally, and at last came her big moment. She met Hitler. At that time, the National Socialists were scaring the rich out of such wits as they happened to have by warning them constantly of the coming "Red Tide." It frightened financial contributions out of pockets that, up to this point, had been open only to receive. Magda induced her husband to donate funds to the party.

Magda's pretty little head swam in a dizzy confusion of conflicting doctrines. She became interested in Buddhism and for a while was absorbed in this ancient philosophy. The National Socialist ideology seized her imagination as nothing had up to now, but it mingled uneasily with the remains of Zionist doctrine with which she had been inculcated by her old friend, Arlosoroff, the Zionist. This friendship dated far back to the time when she still had to take dictation and pound a typewriter. She had met the Zionist at a ball of international students, and she had become exceedingly attached to him.

"If rich Guenther Quandt had not come along," remarked

Conny von Frankenberg when Magda entered the stately dining room with Viktoria von Dirksen, "who knows where she'd be now. Probably doing sentinel duty in front of a Palestine *Kibbutz*, rifle on shoulder and an Old Testament password on her lips."

In December, 1931, she married Joseph Goebbels. Adolph Hitler was best man, holding little Harald by the hand. Harald was in Hitler Youth uniform. The pressure used to induce the boy's father to give him up has not been disclosed, but it was obviously effective.

Magda's mother, Mrs. Friedlander, renounced her Jewish marriage. She severed the Hebraic ties of wedlock and dropped a name that might at some future time prove to be compromising. Pressure was not lacking here, either, for the marriage had been happy enough. She is now Auguste Behrendt, which is her maiden name, and runs a drugstore in the north of Berlin, at Borsigsteg. A Nazi success story.

Tonight at the ball, Magda was lovely. No jewels except the string of pearls around her neck. Her golden hair owes nothing to any drugstore or chemist. It, too, is real. Her big eyes, iridescent and ranging from dark blue to steel gray, radiate icy determination and inordinate ambition.

"How do you like her?" asked François-Poncet. And without waiting for my answer, he added: "I never saw such ice-cold eyes in a woman."

December 17, 1932:

Yesterday's charity tea, an orphan benefit, for some reason or other filled me with foreboding that this might be one of my last performances in that line. Mrs. Cerruti brought along the Italian Secretary of State, Fulvio Suvich. He showed his willingness to help the cause by putting a handsome collection of bank notes into my hand. A pleasant person, smart and vivacious, though unattractive.

"What do you do to attract people to these things?" he asked. "You've got them fighting for tickets."

"I get a few of the right people. The snobs, who are much more numerous—those who have a great deal of money—follow as a matter of course. It's just a formula."

December 18, 1932:

This morning, I dropped by to say hello to Schleicher. He had some visitors, and I could not wait because of an early luncheon date. I left my little bunch of lilies of the valley with Bredow. He smiled: "Who told you that these are his favorite flowers?"

"I guess it must be love," I said.

This evening, his orderly delivered a handwritten note of thanks, from Schleicher: "It was sweet of you. Please come again."

I am glad he understood this little gesture. I am fond of him, and I know what a strenuous time he has.

December 19, 1932:

Charity party for the *Cecilienwerk* at the Hotel Esplanade. Although it is usually an affair sponsored by the Crown Princess and most exclusive in its membership, this time the admission tickets were on public sale, bringing a crowd more colorful than actually distinguished.

Viktoria von Dirksen again brought Magda Goebbels. It is stomach-turning to see how people abase themselves to enter her good graces. General von Witzendorff, the corpulent former Berlin Town-Commander, as well as the Potsdam Town-Commander, Colonel von Pogrell, behaved in a way which revealed more than a slight Nazi inclination.

The Crown Prince appeared in the uniform of his old regiment, the *First Leibhusaren*. His brother Oskar was present, also the Duke Adolf Friedrich zu Mecklenburg, the Mayor of Berlin Dr. Sahm, and the Papens.

The Hugenbergs were also there, sturdy Alfred as funny a sight as ever with his military haircut, full-spreading mustache, small eyes hidden in rolls of fat, and a perpetual leer on his face.

December 22, 1932:

Reception at the Messersmiths, given by the American Consul General in honor of the American orchestra conductor, Howard Hanson. He is here as representative of the Oberlander Trust of the Karl Schurz Memorial Foundation in Philadelphia. I had a chance to talk to the host alone while examining a new piece in his china collection. He expressed himself as being worried about the political situation:

"The German government had better act quickly, and strongly," he said. "It's really upsetting to find so many people of importance in the National Socialist party. There are going to be fireworks here pretty soon, unless I'm badly mistaken."

I do not think that my friend Messersmith is mistaken.

December 23, 1932:

The Rotters sent me the traditional invitation for their Christmas performance. It was the opening night of *Catherine I*, with Gitta Alpar and Gustav Froehlich. *Tout* Berlin had been planted throughout the orchestra and in the boxes. To my pleased surprise I found the Schleichers in the box next to mine. Captain Noeldechen and Commander Hans von Langsdorff were with them.

Both were in uniform. "It is our private demonstration against 'private armies,'" said Langsdorff.

Schleicher was in mufti. When he kissed my hand, I said: "Kurt, you promised me you would always wear your uniform. You know mufti is most unbecoming to you." Elisabeth gave me a grateful look. "He won't listen to me," she said.

She told me he was overworked, being at his desk until 2 A.M. and later night after night. This was the first exception he had made in ages.

After the show, the Rotters gave a brilliant reception in their Grunewald villa. A bit superelaborate. Floods of champagne, gigantic lobsters, a fantastic cold buffet. I was at a table with the Meissners and the François-Poncets. Meissner, known for his greediness on such occasions, darted away and returned with a huge plate of lobster. He and Madame set to work as if they had been starving for weeks. François-Poncet nudged his wife, grinned, and, with obvious malice, helped himself and Mme. François-Poncet to a very moderate little snack.

I think the gesture was lost on the Meissners.

December 28, 1932:

Intimate dinner at the Schleichers. Twelve guests. The talk almost exclusively on domestic politics. I told Schleicher about my conversation with Karl von Wiegand. I emphasized Wiegand's opinions, because I knew Schleicher wouldn't listen to my own thoughts on such subjects.

Schleicher laughed. "You journalists are all alike. You make a living out of professional pessimism."

"These aren't just Wiegand's ideas, or mine alone. Everyone knows that Papen and Hugenberg, with their *Herrenklub* clique, are trying to bring the National Socialists to power."

"I think I can hold them off," said Schleicher.

"As long as the Old Gentleman sticks to you," I said.

Later we happened to be alone in his study. "In confidence, Bella, I think a lot of Gregor Strasser. National Socialist, but far over on the Leftist side of it. Maybe, if I had him in the cabinet..."

"How about the church and Jew-phobia of the party?" I inquired.

"You ought to know me better than that, Bella," he said. "All that will be dropped entirely. I'd like to have your friend Bruening back, sooner or later."

The National Socialist party is not in the habit of dropping anything that suits its purposes. They scuttle men quicker than they scuttle doctrines.

1933

Contemporary Events

January	4	Hitler, Von Papen and Joachim von Ribbentrop meet at a dinner party at the house of von Schroeder, Cologne banker, to discuss further steps.
January	28	Schleicher and his government resign.
January	30	Hindenburg asks Hitler to form the new government.
February	1	*Reichstag* is dissolved.
February	10	Diplomatic dinner at Hindenburg's. Hitler appears for the first time in international society as Chancellor.
Feburary	27	*Reichstag* fire.
March	5	Election. Hitler wins 288 seats.
March	10	National Socialists occupy Bavarian government offices. The black-red-gold flags of the republic are ordered burned.
March	14	Hitler's propagandist, Dr. Paul Joseph Goebbels, is appointed Minister of Propaganda and Public Enlightenment.
March	21	The "Day of Potsdam." *Reichstag* convenes in Garrison Church, Potsdam. Hindenburg invokes return of historic Potsdam spirit.
April	1	Streicher organizes boycott-Jew day all over Germany.
May	1	Celebration of the May Day on the Tempelhof Field.

May	10	Goebbels orders the burning of 20,000 books to "cleanse German literature of alien element."
May	17	Hitler confirms his peaceful intentions and readiness to sign any nonaggression pact.
June	7	Four Power Pact between Germany, England, France and Italy accepted.
June	22	Social Democratic party suspended. Funds and possessions of the unions confiscated.
June	27	Alfred Hugenberg resigns as Minister for Economic Affairs. The first opportunist falls.
July	9	Von Papen reaches concordat between Holy See and Germany.
July	15	Four Power Pact between Germany, England, France and Italy is signed in Rome.
July	18	Arthur Henderson, the English labor leader and president of the Disarmament Conference, visits Berlin.
August	7	France, Italy and Great Britain protest German activities in Austria.
August	20	Hitler orders *Reichsautostrassen* ("auto highways").
August	20	Start of *Reichstag* fire trial in Leipzig.
October	14	Germany withdraws from Disarmament Conference and from the League of Nations.
November	12	New *Reichstag* election. All parties suppressed.
November	13	"Fighters League for Austria" is founded in Germany as a substitute for the Austrian German Peoples League which was dissolved by Austrain Chancellor, Engelbert Dollfuss.
December	1	Hitler declares state and party as one unit: *"Partei und Staat sind eins."*

January 17, 1933:

Foreign Minister von Neurath sent out five hundred invitations for a soirée at the Friedrich Leopold Palace. His own private quarters in the garden of the A.A. are too small for such a reception.

Konstantin von Neurath, a heavy but good-looking man and outwardly jovial, comes from conservative circles. He has been German Ambassador to Rome and London. In June, 1932, when Von Papen became Chancellor, he called Von Neurath to Berlin as his Foreign Minister. He is well liked in diplomatic circles, but I don't think he has much character. He is covetous and self-interested, wealthy and mean. Mrs. von Neurath matches the heavy appearance of her spouse, being proud and fully as mean. She poses as a "Queen Mother," Rolf says. Last night, she wore a gown of dark red velvet, her famous pearls hanging around her neck, a priceless tiara glittering in her graying hair, and several medals pinned to her considerable bosom. She was the very picture of haughtiness.

Although the evening was a glittering, elaborate affair, there was an almost visible tension. The daily battles between the National Socialists and their antagonists have strained everyone's nerves.

The Chancellor of the Reich was, once again, unable to accept the invitation. Bad omen!

Colonel von Bredow, his right-hand man, was there. He told me about the almost inhuman strain weighing upon the Chancellor, who has endless conferences and sessions. "He seems to have made up his mind that, at this point, it would be wise to embody the National Socialists in the government. In his opinion, it will be easier to keep them under control when their activities are legalized. He also is confident that by letting them have a share in the responsiblity, their rowdyism will subside.

"Lately he has been having frequent talks with Gregor Strasser. He thinks him a very able man. Schleicher said to me this morning: 'I'm sure Papen dislikes the National Socialists as much as I do. But he doesn't mind using them for the purpose of getting rid of me.' Schleicher suffers from the almost hostile coolness of the President."

"Why doesn't he do something about it, then? To me he seems hypnotized," I said.

"Von Schleicher thinks it wiser to have them bring about their own ruin. It would be wrong to hold them back by force at a moment when the majority of the German people seem to favor them. The Chancellor also knows that Hitler saw and met Gregor Strasser in Weimar last Monday—no doubt for the purpose of conciliation. From Weimar, Hitler phoned to Von Papen asking him to get an appointment with Schleicher."

It has been arranged.

January 19, 1933:

At Frau Schleicher's tea for the benefit of hospitalization funds. Many of the "old elite" were around, very worried and concerned. Everybody seemed puzzled by the address Papen delivered last Tuesday in Halle.

Rolf remarked: "It's characteristic of Papen to work both sides of the street. He praised Schleicher's speech at the *Kyffhaeuser Bund*, in which he had proposed conscription. At the same time, he is waiting to kick the props out from under him."

For a whole month, Gregor Strasser and Hitler have been at each other's throats; it is good to know that they are weakening the party by their constant friction.

Papen is said to have established close connections with Hitler. The two of them, with Joachim von Ribbentrop, have been asked to dinner with the banker, Von Schroeder, in Cologne on January 4. Hugenberg and Schacht have also had parleys with Hitler. The *Herrenklub* lunchers have debated nothing but one problem lately. "Should Hitler be given a chance?"

It's maddening to watch this mass blindness.

January 22, 1933:

Gala performance for the Berlin *Winterhilfe* under sponsorship of Hindenburg. He, of course, was not present. An exceptionally glamorous affair with the general mood at freezing point. People are slowly waking up to the shocking realization of their blunder in having elected Hindenburg and, what is worse, in reelecting him. They understand now that Hindenburg has been lulled to sleep by his staff. That he is too weak and senile to resist their influence and their plotting. And that a crash is inevitable.

I heard that Dr. Schacht has definitely hitched his horse to the National Socialist star. If things come to a climax, he'll be seated nicely. If not, then there is still the lenient republic, and absolution will be granted.

Papen watched with growing jealousy the deliberate attempts at a Schleicher-Gregor Strasser coalition. He began to conspire in several quarters to prevent it, for he visualized his final success as being in a government that included the radicals. He had no objections to playing his dirty game with Oskar von Hindenburg, and even with Goering and Goebbels. All of these see danger to themselves and their power, should Schleicher be able to work out a smooth solution for forming a cabinet that was less radical.

Goering has had talks with Von Papen. Hitler has named him his political representative. After Papen, he saw Seldte of the *Stahlhelm*, Hugenberg of the Nationalist party, and Secretary of State Otto Meissner, to discuss the future political management of the German republic. Papen has the important task of mediating between the various camps. He avails himself fully of Hindenburg's good graces and affection. Gossip at the *Herrenklub* has it that Seldte has given his pledge to side with Hitler if and when necessary.

Hugenberg seems to be waiting for the right moment to merge the German National with the National Socialist party. I am afraid Hitler is just ready to leap, smash the whole lot of them, and grab power himself. The old to and fro between Wilhelmstrasse and Kaiserhof is in full swing.

January 23, 1933:

Dropped in at Schleicher's. He knows by now that he has been excluded from the palace intrigues. He has no access to Hindenburg. The slanderous whispers against him have persuaded the childish old man that a revolt in the *Reichswehr* will break out soon, if the appointment of a strong man is postponed much longer. The President is deliberately misled by his "devoted" staff. I am afraid Meissner's anecdote about a remark Hindenburg made in reference to Hitler has lulled Schleicher's alertness. Meissner has put this verdict into Hindenburg's mouth: "What is the use of that breech-loader!"

I tried being coldly realistic, for I get to hear a great deal of palace gossip. I told Schleicher I heard that Hitler was just waiting at the Kaiserhof for Papen and the staff of the Hindenburg household to get ready. Then the revolution!

Perhaps I was talking out of turn. But I could not spare him. I had to tell him what was being said among people who should

know what they are talking about. It seemed to me Schleicher
knows, too.

January 28, 1933:

There was so much excitement and speculation going on at the
office that I couldn't stand it any longer. I jumped into my car and
drove over to Schleicher.

"Don't worry so hard, Bella, dear," he coaxed. "I'll see you
tonight at the Press Ball. I'll come to the Ullstein box to have the
second dance with you."

It is two o'clock now. Lots of things can happen between now
and ten!"

January 29, 1933:

An anguish of suspense and waiting hung over the Press Ball, a
Chancellor-less vacuum waited to be filled. Schleicher was out.
Hitler, Papen, Hugenberg...who was to take his place? Will the
inevitable really be inevitable, and will Hitler...try not to think,
Bellachen...

When I left Schleicher this morning, I thought for a moment
that perhaps he was right about me being too pessimistic. But in
the early afternoon Schleicher resigned. Hindenburg did not
support him. Rumors began to spread.

I had to cover the Press Ball. Who flirted with whom, who wore
what, who escorted whom, and who shared which table with
whom...that's what the readers want to know in the morning. I
kept a proper smile beaming on my face, in accordance with my
festive appearance. I felt very gala in a pale rose velvet affair, with
a sweeping train, trimmed with chinchilla. Specially ordered from
Paris for the occasion.

My heart was heavy, however, with foreboding over what might
be in store for us. The only guest in the official box who seemed to
feel at ease was Meissner. He glowed with the conceited affability
of a man who has achieved his work.

January 30, 1933:

At 11:00 this morning, Hitler was appointed Chancellor of the
Reich. It took him another ten minutes to form his cabinet. The
ministers had been waiting for his call. Everything ran according
to schedule.

Hitler certainly loses no time. This afternoon, he had already convened his first cabinet session. It seems an ironic foreboding that the new Hitler cabinet should start off without a Minister of Justice.

Frau von Papen said at a tea party: "The Old Gentleman seemed very relieved. Franz told me that Hindenburg, on leaving the new cabinet, remarked: "Now, gentlemen, go ahead, and God be with you!"

Strange coincidence: Kurt von Schleicher's favorite horse, the thoroughbred "Farewell," is the first one to start this afternoon for the horse show and tournament. "Farewell" was registered three weeks ago. His owner will not be present at the horse show...Farewell...

January 31, 1933:

Grandmother is dead! This was the prepared password for the Nazi armies. When the word was given, they leaped into action. In the flickering light of a sea of torches they paraded...from the West to the *Knie*...through the *Tiergarten* to the *Wilhelmstrasse*. An endless sea of brown. An ominous night. A night of deadly menace, a nightmare in the living reality of 20,000 blazing torches.

Hindenburg stood with Meissner at his special window on the first floor to the left. I don't know whether it was my imagination or not, but as the brown and black masses thudded past, his face, like cast bronze, seemed bewildered and somewhat startled.

This morning at the office, the report was around that Hindenburg, a bit dazed, had asked Meissner: "Did we really take all these Russian prisoners at Tannenberg?"

February 2, 1933:

The *Kurmaerker* Ball, the annual festivity of the old nobility, was the scene of general excitement. Wild rumors circulated. Adherence to the new masters of the Reich was confessed. More than one mask was dropped for good. There were a great many foreign diplomats there, all anxious to find out just what is going to happen in German domestic affairs.

Heard how the "go ahead" signal had at last been extracted from Hindenburg. It was so simple that it's hard to believe, but then this whole business is pretty hard to believe if your mind has a leaning toward sanity. Well, anyway, it seems that Papen called on the Field Marshal. He painted for him a highly colored story of an imminent army revolt and a plot to assassinate Schleicher. It was urgent. The tension was so high that it would happen any moment! They worked the Old Gentleman up into a really panic-stricken state, calculated their moment well, and snatched the decision from him before he had a chance to pull himself together.

February 10, 1933:

Last night, at Hindenburg's formal dinner reception, Adolf Hitler made his debut in diplomatic society. When the foreign diplomats received their invitations four weeks ago, it was just routine. No one dreamed of the importance this dinner was to assume. Strict observance of prewar etiquette began with the invitations, which bore at the lower left corner the warning: "Carriages 11 P.M."

Everyone watched Hitler. The Corporal seemed to be ill at ease, awkward and moody. His coattails embarrassed him. Again and again his hand fumbled for the encouraging support of his sword belt. Each time he missed the familiar cold and bracing support, his uneasiness grew. He crumpled his handkerchief, tugged it, rolled it, just plain stage fright.

The scene was a brilliant one, and in all the large company there were but two Jewish women. Maria Chintchuk and Elisabeth Cerruti, the wives of the Russian and Italian ambassadors. The former was seated next to François-Poncet, French Ambassador. The other—call it the playful malevolence of fate, if you wish—found herself seated next to the *Reichskanzler*.

Hitler had a pleasant time with Elisabeth Cerruit. She is enthusiastic about Facism. It's going to be interesting to learn whether this enthusiasm extends to Nazism also.

February 15, 1933:

Rolf got a position at the Home Office.

"I saw the way the game was to be played as soon as I was introduced to Frick," he said. "He asked me why I was not a party member. I said I had lived in South America since 1924. That apparently was satisfactory. 'Where were you on November 9, 1923?' he asked me then. That could have tripped me up, but I have recently become trained to deceit.

" 'Marching toward Munich,' I replied without the slightest hesitation. That contented him. I got the job. He did not ask which side I had marched on. That would have been embarrassing. It doesn't look to me as if they were all party members in the Office. I guess that will be taken care of pretty soon, though...."

I hear that neither Hitler nor Goering make decisions without consulting their astrologers. Hitler's is Jan Hanussen, known in certain circles to be of Jewish origin, but he manages to conceal his origin successfully in the places where concealment is considered necessary. He is a close friend of Count Helldorff.

February 26, 1933:

Musicale at home of Count Rudolf von Bassewitz, Chief of Protocol. The talk was all about the stories in the morning papers about the fabulous party given by "Court Astrologer" Hanussen. The story read that the host put himself into a trance at midnight, and uttered Delphic and ambiguous prophecies.

"I see a bloodcurdling crime committed by the Communists," he said through frothing lips. "I see blazing flames. I see a terrible firebrand that lights up the world."

When Hanussen was once asked his impression of Hitler, I was told by Major von Ohst that he said: "Adolf looks more like an unemployed hairdresser than a Caesar."

February 27, 1933:

What a flurry last night, caused by the sudden appearance of the Town-Commander's adjutant at the Esplanade Ball!

Colonel Schaumburg happened to be in the same party with me, at Signora Cerruti's table. He got a short report from his aide, jumped to his feet, and with the staccato explanation, "I am sorry, the *Reichstag* is in flames." He dashed off.

One after another stole away. It was impossible to get near the scene of the fire, however. Everything was roped off.

February 28, 1933:

The *Reichstag* fire has released torrents of speculation. Everybody was in a state of excitement at the Sacketts' today. A crossfire of accusations, information, and statements whizzed across the reception room.

"Did you know about that underground passage leading from the National Socialists to the villa of the *Reichstag* presidency, where Goering lives?" somebody asked. "Hitler convened his cabinet during the night between yesterday and today. Papen said at a luncheon today that a decision was made during the night session, to set the S.A. on the opponents' heels. Now Hanussen's star will rise high."

At that point, Frau von Papen, with her daughters, made her entrance. The comments in English, French, German, and Italian came to an abrupt hush.

Sackett has asked his government to recall him. He is too disappointed about the failure of the Hoover plan and deeply displeased with German domestic politics.

March 2, 1933:

Every day brings many casualties, wounded and dead, in "political clashes."

"The people object more violently than anticipated against the Hitler regime," said Rolf.

"In Bavaria, they're making another try at regaining their independence. Hitler is going to get tough now. After the election comes the abolition of the state governments."

The *Reichstag* fire was the pretext for mass arrests of workers and Leftist voters. There is little question, of course, as to how the voting will turn out. Goebbel's collaborator, Dr. Brauweiler, is known to be an expert in correcting "defective" ballots.

March 4, 1933:

Reception at the Russian Embassy.

The People's Commissar, Maxim Litvinoff, was the center of attention. He stopped here en route to Russia from Geneva.

There is something very reassuring about Litvinoff's well-composed affable appearance. Seeing him standing there, his feet solidly planted apart, sturdy, well-rounded, he seemed the very image of a personality well adjusted to reality. The comfortable creases of his substantial pinkish neck harmonize perfectly with the good-natured expression of his clean-shaven face. His correctly cut tailcoat may well be a contrast to Stalin's blouse, but somehow one does not think of it. He speaks English, French, and German, has a good sense of humor and, obviously, a strong appreciation for well-cooked food.

One of the younger members of the embassy asked me: "Frau Bella, do *you* believe the Communists set fire to the *Reichstag?*" The topic is endless. They come back to it over and over again.

"The fire was very badly managed. You Germans are generally

more thorough. The incendiary lubrication was applied so economically that the building refused to burn," he said.

March 7, 1933:

The Minister of Venezuela discussed the electioneering terror
system today. He said that Hindenburg had stopped for several
minutes inside the poll booth. "He evidently couldn't decide up to
the very last minute whether or not to vote for the National
Socialists..."

My friend, Poulette, gave a big tea at the *Garde Kavallerieklub.*
The club includes the members of the eight former Guard Cavalry
regiments. The clubhouse is kept in prewar military style: pictures, etchings, old prints and paintings representing the Prussian
kings, the German emperors, the famous army commanders. The
heavy old silver and the china come from the eight exclusive
regimental casinos.

The elderly servants, too, are leftovers from olden times. They
served tea and gave the dignified atmosphere the exact finishing
touch.

I was a little late. "Poulette was worried that something might
have happened to you," were François-Poncet's words of welcome.
"But I told her nobody is going to do any harm to our Bella. They
know that the diplomatic corps protects her."

"Let's hope you are right, Your Excellency!"

He was in high spirits, sparkling and sarcastic. It is not easy to
label him. Such a conflicting personality.

I have been studying the French Ambassador more closely than
any of the other diplomats. He interests me extremely, and I have
tried hard to pierce through the diplomatic varnish. He gives the
impression of a human icicle, whether at the conference table or
on other formal occasions. In his morning coat, as well as garbed
in the gold-braided diplomatic uniform, his "three-master" tucked
under his arm, his face is set in a mask. But his eyes seem to have a
life of their own, scrutinizing, observant, quick. The glitter of his
monocle, now dropped, now pressed back into position, stresses
the frozen aloofness of his expression. He is unyielding in
discussions, inexhaustible in his arguments.

The picture changes, seen from the angle of informal gatherings at Mme. Jacqueline's. He is likely, in the midst of the most
stimulating topic, to turn to his four boys and sit on the floor with
them, engrossed in the repair of a toy train, or in the construction

of a miniature church steeple. The Ambassador of *la grande nation* sits there with glowing cheeks, a big warmhearted playmate.

It would be easy to classify him as professionally cold-blooded and privately warmhearted. It isn't as simple as that. His sudden whims complicate the analysis. Intensely discussing a subject, something, almost tangible, passes his mind in a flash; the conversation is dropped. His face becomes inscrutable.

Now he speaks scornfully, sarcastically about the Nazis. A little while ago, the tenor of his words seemed to betray concealed admiration, secret approval for the masters of the Third Reich. No doubt, he has studied the big and the small Hitlers. He knows what they are and what they stand for. I can't even help feeling that he foresaw their coming approvingly! Now, however, he recognizes the danger. Now he sees there is no way to stop the monster which, so foolishly, has been turned loose. He hides his reactions behind an elegant Latin flippancy. No way to sound out how worried he really is, or how pleased.

March 8, 1933:

The reappointment of Dr. Schacht as president of the *Reichsbank* has aroused scorn, including my own.

Way back, in November, 1923, the Stresemann government, backed by Jewish bankers and energetic democrats, hoisted Schacht to his position. But this ruthless opportunist does not care whose hands deal the cards of power and position. He sided early with the coming winners. This time Thyssen and Stinnes were his stepping-stones. I heard that these two gentlemen again financed the Nazis last November to help them recover from their blow. The reward exacted was the *Reichsbank* presidency for Schacht as soon as the party seized the power. Hitler has now had to make good the note he endorsed.

"Schacht is going to be reappointed," Schmidt-Pauly told me.

"How about Luther?" I asked.

"Luther," commented handsome Edgar, "is going to be Ambassador in Washington. His is one of the pliable natures. Besides, he has 'connections' over there. He will succeed with his display of good-natured joviality. He's an excellent shoulder-slapper."

Luther is the personification of the small middle-class. Sturdy, cheerful, with an eternally amiable smile.

"But Luther is no National Socialist, Edgar!"

"Wouldn't be any good if he were, right now. We have to reassure the people over there."

March 10, 1933:

Midnight. I am still so upset that there is no chance of my falling asleep, anyway. I may as well sit up and write this out.

For years I have given a cocktail party once or twice a month. As the diplomats count me not only as a reporter but also as a friend, I feel I should repay their numerous invitations by entertaining in my own house.

The invitations for today's cocktail party had been sent out quite some time ago. At that time, political and social pandemonium had not yet broken loose. There was no reason for me to expect any such acts of imbecility at today's.

Early in the morning, apparently acting on official party order, groups of young S.A. men, almost children most of them, swarmed through the streets, dragging their loot of black, red, and gold flags through the dust of roads and sidewalks. They seemed to have conducted a thorough house-to-house search. Passersby, especially women, in their easily kindled outbursts of hysteria, went out of their way to trample the soiled flag cloth. Rags of black, red, and gold material were seized and burned in the streets, while howling mobs yelled "*Heil* Hitler!"

Even in our secluded suburb, with its private family homes, the excitement ran high. Shortly before the arrival of my guests, a troup of S.A. men had discovered a forgotten flag of the Weimar Republic, an especially gigantic specimen, in the attic of the nearby hospital. They dragged it through the boulevards and stopped a stone's throw from my house to build a cozy little fire, right in the middle of the driveway, to burn the banner.

Just then the first limousine, with its little foreign flag flapping cheerfully in the breeze, drove up.

Among the guests I expected today were the French Ambassador, François-Poncet and his wife; also Signora Elizabeth Cerruti, wife of the Italian Ambassador. The latter is the only one, so far, within the circles of the foreign diplomats, to have been "honored" by Adolf Hitler's presence at her dinners. I expected the Czech Envoy and his wife, Mr. and Mrs. Voijtech Mastny; the Belgian Envoy Baron de Kerchove de Denthergem and his wife; the Rumanian Envoy and Mrs. J. P. Comnen, famous in diplomatic circles for her beauty. The Comnens brought their house guest, the Marquis Giovani Maurigi di Castelmaurigi, Mayor of Palermo.

Maurigi has been a friend of Benito Mussolini since his early days. The Marquis did not seem to think very highly of the German "Fascisti."

There was my old friend Hassan Nachat Pasha, Envoy of King Fuad of Egypt, and the French Naval Attaché, Jean Tracou. I was informed tonight that Tracou reported the whole event to his chief, who never stops longer than a few minutes at any reception held in daytime. Mostly he cannot even attend at all. There were some other members of the corps with their ladies.

Baron and Baroness de Gruben of the Belgian Legation had, as I found tonight, been unable to drive to the house. They had been a little late. The National Socialists hordes had grown to such dimensions that the traffic was blocked. The de Grubens had with them the wife of a diplomat who lives in Bucharest. When their car got into the traffic jam near my house, this lady was molested by the National Socialists. They took her Mediterranean appearance and dark hair for Jewish features. These are now becoming criminally dangerous to possess.

Among my German guests were Frau Meissner, wife of the Secretary of State. He is a leftover from several former regimes which he has survived in true opportunist fashion. Hitler, too, accepted his services because of the zeal Meissner had shown the party before it came to power. Vice-Chief of Protocol Herbert Mumm von Schwarzenstein; of course, Wera von Huhn. I wouldn't have wanted to miss Poulette at any of my parties.

It is still too early in the year to sit in the garden or on the terraces, so I had gathered my guests in the music room, which extends almost through the entire ground floor of the house. The windows look to the east and west. A vaulted south door leads to one of the terraces. As usual at these diplomatic routs, people stood around in little groups, chatting, juggling cocktail glasses and pastry plates, the whole scene in constant informal movement.

Hassan Nachat Pasha had brought faithful Ali, one of his native servants. We had posted him at the door. Upon arrival of the last guest Ali, quaking with fear and turning pale under his dark brown skin, tiptoed into the room and whispered into my ear: "Madam, thou must come outside, great mishap going to happen."

I tried to leave the salon quite "casually" and dashed through the hall to the entrance door. Outside I noticed a menacing mob of Brown Shirts. In an alarming attitude, they kept an eye on the entrance and on the cars waiting outside.

I was panic-stricken, but managed to pull myself together.

I shouted at the S.A. man who stood closest to the scene: "What's going on? What do you want?"

After a stubborn silence, and after my repeated question, one of the roughnecks replied: "Passersby have called us here. They have seen that arms and ammunition have been delivered to the house. They have seen spies driving up in these cars. We know very well that this house belongs to non-Aryans. Now we are going to fumigate the place."

At first, this incredible stupidity made me laugh. Then, in a flash, I realized the danger which threatened my guests. I even forgot to worry about myself. I told the roughnecks to get in touch with the nearest police station. There they could find out on the spot who the owners of the cars really were.

"You can place a guard here so that nobody can leave the house," I tried to reason. But I might as well have talked to the moon. They did not budge. In fact, more and more rowdies in brown uniforms joined them. Of course, the crowd of onlookers grew, too.

I told Ali to hurry and turn on the lights in the music salon, draw the curtains and close the shutters.

Then I made a renewed attempt to parley with the "enemy." When I was still conferring with their leader, the next blow crashed down on my poor head in the shape of a police captain. He was accompanied by five officers. Although the captain recognized the low plate numbers of the diplomats and government members, he took an important and bullying attitude.

"I am from station Kreuzberg. We have word that this is a meeting of political agitators. I have orders to search your house." That was just what the Nazis had waited for. Their attitude grew twice as threatening.

The police captain finally agreed to wait until the guests had left. He had surrounded the house for the time being. However, he refused to disperse the mob. "I have orders not to interfere with the S.S. or with the S.A.," he said.

All I could do, I reflected, was to phone the Chief of Protocol.

"Ru" Bassewitz was very shocked to hear my terse report, which, at first, he did not believe because I "did not sound upset." He promised to go over immediately to see my patron, Secretary of State von Buelow, to report the case. Buelow seemed duly impressed. He phoned me after a few minutes to keep my chin up, as he had already sent word to Vice-Chancellor von Papen. "I am going to rush over to Hitler's office for advice, too."

I returned to the gate and assured the crowd they would not be cheated. They would have the pleasure of setting fire to the house once the guests had left. But that they had better await the word of their Fuehrer, whom I just informed through the Foreign Office.

They muttered in protest. "Everybody can say that. Give us proof that Hitler really has been informed." I promised to be at their disposal after one hour.

Somewhat relieved, I returned to my guests. With one glance, I noticed that almost nobody had paid any attention to my absence. I discovered, however, the French Naval Attaché, together with the Czech Envoy, on the terrace. They peered through the bushes into the street. We winked at each other, and I was glad to have somebody to share my secret and face the danger with me.

Again somebody came to call me to the phone. Secretary of State Meissner wanted to talk to me. Bassewitz, in his panic, had hurried to the Presidential Palace. The Old Gentleman was informed and is said to have cursed and thundered. I assured him that with the exception of Tracou, Mastny and myself, nobody had noticed anything so far. Meissner asked me to be brave. Help would be here any moment now. He felt a little uneasy, his darling wife being in the mess.

The second phone rang, Papen himself lisped from the other end: "Frau Bella, fifteen mounted police are on their way out to you with orders to shoot; tell the crowd."

"Shoot at whom?" I asked tartly. My question remained unanswered. Well, I didn't tell them anything of the kind. I returned to my guests instead. I used Papen's message, however, to reassure the Frenchman and the Czech. I then asked the two gentlemen to assist me in keeping the affair from being perceived by any of the other guests. I preferred to stay outside to prevent possible incidents.

I arrived just in time to see one of the S.A. men tear the little flags from the radiators of the French and Rumanian cars and shove them into his pocket. The two foreign drivers rushed the S.A. idiot, and in a moment they, together with the trooper, were rolling in the dust of the road.

Then in a clamor of hooting and hornblowing, the "saviors" sent by Adolf Hitler drove up in four shining black cars, five men alighting from each one. I recognized Schaefer, a group leader with his gang. He came to the foot of the staircase and asked what the trouble was.

I refused to explain: "There are plenty of your party comrades present. I can't very well assume the right to testify against S.A. men."

This took him aback. He turned around in a rage and grabbed the nearest Brown roughneck by the throat. The little S.A creature turned purple. He spluttered out the familiar tale of the arms, the spies and the non-Aryan house.

Schaefer lost his temper. He became increasingly infuriated. He knew these license numbers. When the chauffeurs, in their broken German, had complained about the stolen flags, Schaefer's hand closed once more around his victim's throat. He happened to be the very one who had taken the flags. Reluctantly, he pulled them out of his pockets.

Schaefer asked me whether my guests had been molested. He was apologetic. "It's too embarrassing that these rascals, who have just been ordered here from the country, behave so idiotically." He wanted to come in to be introduced. He wished to apologize and explain the mistake to the foriegn diplomats. I advised him to postpone it until tomorrow. I cannot very well ask you to enter my house," I said, "You are wearing the S.A. uniform." He was astonished to find himself turned down.

I excused myself: "I suppose my presence here is no longer necessary. I am sure you will take care of everything. I must return to my guests."

I heard him bark, "Police Captain, take over the protection here. I forbid the searching of the house. I am leaving three men of my staff behind."

Bullied into obedience by the young Nazi, the old police captain with the Iron Cross First Class, clicked to attention and acknowledged, "*Zu Befehl.*"

Returning to my guests, I saw that everything was proceeding smoothly. My two friends outside on the terrace had stayed at the observation post. Nobody else had got wind of the affair. I teased them about it.

Mastny kissed my hand and grinned, "I am most obliged. I have just now experienced a page of world history. I have had the chance to study the Nazi soul."

He was overheard. There were excited demands to be told what had happened. The ladies paled when the Czech Minister gave a detailed survey of what had happened during the last half-hour in front of the house. Mrs. Meissner rushed to phone her husband. Mrs. François-Poncet fainted.

Just then the "mounted police," who were sent upon Von Papen's order, were announced by Ali. There was nothing for the fifteen horsemen to do. They returned to their quarters, order having been restored by the motorized Nazis.

When I had seen each guest to his car, I went down to the basement. In the kitchen, at the coffee table with my servants, I found the three Nazi guards cozily settled. They praised the coffee and cake, which was better than any they had ever tasted before. I could not help replying how proud I was that they considered the food of a non-Aryan household so palatable.

I found it was time to get dressed for the farewell dinner given by Vice-Chancellor von Papen for the Sacketts. When shortly after seven o'clock, I came downstairs in full evening dress with orders and decorations, the police captain was there clicking his heels again. He had just wanted to come in to bring me his apologies. I insisted that he should search the house for arms and ammunition.

"For God's sake, *gnädige Frau*, you heard that group leader Schaefer forbid anything of the kind." He led me to my auto, clicked to attention again, and returned to his post. He and his people had orders, together with the Nazi guard, to stay on duty all night long.

Driving in the direction of the Brandenburger Tor on my way to the Hotel Adlon, I retraced in my mind the events of the afternoon. I must admit that I entered the lounge with slightly wobbling knees. To my surprise, Louis Adlon came to welcome me. "You are a hero, I am told. The Vice-Chancellor is expecting you in the writing room."

"Franzchen" put on his best face when I entered and kissed my hand. "May I express my gratitude for this afternoon? After all this unpleasantess I have one favor to ask, in the name of the government. I am referring to the incident with the two flags torn from the cars of the French Embassy and of the Rumanian Legation. The two diplomats will probably undertake a *démarche* because of the disrespect shown to their national colors. We are very anxious to avoid such action! I know you have influence with them. Ask them to forget the incident. You may be assured of the gratitude of the government."

My neighbor at the table was Dr. Hans Draeger, secretary of the *Karl Schurz Vereinigung*. When I told him about this afternoon, he laughed. "I hope the diplomats spread it all over the outside world. What a pity you did not invite me!"

Growing uneasy about my frozen reaction, he started to tell me anti-Nazi jokes. He said nasty things about Hitler and Goering. He referred to Goebbels as "the ugly dwarf with the Jewish grandmother," "the vicious cripple," and "the synthetic Jew." He ridiculed Goering on account of his passion for uniforms and decorations. He said Goering even pins rubber replicas of his medals to his bathing suit. Then he wisecracked about Hitler's inferiority and that he was greatly impressed by "people of high social standing." The office staff is highly amused at the spectacle of Hitler addressing Prince Phillip von Hessen as "Royal Highness," an incongruous way for a leader to speak to a party member when, according to party etiquette, he should have been addressed simply as "Party Comrade." Prince Phillip is a war comrade of Goering's and was on the side of the Nazis as early as 1925. In that year, he married the daughter of King Victor Emmanuel of Italy, who presented him with the title of Royal Highness, since the revolution in Germany in 1918 had cancelled and abolished titles.

Draeger spoke about Goering's comrade-in-arms, Erhard Milch. "He is the son of a Jewish druggist from Breslau. For years he has done well in the motor business and has given many a break to Goering.

"Goering is now showing his gratitude and has appointed Milch his Secretary of State. He advised him to declare officially that his father was a Gentile, an army officer by the name of Von Bier, with whom his likewise Gentile mother had deceived her Jewish husband. In the Air Force when the gossip concerning Milch's Jewish origin grew to unpleasant proportions, Goering stamped his foot. He declared despotically: '*I decide* who is Jewish.' But even that is not original. Long before the war, some Viennese mayor coined that bon mot..."

Draeger could not break the ice. He had tried hard. I remained careful. I don't trust him. I felt that he was acting as a *provocateur*.

March 12, 1933:

Hitler was given his start in Bavaria. Now having conquered Prussia, the Bavarians are beginning to feel that they have assisted at the birth of a Frankenstein monster. In their insularity, the Bavarians did not pay too much attention to the January change of the Reich government.

Well, they're going to begin to pay attention from this time forward. Dr. Wilhelm Frick, Minister of Home Affairs in Berlin, has just named General von Epp to be National Socialist Commissar for Bavaria. Police President in Munich is now Heinrich Himmler. He was once secretary to Gregor Strasser and before that was co-spy with Hitler for the *Reichswehr*.

Von Buelow told me this morning that François-Poncet kept his promise. He did not complain about the mistreatment of his flag. The Rumanian, however, had not kept his word. The Foreign Office, which insults well but apologizes badly, had to apologize.

March 13, 1933:

The Nazis act more and more ruthlessly. Now they have promised Hindenburg, after the ban on black, red, and gold flags, that the prewar black, white, and red flag will take its old place of honor. It will be displayed side by side with the swastika flag.

On January 30, Goering, who already held the office of Prussian Minister of Home Affairs, was also appointed Prime Minister. He waited barely twenty-four hours before ordering the swastika to be hoisted at the Home Ministry. An honor guard of police, S.S., and *Stahlhelm* was commanded to attend the affair. In further celebration of the day, he dismissed twenty-two out of thirty-two colonels of the *Schutz-Polizei*. Thousands of police officers and sergeants were thrown out next. They were replaced by men recruited from the S.S. and S.A. A special personal bodyguard of police forces was appointed, crack troops, under the command of Colonel Wecke, and named after him.

He has ordered rigorous measures taken against "subversive elements." According to the Nazi book, these are members of any party or organization other than those that fly the swastika.

Goering adopts a somewhat murderous mood. In an address delivered last week at Dortmund, he said: "Each bullet fired from the gun of any of my men is *my* bullet. If it is murder, I am the murderer. I give the order to shoot, and I assume the responsibility."

Rolf heard him ranting at a dinner party about the things he has done, the things he intends to do.

"I know exactly what is happening all through the Reich," Goering said. "Information keeps coming in continuously. The remotest hideout of the Communists is known to us. There were eight million Communist votes at the last election. We won't forget them. We're building concentration camps now."

There were foreign diplomats listening, and they must have been interested, to say the least, when Goering continued: "You must not be shocked by what some people call excesses. Flogging, general cruelty, even deaths...these are inevitable in a forceful, sweeping young revolution."

His fat chest gleamed with decorations. His eyes had in them a beatific blood lust. I wonder what Germany has in store for itself. Or what the Nazis have in store for Germany?

March 15, 1933:

Dr. Joseph Goebbels was appointed Minister of Propaganda and National Enlightenment this week. The new ministry is going to be elaborately established in the old Friedrich Leopold Palace. Goebbels, although the shrewdest and most brilliant of the Brown leaders, has not been too prominent up to this point. Now, he has suddenly been given important powers by Hitler. Supremacy over the press has been taken from Goering's cushioned paws and placed in the cunning clutches of the limping monster.

Mammi von Carnap was at luncheon with Baroness von Neurath yesterday. The Baroness appeared displeased with the new masters. "That," speaking of Goebbels, "can boast of the same rank as my husband."

I couldn't help being sharp with Mammi. "None of you have any right to complain. You and your entire aristocratic clique, the Nationalists, the *Junkers*, most of the generals, and the industrial magnates, all of you are to blame for the catastrophe. You undermined the republic. Now let's see what a Hitler government will do for you."

"I hope we won't have to accept them socially," sighed Mammi. There isn't much you can answer to that.

March 16, 1933:

We had our fourth charity tea. I can't put my heart into the work any longer. A Nazi "lady" at every table. Mrs. Meissner basked in the presence of so many Brown stars. She just loves to raise her arm in the Hitler salute. She is not aware how unbecoming the gesture is to her.

Colonel Schaumburg sat at my table. Baroness von der Heyden-Rynsch, the "tea pest," as François-Poncet dubbed her, tried to pump the Colonel about the *Reichstag* fire. Schaumburg, a huge, bearlike individual, has never been a very chivalrous, suave-spoken ladies' pet. Now he reacted rudely.

"Baroness, don't you read the papers?" he barked. "The papers report everything."

But the Baroness wanted to know what the papers do not report. "I am an officer, not an information bureau," said the Colonel curtly.

Frau Helmuth Wohltat, wife of the new Cabinet Councilor, was present. I hated to see her at my tea, because she is a National Socialist. She and her husband are notorious climbers, and I wouldn't care to be of assistance to her in her attempts to squeeze her way into international society. She is very blunt in her aims and most unattractive and unpleasant. She is an American and, it is said, related to Dr. Schacht.

March 17, 1933:

Since the "Court Dinner," the Chancellor of the Reich has not appeared in society. It has been made known what a wonderful and hardworking father he is to his people. He spends most of the night at his desk. He goes from conference to conference. He keeps an eye on the construction of new driveways, on the erection of buildings, the construction of playgrounds.

Last night, however, he neglected his manifold duties. He interrupted his voluntary seclusion to accept an invitation to the home of a non-Aryan. Again he was Mrs. Cerruti's partner at her table. Again he seemed to find her conversation most stimulating.

Another Jewess was the success of the party. Blonde Susanne Renzetti, born Kochmann from Gleiwitz, wife of the president of the Italian chamber of commerce, friend of Mussolini and Goering. She stole last night's show and ravished Hitler with her sparkling beauty, charm, and manner. I was non-Aryan number three. I avoided the spotlight and managed to keep in the background. I did not want to be "honored" by a presentation to Hitler.

The Cerrutis also had after-dinner guests. A merry hodgepodge of prewar and postrevolution society, of foreign and domestic statesmen. Hitler had brought a small army of brown-and black-clad boys. According to their rank and merits, they were either seated at the dinner table, their stripes and bars proving that they were high officers and "society," or, if still low in the ranks, distributed around and inside the house, watching doors, gates, and street corners. The Chancellor is said to be a jittery man and concerned about possible attempts on his life. He rides in a car with a bulletproof windshield, preceded and followed by heavily armed bodyguards of elite S.S., driving along in his wake in open black Mercedes cars. Nobody is allowed to throw flowers into Adolf's car.

Another guest was the absurd-looking giant, Dr. Ernst Hanfstaengl. His hands, of almost frightening dimensions, accompany every phrase in violent gesticulation. A jerk of his strangely distorted head drives every point home. The party members love him as a court jester is loved. "Putzi" is Nazi-struck. He has neglected family and business for years to follow the trail of his master like a faithful hound. It is said his American mother has helped the Nazi cause with donations of no mean dimensions.

"I play the piano for Hitler late into the night," he told proudly, "when he has his insomnia spells."

I did not say, "Who cares?"

I was told that Hitler has some sort of emotional fondness for the giant with the oversized hands. Just as he has for his old friend, Ernst Roehm. The household staff and adjutants say: "Putzi was with Hitler all night. Piano playing, they say..."

I have never believed the rumors of homosexuality that have been spread about Hitler. I rather believe, and many people have felt the same way, that he is asexual, or perhaps impotent, finding a sexual sublimation through cruelty. They take private films of an especially gruesome nature in concentration camps. Films that only the Fuehrer sees. These are rushed to him and shown, night after night.

Occasionally Hitler's interest in a woman may be aroused; he may feel attracted by her charm—but that is all. His emotions culminate in a kind of jealousy caused by his sense of frustration, in the knowledge that he cannot respond normally.

Each woman crossing his path has been frightened out of her wits by Hitler, whose reaction to the woman of his choice is a morose effort to hurt her feelings. He screams at her, he rages. He provokes scenes about a trifle. He tortures the woman, treating her as if she were his personal prisoner. The case of his niece, Geli Raubal, is the perfect example. Aware that he could not love her as a normal man would love a woman, he kept her locked in a room, treated her as if she were a dangerous criminal, and finally shot her down one night in a fit of mad jealousy against a phantom rival.

Hitler is inordinately fond of motion pictures. He spends many hours every night in his private movie room. It takes two or three full-length pictures a night to satisfy him. Once after seeing a picture in which Felix Bressart appeared, the Fuehrer said: "This fellow is wonderful. A pity he is a Jew."

March 20, 1933:

This week Bruno Walter and Fritz Busch were stopped from giving their concerts.

Goebbel's "inauguration" speech to the press was interlarded with new words. *Gleichschaltung, Rassenschande, Belange, Artfremd*...words which you can hunt for in vain in a dictionary.

Rolf said: "Goebbel's propagandistic method sweeps away the minds. It dopes the masses. It will be too late when they return to their senses. The German people are, temperamentally, made to order for just that kind of mental poison."

March 23, 1933:

Evening reception at the Peruvian Legation. While there, I got a most peculiar proposition from Dr. Felix Tripeloury, Secretary of the Reich Press Office. I was given to understand that this mission originated in the brain of Foreign Minister von Neurath.

It appears that the Foreign Office is perturbed about the "Jew boycott" scheduled for April 1. Not on account of the Jews, but because the thing is disastrous for Germany's foreign prestige. The idea was for me to call on Goering with a petition for a transplantation of "undesirable" Jews. The Jewish population of long standing should be permitted to stay here with some minor restrictions on their general rights as citizens! As a front, a couple of "good-looking" Jews, if possible, heroes with the Iron Cross First Class, should accompany me.

I thanked him. I would get in touch with the Jewish community. I was certain that no one would accept any privileges at the expense of others.

March 24, 1933:

Hitler pulled a fast one. He opened the *Reichstag* on March 21 in Potsdam, the burned *Reichstag* building being not yet tenantble. It was a first performance for the Potsdam garrison church, never before the scene of such a ceremony.

It was very shrewd to execute this curtsy to tradition! Very cunning to drag the old President out to Potsdam; to set up a cheering crowd of more than 100,000 people. Army and other high officials and diplomats were there. Black-white-red banners side by side with swastikas. Flowers, wreaths, and posters adorned the streets. Made one think of the jubilant welcome for a military victor. The entire population of Potsdam, half of Berlin, and thousands from all over the Reich crowded the streets. The garrison was mobilized. An army of police and auxiliary police forces stood ready. More than sixteen hundred "Schupo," two thousand plainclothesmen were on duty for public—and Hitler's— security. Every kind of precaution was taken against possible air raids as well as other assaults. Outposts were placed on the roofs of the houses, with machine guns and rifles. *Reichswehr* detachments for mine sounding were on underground duty.

Hindenburg and Hitler were the speakers. "The Chancellor," Ernst Udet said to me, "was extremely tame. He will eventually let off the steam at the first session." Which, indeed, he did sufficiently today, three days after the Potsdam celebration.

Scornfully he assailed all parties, especially the Leftists. He demanded uncompromising decisions in matters of proxy and authorization. "Fight against Communism." "Public execution of the *Reichstag* incendiaries." "Abolition of the peoples' class divisions."

He was particularly aggressive against the former President of the *Reichstag*, Paul Loebe; against the leader of the Social Democrats, Otto Wels; against Torgler, Thaelmann and, of course, against the Jews.

"Your leader is settling general accounts," said the Danish Minister Herluf Zahle.

"All the rumors about the persecution of Jews and the mistreatment of Catholics are cheap lies and absurd tattletales," said Putzi Hanfstaengl during today's tea party at the Italian Embassy.

March 25, 1933:

Dinner, with following bridge tournament, at the Belgian Minister's and Countess Kerchove Denterghem. There was not much of a bridge game. People were too preoccupied and excited to concentrate on card playing. There is much speculation and guessing as to the nightly "liquidation" of human lives. Yesterday's *Reichstag* session must have been ghastly. The deputies had to pass through a cordon of S.A. men flanking the way to the session room. A most unpleasant passage for the non-Nazi deputies.

March 26, 1933:

Last handclasp for the Sacketts at the Anhalter Railway Station. An entire railway carriage had been reserved. One compartment alone was filled with costly flowers, Mrs. Sackett's farewell gifts from numerous friends. The entire diplomatic corps waved them good-bye.

March 27, 1933:

Dr. Goebbels announced "mass action."

"We are going to take our revenge. The Jews in America and England are trying to injure us. We shall know how to deal with their brothers in Germany."

March 29, 1933:

Some of the Hohenzollerns have not found it beneath them to goose-step aboard the Nazi bandwagon. I heard the Lithuanian Colonel, Skirpa, say that Prince August Wilhelm is giving up his salary as a *Reichstag* deputy for the benefit of wounded S.A. comrades. "Doesn't that impose something of a hardship on you?" he asked the Brown Prince.

His brother, the Crown Prince, also does what he's told. He has written to George Sylvester Viereck, asking him to enlighten the United States about the fake Jewish atrocity stories. It is said that he is a relative of Kaiser Wilhelm II, and it is true that the Munich-born American citizen and writer is on friendly terms with the former Kaiser and his second wife, whom he visited at Doorn on several occasions. He also had met Adolf Hitler as early as 1923 and had predicted that Hitler would one day make world history. "There is absolutely nothing in them. The Jews in Germany are not even aware of any change in their regard," said the published letter.

I wonder if they'll believe that in New York. Here the baiting of the Jews continues incessantly. It has become accepted practice for Jewish victims to be dragged from their beds before dawn and taken away.

The German states are now "coordinated." The newspapers are unanimous in their praise of the Fuehrer for this.

They are starting to work on the German mind. It is to be coordinated also, or else it will be legislated out of existence. And don't think it cannot be done, either.

March 30, 1933:

"Vice-Chancellor and Frau von Papen request the pleasure of Frau Bella Fromm's company, Wednesday, March 29, 1933, from 9:30 P.M. on, at the Palais Prinz Friedrich Leopold."

The pasteboard has been on my desk for three weeks. I felt uneasy whenever I looked at it. The date rolled around yesterday, and I felt I had to attend. I didn't like it. I cannot just say why.

Rolf and I had dinner at the Kaiserhof. Rolf's tall slenderness was emphasized by his perfectly cut evening clothes, adorned only with the Iron Cross First Class and the order of the princely house of his mother's family. "Evening suits have to be made in Bond Street," he laughed, when I told him that he looked like a million dollars. Around 10 P.M., we walked over to the palace. I love the historic old building. It saddens me to think of the barbarians from the Ministry of Propaganda housed in its aloof and lofty dignity.

So far everything seemed unchanged. We climbed the white marble steps. In the stately reception room, people were already gathering, the crystal chandeliers radiating a flood of light on the brilliant uniforms, the medals, the evening gowns, the jewels. The scene was spoiled only by the ugly smudge of brown and black uniforms scattered throughout. The horrible high boots preferred by most uniformed Nazis were an offensive dissonance in the general color harmony.

Word had spread that Adolf Hitler had been invited. This is

only hearsay. There is a general taboo concerning the discussion of any of sacred Adolf's movements.

Mammi von Carnap and I stood in a group with Frau von Papen right under the center chandelier. Suddenly our host, "Franzchen," appeared from somewhere. He dashed up to his wife, whispered hastily into her ear, and hurried off.

She turned pale, trembling in every limb. She clung to Mammi's arm and mine.

"The Fuehrer has just entered the palace," she said. When I saw the skinny and unattractive creature, dressed in her shabby silk Sunday best, so excited about the arrival of the Fuehrer, it flashed through my mind that here was still another of the countless females who fell into hysterical rapture at the mere approach of the divine Adolf and who helped him into power.

Suddenly, God knows where they emerged from, black-clad S.S men studded the place. I looked on in amazement. They had not been there a minute ago.

Now things went on as though on a revolving stage. Folding doors were flung grandly open. There was a moment's silence, and Adolf Hitler made his entrance. Meissner and his wife raised their arms in the Nazi salute.

Adolf paused. A plain-looking little man. The coattails well-cut, in fact, better cut than the head, which seems out of drawing, as if it did not belong with the rest of him. The last time I saw him, his suit was not so well-fitting. New tailors go along with new jobs. The better the job, the better the tailor.

Behind Adolf loomed a huge, uncouth figure—his Adjutant, Oberleutnant Brueckner. At the Lieutenant's side appeared the elegant figure of Hans Thomsen. His suave elegance threw the clumsiness of the Fuehrer and his Adjutant into rather tawdry relief.

Papen, in his flustered state, had been neglecting his duties. He was dashing from group to group to spread the news of the Fuehrer's arrival when he should have been at the door to welcome the illustrious visitor. I saw Adolf throw a glance in "Tommy's" direction for a cue as to just what to do next. Then I saw him try out the slippery floor with a tentative Nazi toe. Gathering his resources, his coattails flapping and his body moving forward dynamically, he dashed right in the direction of our group.

My first impulse was the animal one of self-preservation. I wanted to scramble away. But already the Fuehrer was bent over

Martha von Papen's shaking hand. I could see Mammi trembling
in anticipation of her turn. My actions spoiled it for her, however.
My attempt at a retreat had attracted Adolf's attention from
Mammi. He came to me. I was rooted to the spot.

"May I have the pleasure of bidding you good evening, *gnädige
Frau?* he cooed. He seized my hand, pressed it to his lips, and
presented me, gratis, with one of his famous hypnotic glances.

It did not seem to work on me. I felt only a slight nausea. The
fact is, I could not even feel that he was a member of the other sex.
A glance around, out of the corner of my eyes, showed me some of
my foreign friends grinning more or less openly.

Weird ideas flashed through my mind. Why did I not have my
little revolver with me?...Then I realized that he was asking me
polite questions. That I really ought to give him polite answers.

"Are you having a good time?" I was, I told him. "Where did
you gain these decorations?"

They were from the World War. For my services with the Red
Cross.

"You enjoy being here?"

I said that I did, but that, in addition, it was my job, as I was
diplomatic columnist for the Ullstein papers.

I saw Hitler wince. The word "Ullstein" rang an unpleasant bell
in some noisome depth of his mind. Another kiss on my hand.
"Hope to see you again soon." He was off. He forgot to pay
attention to Mammi. She was furious. "Thyssen says that often
when Hitler is attracted to a woman she turns out to be racially
undesirable."

"Well, Bellachen, are you going to allow anyone else to kiss your
hand tonight?" one of my foreign friends bantered.

I rubbed my hand against his sleeve, as though to remove a
stain. "Perhaps it needs fumigation," I said.

When I joined Lammers and Thomsen, I couldn't help a
slightly catty remark. "Your Fuehrer must have a cold," I said.

"Why?" Thomsen asked.

"He's supposed to be able to smell a Jew ten miles away, isn't he?
Apparently his sense of smell isn't working tonight."

They couldn't help laughing...though not without a quick,
furtive glance around to see who was listening.

I followed Adolf with my eyes everywhere, not wanting to miss
any of his debut. There comes a sudden flash into his eyes that
leaves one chilled. It reveals the diabolical and sadistic streak in

Hitler's twisted makeup. A glimpse of this expression leaves one no doubt as to the hopelessness of expecting any humane understanding or mercy from this bellowing, blustering, dangerous egoist who obviously cloaks his inferiority complex with his cruel despotism. In talking to people you got the impression that he was addressing an audience. The most casual remark was delivered as though to a mass meeting. His gestures appeared as studied, and as unnatural, as those of a ham actor.

He was no awe-inspiring personality. He gave no impression of dignity. He was indifferent to whom he talked or which group he joined. He was self-conscious and inferior in attitude. He did not know what to do with his hands. He clung to his handkerchief or pushed his greasy forelock from his brow. The forelock glistened under the elaborate care of his Major-domo, fat Gustav Kannenberg—formerly owner of a famous Berlin wine tavern.

Hitler's eagerness to obtain the good graces of the princes present was subject to much comment. He bowed and clicked and all but knelt in his zeal to please oversized, ugly Princess Luise von Sachsen Meiningen, her brother, hereditary Prince George, and their sister, Grand Duchess of Sachsen Weimar.

Beaming in his servile attitude, he dashed personally to bring the princesses' refreshments from the buffet. He almost slid off the edge of his chair after they had offered him a seat in their most gracious company. Papen found the most exquisite delicacies to feed his Fuehrer. Hitler nibbled a lettuce leaf. He sipped orange juice. Everything else remained untouched. Of course, Hitler is known to be a vegetarian. But is there another reason for his public abstinence? Kannenberg told me recently: "The Fuehrer does not eat a bite unless my wife has prepared and cooked it. And even then one of us has to taste it first before his eyes."

Upon the arrival of the immensely rich Prince Ratibor-Corvey and his two daughters, Hitler was again overwhelmed. The princesses' mother is the granddaughter of Pauline Metternich. Ratibor is one of the best-paying members of the party. The young princesses reacted with a proper show of pleasure to his hand kissing and his piercing glance.

The evening had further trouble in store for me. I had the bad luck to be placed at a table with the Propaganda Minister. There were a few foreign diplomats at the same table. With the first spoonful of food lifted to his gigantic mouth, Goebbels started to discuss his pet topic: Jews and Communists. I was somewhat surprised, because I knew that the Propaganda Minister usually tried not to come into close contact with foreigners. The diplomats reacted in violent protest. The Rumanian Envoy, Petrescu Comnen, tried to prove that Communists were to be found in all creeds and races. "There are also Jews in conservative circles."

The clubfooted dwarf shrieked hysterically: "There is nothing worse than Rightist Jews! It would be preferable if they were all Communists." Comnen led me away. I was glad. Sometimes I can't keep my mouth shut.

I was fed up with the whole evening and wanted to go home. Just then I came across Baron von Brandenstein. He, too, had seen the Fuehrer kissing my hand. "Wait a year or two," he began, "he won't kiss your hand by then." His voice is thick and loud, and his appearance brutish.

"Well, I can easily dispense with that memory," I said. Brandenstein shrugged in disdain: "Better try to get out of Germany. I know the aims of the National Socialists. As soon as they have sufficient men to replace nonmembers, antagonists of the party are going to be dropped. They will pass laws to bar non-Aryan children from German schools. Jews will be permitted to employ only Jewish servants. They will not be served in restaurants nor in shops. They will have to establish their own theaters, their own newspapers. They will have to live in ghettoes." Brandenstein admitted that he saw quite a few acceptable points in the Nazi doctrines. He did, however, condemn their Jew-baiting, "as every decent German condemns it," he added. He also disliked their antichurch attitude. But seemingly, they had not prevented him from joining the party.

I had to be careful with my column, as Hitler had to be mentioned, and yet I did not want to flatter him. However, he was news, social and otherwise. Finally, I solved the difficulty by giving him a little extra paragraph:

> Very much to the surprise of the guests, Adolf Hitler appeared at about ten o'clock. This constituted his first formal social appearance at a large party since his assumption of his duties as Chancellor. He was warmly welcomed by the hosts. They used the occasion to present those diplomats whom he had not yet met, especially the ladies of the international set.

March 31, 1933:

This morning, a frantic call from the Foreign Office. They are terribly upset. The Chancellor's first appearance in high society was not mentioned in the *B.Z.* "Your noon paper is first to appear on the stands," came the excited accusation from the other end of the wire. "You should have taken care of that important item, Frau Bella!"

"I'll be there in twenty minutes. There must be a misunderstanding," I said. I was absolutely sure that within twenty minutes I would be able to put my column with its little extra paragraph about Adolf before Von Neurath. I dashed to the Ullstein office. Upon checking, I found that Paul Wiegler, editor in charge, had omitted my painstakingly conceived Hitler paragraph! Raging, I dashed into his office and called him to account.

He was unruffled: "I didn't think the fact of Adolf Hitler's presence important enough to give it special mention."

I was speechless. Finally I spluttered: "Are you *that* dumb; are you trying to get me into trouble, or are you trying to annoy the Nazis?"

I banged the door, jumped into my car and sped to the Foreign Office. The Foreign Minister believed my statement. He promised to see Goebbels right away and straighten everything out.

Well, I know now why the mere sight of that invitation gave me the creeps for weeks!...

Employees are fired daily. Yesterday three hundred seventy-eight dismissals alone in the municipal offices. Inferior clerks got the sack. Even the garbage must be taken care of by party members.

Goering announced the Jew boycott, scheduled for tomorrow, over the radio. I heard him roar: "I have been appointed to destroy..."

Said good-bye at the Friedrichstrasse Station to friends who preferred to leave before the boycott started and before a possible closing of the frontiers. The Venezuelan Envoy, who was awaiting the arrival of his daughter, said to me: "Won't you move into our house for a time? Things may be pretty nasty the next few weeks. I was in Rome when Mussolini upset things. They may be worse here. The Germans are tougher. They're bent on destruction of free labor, intellect, and Judaism."

I thanked him.

International expresses make strange bedfellows. S.A. Chief Roehm was a fellow traveler with my departing anti-Nazi friend.

"Good luck," I said. "Don't encourage Roehm. Send me a post card."

April 1, 1933:

My secretary tried to keep me at home today. But I set out for the office. Exchanged, as always, a few words with the doorman at the Markgrafenstrasse entrance of the Ullstein office. I entered while the doorman, in his impressive gray uniform with the gold-embroidered "U" on his coat, took my car to its parking place.

"Business as usual," was the impression I gained in the editorial offices. There was, however, a noticeable tension in the air. The Gentiles of the staff, especially, were jumpy.

The *B.Z.* was just off the press when hell broke loose. The stamping of heavy boots resounded from the pavement. Ever since the Brown parade in Berchtesgaden, the heavy steps of the Nazis' boots put my nerves on edge. Now voices rose in carefully rehearsed group recital: "To hell with the Jews," followed by a lusty chorus of the *Horst Wessel* song.

Stepping outside, I saw a strange sight. In front of the whole gang, their company leader, so to speak, marched our big, fat doorman, his gray uniform exchanged for the ominous brown garment of the ruling mob. I caught his eye. He couldn't stand my glance and blushed to the roots of his hair. He, too, was probably thinking about the coat I had brought him a couple of days ago. A gift for his wife he had asked me for.

Half an hour later, they had vanished. They had not had the impudence to enter the offices. I had, however, found out during this half-hour who of the staff was pro and who contra the republic.

On the pro side was Conrad Conradus, political editor of the *B.Z.* Only yesterday morning he had said: "What difference does it make, Bella, if Hitler was mentioned or not at the Papen reception. It won't be long before nobody mentions him any more."

I felt a slight dizziness. I needed fresh air. The big, fat doorman, once more in his dignified gray Ullstein livery, brought my car. He held the door open and clicked to attention when I started off, his face a full moon of good-natured innocence.

Near the Hallesche Tor, I almost crashed into my pet police-man, the tall *Oberwachtmeister*. I was so absentminded, so torn by doubts, that it's a wonder I managed to reach home without serious accident.

I tried to think it out clearly. Why is all this? Are the German people acting under pressure? Is the entire nation in a state of trance? The fat doorman haunted me as a kind of symbol of the German people. Twice within two hours he had changed color!...

In the evening, I drove to the Anhalter Railway Station to fetch my Gonny. She was coming back from a skiing trip. Just before the train moved in, there was the dreaded stamping of boots again. A company of S.A. came to a halt right in the middle of the platform. Commands were shouted. I wondered what important personage would be in the train that was to bring my daughter. But no important personage arrived. The group of ruffians was there merely to receive the train with a repetition of their same old recital.

"To hell with the Jews! Shameful death to the Jews! We won't have any more Jews!" Their lesson intoned, the rowdies started for the next platform to welcome the next train with their animal cadences.

April 2, 1933:

Had a talk with Secretary of State Dr. Bernhard von Buelow at the Rumanian Legation Ball. He seemed seriously concerned.

"Our relations with other nations had just been restored," he complained. "These medieval methods here have again torn down the bridges. The whole world is against us.

"I am glad that the people were unanimous in protest against yesterday's violent measures," he continued.

"I am afraid, in the long run, they are likely to give in," I said.

"Don't lose courage, Frau Bella," he said reassuringly.

Buelow is one of the exceptional men who will remain true to their convictions, I believe.

Mussolini's friend, Marquis Maurigi, asked me whether I had been duly impressed by Goering's new uniform. Thinking of the appearance he had presented, I burst into laughter. He had been sitting in front of me at the recent musicale in the Italian Embassy. The little monkey coat of the new light gray air force uniform did not conceal much of Hermann's bloated opulence. The little gilded chair groaned under his weight.

Lucky for the Cerrutis that the chair did not break. Goering, following the new ethics of National Socialism, might have claimed indemnification.

How complicated the routine in diplomatic circles becomes these days! Dr. Goebbels has stubbornly refused to admit "that Russian" to his sanctuary. "That Russian" happens to be Maria Chintschuk, wife of the Soviet Ambassador. She is substituting for the *doyenne* of the diplomatic corps, Madame Kemalettin Sami Pasha, who is on a trip. The duty of the *doyenne* was to introduce the diplomatic ladies to the new Nazi Minister's wife.

The Goebbels dilemma was settled by having Madame François-Poncet perform for "that Russian."

April 3, 1933:

Baron von Behrenberg, a convinced monarchist, entertained at a musicale in his Tiergarten Villa. The international society has always made it a point to attend his very exclusive and attractive receptions.

The host's son, member of the board of directors at Krupp's, was next to me at table. As usual he joked about the Nazis. He said how much the boycott against the Jews is resented in his circles.

"Most people refused to join in. I am glad that the Nazis were obliged to give the 'stop' signal the first night. However, I hope it has taught the Jews a lesson. They should all leave Germany and bide their time outside."

All of a sudden I discovered the party badge under the lapel of young Behrenberg's tail coat. Unable to hide my bitter disappointment in his hypocrisy, I seized his coat lapel and pointed to the badge. "Too bad you changed your mind," I said.

He laughed. "Haven't you ever heard of 'Nazi by force?' I have to play along because of my position. One member of the family has to sacrifice himself. Father would rather have every bone in his body broken. So I had to play the part."

Jan Hannusen, the stargazer and astrologer, fell into the hands of the self-styled "sizzling souls of the people." He has been slain. Goering's order. He has paid for his treachery in lending his hand to bring about the destruction of innocent people. When they had no more use for him, he was ruthlessly liquidated.

It's strange that his familiar stars did not tell him that.

April 4, 1933:

The assault on my cocktail party did not stop me from inviting my friends again. After the embarrassing incident last month, the protocol of the Foreign Office had asked me to let them know whenever I was entertaining. I kept my promise, and I went to talk it over with one of the officials at the Foreign Office. He sat there gasping when I told him, quite innocently, whom I expected. I had invited the Russian Ambassador and his wife, as well as their Secretary of Embassy, and they had accepted.

"What a foolish thing to do! At a time of such tension you simply can't have the Soviet people in your house. It may be dangerous for both you and the Russians. You'll have to cancel the invitation."

Nothing for me to do but to spend two days of voluntary house-arrest. Tilla Kraus, my secretary, had to phone and tell everybody that I was running a bad temperature, had to stay in bed, and would be very much obliged if the party could be delayed until after my complete recovery....

With the steady flow of new bills drafted daily, the legislation of the "secret police as independent authority" was passed today. From now on, every "state-endangering" enterprise will be closely studied, in the premises of the public art school at 8 Prince Albrecht Strasse. This former setting of Berlin's most charming costume balls is now going to be turned into the grim theater of the Third Reich's secret "Justice."

Richard, my friend and colleague, has joined the Party. It was that, or be dismissed. "I have a wife, a mother, and two children to support," he said. "If they keep firing newspapermen at this rate, the leaves (newspaper pages) will turn brown this spring, instead of green."

Dr. Goebbels has planted a horde of "reliable" journalists throughout the German editorial offices. These men are picked on account of their party affiliations. Because they feel inclined to do newspaper work, not because they have the slightest journalistic ability. It makes things difficult in every editorial office.

The Party comrade we got, along with those Nazis we already employ, is a tiny dark insipid illiterate named Brecht. He is an intimate friend of Goebbels', and looks enough like him to be his twin brother. The Propaganda Office stipulated his salary. One of the old and efficient members of the staff has been told to "translate" this man's scribbles into decent German. He hasn't the slightest idea of newspaper work.

His opening gun was:

"Well, folks, better try to get along with me. What kind of photos do you need? I want to cover the press photos, too. I'm going to borrow some money from Doctor Goebbels today, buy myself a Leica, which I've always wanted, and try my hand at it. The Doctor receives me whenever I want to see him. Frau Bella, where are you going this week? I think I'll come along to the dinner party at the English Minister's."

I tried to make it clear to him that the King of England is represented by an ambassador in Berlin. Also, that one cannot attend diplomatic dinners without invitation.

From now on, twice a day, one of the editors must be sent to the Propaganda Office, where the newspaper is instructed on what to think and how to say it.

There the editors are instructed in Nazi newspaper technique. They are given precise instructions as to the length of the captions, how many words the headings should contain, and how to phrase them. The editor is at liberty to decide the sequence of the words.

Goebbels appointed Dr. Funk Secretary of State, not only because he has a most docile and pliable nature, but also because he has good connections with the Thyssen, Voegler, Stinnes, and I.G. Farben concerns. That makes him a good Secretary of State.

When Schacht heard about the rising star of Dr. Funk, he took the occasion to be quite scornful. "Clever timing. He took up with the homosexual clique around Roehm in time to get his reward."

Individuality and personality, the foundations of good journalism, are now about to disappear.

April 8, 1933:

Recovering from my "grave illness," I attended two parties today. At the tea reception given by the Omer Wilhelm, the Secretary of the Russian Embassy greeted me with a wicked smile: "We are so sorry that you had to cancel your party because our Ambassador accepted your invitation!"

The numerous international guests talked about the establishment of the "Foreign Office of the National Socialist Party." Alfred Rosenberg, the Baltic apostle and originator of the new paganism, editor-in-chief of the *Voelkischer Beobachter*, has been reappointed chief of the Nazi Foreign Office. Putzi Hanfstaengl, composer of the Brown marching tunes, is chief of press.

April 9, 1933:

Lunched with Eduard von der Heydt, director of the Thyssen bank.

"The Brown Shirts won the first round. They have conquered Germany," he lamented.

"Obligingly assisted by your idiotic Thyssen," I threw at him. "Don't you think it would be decent of the pious Herr Thyssen to speak up for persecuted minorities, both racial and religious, before making further payments to the Nazis?" Heydt did not answer.

Had to interview the new Japanese Ambassador, Matsuzo Nagai. He seems the product of a brilliant Western education with a complete command of both the English and the French languages. His inclinations are evidently on the Brown side.

He uttered his polite regret concerning the Japanese resignation from the League of Nations. "Unfortunately, they had no understanding of Far Eastern questions, although Japan was willing to reinforce its good-neighbor relations with other nations. We have no intention of playing power politics in the Far East," he asserted.

He then went into a detailed comparison of Teutonic and Japanese virtues, aims and doctrines.

I looked at him without too much amazement, being familiar with the convolutions of the diplomatic mind by now. Nagai knows very well that this Germany, which he calls "so congenial to the land of the Rising Sun," considers the Japanese inferior to the German master race.

April 10, 1933:

Palm Sunday in the *Dreifaltigkeits* church. I arrived rather late. Entered the church at the same time as President von Hindenburg and his shadow, Colonel Oskar von Hindenburg. A chivalrous caprice made the Old Gentleman insist that a lady must be helped to obtain a seat. He charged Oskar to invite me to their family pew. So, surprisingly, I found myself seated one chair removed from the Field Marshal. The chair between the President and me was occupied by the President's top hat. Behind us, the inevitable Oskar.

For a moment I had a wild idea: This is *the* opportunity. Tell the old man that he is being deceived. Convince him of his terrific blunders....But a look at the vague expression in his dim eyes discouraged me. What was the sense in whispering a hasty warning to this slow-working mind?

April 15, 1933:

The Cerrutis invited a nicer crowd this time. Not too many Nazis.

Secretary of State Erhard Milch was there, and his wife. All his energies are devoted to military success. He is a plain-looking man. Short, with pale blue, watery, protruding eyes that remind you faintly of a frog.

April 27, 1933:

I found my dear friend, Secretary of State von Buelow, among the guests of the Japanese Ambassador. We had a very stimulating talk with Edgar Ansel Mowrer, an American who has a brilliant mind and a striking personality.

"This man is one of the few who write as they honestly feel," said Buelow.

May 3, 1933:

The Papens entertained at an intimate luncheon. How uncomfortably they live when they are in Berlin! They have no quarters of their own but occupy a flat in one of the ministries. Numerous rooms on a long corridor, with many windows opening on a court. It has almost the aspect of a rooming house.

Frau von Papen received in a light-colored Empire salon. The next room is old English country-seat style. Etchings of the period of 1800 on the light-colored walls. From there she took us to the host's study. The bright yellow walls fit the poisonous character of the tenant, I couldn't help thinking. A mighty baroque closet fills almost one entire side of the room. Hunting trophies everywhere, neatly furnished with date and location on a little silver plate. On the desk, proudly displayed, Hindenburg's picture, inscribed *"Ich hatt' einen Kameraden*—November 1932."

Frau von Papen is being helpful to the new Minister of Propaganda: "I am old-fashioned. America, England, all the countries who gave women the right to vote certainly have no important changes to show for this step."

Herr Hitler would have had a much harder time had it not been for the woman's vote, to which he owes his victory! In reward for their enthusiasm, equal rights, which they had finally obtained after 1918, were erased as soon as Hindenburg signed the decree of Hitler's appointment.

With but a few exceptions, the German woman in the Third
Reich is relegated to the function of a mere breeding machine.
Her duty is to present the Fatherland with a child each year.

* * *

The general atmosphere at the Italian Embassy dinner was
grim, indeed. They invited Minister Alfred Hugenberg, who has
practically been written off the National Socialist books. Also
asked were Dr. Goebbels and Alfred Rosenberg. To make the
disaster complete, Gottfried Treviranus, Hugenberg's opponent
from the former Nationalist camp, was there.

"Trevi," or the Cadet, as they call him, has been out of the
government since January. He and Hitler had stormy words way
back in 1931. They say Hitler never forgets an adverse word or
opinion.

Everybody behaved well, which is unusual with so many National Socialists around, because they seem to have a code of
manners all their own. The dinner was an ordeal, and everyone
was glad when it was over. After dinner there was the usual influx
of guests, including Labor Minister and *Stahlhelm* leader, Franz
Seldte. This did not help matters a great deal, because it appears
that Rosenberg cannot stand him. The "Party Pope," as usual
hung around in obvious ill humor.

On our way home with Marchese Antinori, chief of the Italian
Protocol. He wiped the cold pearls of perspiration from his brow:
"Thank God, it's over."

May 5, 1933:

Today, I met Prince Wilhelm, the eldest son of the Crown
Prince. He is engaged to be married to Dorothea von Salviati
from Bonn.

"Grandfather and my parents were mad at me. But I shall
marry her anyway," he said. "I renounce my rights. You know,
Grandfather really lives in the illusion that the Nazis are going to
restore our throne!"

May 6, 1933:

I met my famous colleague, Frederick T. Birchall, at the
Netherlanders today.

"Frau Bella," he urged me, "go away for an extensive vacation.
You are headed toward a lot of trouble here. And you can't do

anything to change matters. The *Reichstag* elections have shown that Hitler still has to reckon with many opponents. He will have to take more and more violent measures."

"Thank you, but I really feel I have a duty to stay here."

Magda Goebbels sent me a personal invitation for the birthday celebration of the "National Socialist People's Welfare."

I did not feel like going, but Eva von Schroeder, head of the committee, advised me to accept. Although a convinced Nazi, she is also warmhearted and fair. A contradiction, but true in this case.

"As long as you are a member of the press and as long as you want to keep your job, you simply have to play along. And you know that we want you to stay!"

"Well, I don't think there is anybody on earth able to save my position the moment Goebbels decides to get rid of me," I said.

Again I had the bad luck to come into contact with Hitler. He entered the big room, escorted by his giant adjutant, Brueckner. He headed straight for the two empty seats available—right next to me!

He strutted across the room, sat down, and said: "We have met before, *gnädige Frau*, haven't we? I hoped he would raise his arm and say "*Heil* Hitler!"—but my hope was in vain.

Instead, I had to raise my arm in the Hitler salute for the first time. There was no escape. The entire audience had to stand at attention when the *Horst Wessel* song was played. Each verse makes my hair stand on end. Hitler has decreed that this song is to be the official party anthem. It has to be played right after *Deutschland, Deutschland ueber Alles* at all official events, the "National Anthem Number Two."

The deferential salute to the Nazi national anthem is *de rigueur* for all creeds and races. Of late, however, Jews have been excluded from the "privilege" of raising their hand to heil either Fuehrer, banner, or song. If they have the bad luck to be present while the *Horst Wessel* anthem is played, they are, however, guilty of *lèse-majesté* and accordingly punished.

May 8, 1933:

Brecht, the Nazi who was forced upon our newspapers, came into the office to have his manuscript edited and put into printable shape. Although he is Goebbels' friend, he hasn't yet managed to get a car for himself. He asked me to give him a lift to the Grunewald. He spills so much party and political gossip that he really interested me, and I took him along.

He spoke a great deal about the rate at which we were rearming and the subterfuges of the *Lufthansa* and the *Luft-Sportsverband*. They have been training intensively for air warfare. Underground airports and factories are being built at a truly astounding rate. An enormous school for pilots will be established near Gatow, only twenty miles from Berlin. "Of course," he said, "those fellows crash like flies. But there are plenty of them, and they get commissioned as soon as they've finished school. They don't know the first thing about the machine."

He spoke about Rosenberg's going to London, driven by jealousy of the wine salesman, von Ribbentrop. Lady Oxford, who intended to use him for the sake of her journalist friends, said that a greater change had taken place in official opinion in England toward Germany than ever before in that country's past political history. Rosenberg's English is not too good. He missed the key words.

"Yes, Hitler has turned Germany into a happy country again," he said.

"The sheep only," his hostess stated. "Not the great men."

The "Party Pope" beamed, thinking she had paid Hitler some compliment. He did not understand how he had been gibed at until they translated the accounts in the papers for him at the German Embassy.

Brecht said also that "Jupp"—Goebbels' pet name—was angry with Goering and Schacht for allocating so much money for planes. He hates Schacht for refusing more cash for foreign propaganda.

May 10, 1933:

The Propaganda Ministry sent word that Goebbels wanted to see me, in reference to the coming fashion show at the race track club. I had staged quite a few of these shows, and I wondered what I was in for now.

I was on the dot for the appointment, but Herr Goebbels gave me ample time to cool my heels before he deigned to call me in for an odd two-minutes' talk.

He muttered his satisfaction with my work. "But," he warned, "from now on I want the French fashion to be omitted. Have it replaced by German models."

I could not help smiling. It was too wonderful to imagine the race track, the elegant crowd. In place of our stylish models, however, the "Hitler Maidens," with "Gretchen" braids, flat heels, and clean-scrubbed faces! Black skirts down to the ankles, brown jackets bearing the swastika! Neither rouge nor lipstick!

May 13, 1933:

Doing a serial about German hostesses for *B.Z.* Couldn't leave out a profile of Magda Goebbels, naturally. Goebbels' idiotic order to put all that was best in German literature to the torch made me so furious that I refused to write the profile myself and had Brecht do it. But I had to sign it. All such material must be checked with Goebbels' office, so I sent a copy there. Got it back with rather interesting additions and a letter from the secretary to the wife of the Propaganda Minister that I thought rather amusing. It read:

> "Dear Frau Fromm:
> "Frau Reichminister Goebbels has received your friendly communication with the enclosed proof of your article and wishes to express her thanks. Frau Reichsminister does not desire the fact to be made public that she is interested in Buddhism. Furthermore, Frau Reichsminister enjoys playing chess, but chess is not one of her hobbies, so Frau Reichsminister asks you remove the last sentence."

May 18, 1933:

Took a little non-Aryan visiting friend of mine to the *Rot-Weiss* Ball. Most glamorous affair! The new honorary president of the club, Vice-Chancellor von Papen, appeared, together with Ernst Hanfstaengl.

Putzi danced with my little visitor.

"You should go to the Anthropological Institute for a consultation," he told her. "I think it is absurd that you should be Jewish. Your skull has the perfect Aryan formation."

May 21, 1933:

Dr. Robert Ley, chief of the Labor Organization of the National Socialist Party, honored the Ullstein office with a visit. Now everybody in the place seems distracted. Of course, we have our "cell," with head men and informers. The Nazi representative on our staff protested because the editorial office is not yet sufficiently coordinated.

Not a day goes by without the arrest of some "unreliable" colleague through the Gestapo. The very ringing of the doorbell has a shattering effect on all of us.

Those among the colleagues who heretofore wore their badges modestly on the underside of their lapels now make a visible display of the decoration. Thus adorned, they were chosen to show the "Leader of the Labor Front" through the premises.

Today, Eva Schubring, a woman editor, told us sarcastically about Ley's visit and repeated an anecdote. "Hitler gave Ley permission to take the *v* out of its place in his name and to insert it before the letter *L*, thus raising him to nobility and changing Levy into V. Ley. Too bad he looks so non-Aryan."

May 27, 1933:

"Ley and his gang were only interested in our cafeteria. We poured gallons of alcohol into them and got them thoroughly drunk. The funniest thing was that Ley drank a toast to the far from Aryan Messrs. Ullstein."

May 27, 1933:

Ascension Day, gala dinner at the Italian Embassy. The event of the evening was Minister Goering. He had donned a new snow-white uniform. Although his spacious chest was already overflowing with medals, he was honored by the award of a new order, the St. Mauritius. Prince Philipp von Hessen said maliciously: "If this goes on, Goering will soon have to pin the medals to his rear."

Mrs. Cerruti had among her afterdinner guests the new "Gretchen" of the *Staatstheater*, Mrs. Emmy Sonnemann.

The hostess introduced me to the newcomer. "Bella, you never can tell how you may use that connection some day."

"What do you mean?" I asked innocently.

"Don't you ever hear anything, Bella? Emmy Sonnemann is Hermann Goering's mistress."

Mrs. Sonnemann introduced me to her friend, Dr. Elisabeth Keimer, who is redecorating Goering's palace. From an immense handbag she fished out a batch of photos and showed them to me. A truly hair-raising display of bad taste in interior decorating, culminating in a monstrous swastika which will adorn the wall over the fireplace in Goering's reception hall.

The swastika is a decorative theme on almost everything nowadays, including dog collars, bed sheets, matchbooks, and the water glasses on the desks of Nazi dignitaries. Julius Streicher drinks wine only from glasses which are politically blessed by a good-sized *Hakenkreuz.*

May 28, 1933:

"Hindenburg Day" at the races. Just as always, and yet so different. Many a familiar face has vanished from the scene. Black and brown uniforms have replaced the colorful pageant.

Conny von Frankenberg turned up with Prince Hatzfeld Wildenbruch. The Prince beamed: "Children, I am rehabilitated. They have hunted up a non-Aryan grandmother in my pedigree. Thank heaven! It really is a disgrace not to belong to the 'outcasts.'"

The President sat in his place of honor. Only once did his impassive features light up. He asked me about an old lady who seemed to awaken some reminiscence in his hazy mind. I told him her name.

"Oh, yes," he said, with relish, "I remember her folks had such delicious plum cake Sundays. They invited me when I was a cadet." And he fell back into his ancient reveries.

May 30, 1933:

I wanted to get away from everything for a couple of days and went out to Heiligendamm to get some sea air. Apparently, there is a brown curse on me. Adolf Hitler, Dr. Goebbels, Magda, the different staffs and the inevitable "secretaries" of the Chief of Propaganda had unfortunately chosen my place of seclusion for a merry holiday interlude. The solitary *Kurhaus* was spotted with the Brown beetles. The beach, the boulevards, the cafés resounded with "*Heil* Hitlers." My little vacation was thoroughly spoiled. This is carrying persecution too far.

Pretty Hela Strehl, fashion editor at Scherl's, was on Goebbels' "staff." She is on rather strained terms with Magda Goebbels. Nobody but Magda seemed to mind, however.

May 31, 1933:

At the Argentine Legation, I met the Reich Commissar for Economy, Dr. Otto Wagener, one of Ley's top men.

"A week ago, Goering called on Mussolini. They negotiated

Austria's fate," he told me. "Goebbels is furious because his rival is now in the limelight. He will appear in Rome, too, one of these days. Whether he will have anything to offer more official than his wife and a couple of sweethearts, disguised as his secretaries, is very doubtful." This, from a party comrade, was pretty good.

June 1, 1933:

Poulette's physician and faithful adviser took his own life.

"He was so pessimistic about the future. From now on I shall collect sleeping drugs," Poulette said.

June 15, 1933:

The press chief of the Austrian Legation, Dr. Erwin Wasserbaeck, called me today with some bad news.

"The Nazis have surpassed themselves," he said excitedly. "Theo Habicht, a Nazi agent in Vienna, was suddenly assigned to the German Legation in order to give him extraterritorial protection for his underground work. But he has been expelled from Vienna. In retaliation, the Nazis arrested *me* and kept me for hours in solitary confinement. Prime Minister Dollfuss and Foreign Minister von Neurath obtained my release after frantic long-distance calls. I must leave Germany within twenty-four hours, however. All this makes me feel greatly disturbed about Austria."

I felt sorry for Wasserbaeck. To divert his mind from his own sorrows, I unburdened mine. I told him that I had received my first Nazi blow. The *Reichsverband* of the German Sport Press advised me that I had been eliminated from their membership list, "because of the new order stipulated by the National Revolution."

"You shouldn't stay in Germany," said Wasserbaeck.

"I will send Gonny away if it turns out to be necessary," I said, "but I will try to stay on if I can."

June 17, 1933—London:

Conference of World Economy. Confederate Hall of the Geological Museum in South Kensington. A conglomeration of outstanding statesmen from all over the world. Journalists' headquarters in the basement. The gigantic study and the telephone rooms were beehives of activity. 110 typewriters! A post office, a bar, a restaurant, a complete little underground city. The most conspicuous among the four hundred newspapermen is Jimmy Walker, former Mayor of New York. I wonder whether his reports are going to be as smart, sleek, and dapper as his fashionable suit, his pale gray shirt with matching tie. His young wife, Betty Compton, never took her eyes off him.

In the upper world, the scene was illuminated by the flashes of the cameramen. They took a picture of MacDonald buttonholing the white-curled Belgian Minister of Finance. MacDonald held him by an upper button and talked intensely.

Colijn, the Dutch Prime Minister, in a comfortable armchair hidden by the huge pages of the *Times*. In a corner of the room, the Japanese snoozed peacefully, exhausted before noon. Coming out of his little nap, he will be surprised to find the first copies of his pictures, showing the representative of His Majesty, the Emperor of Nippon, napping, already in circulation.

Arthur Henderson has ample opportunity to compare the methods of his Geneva Disarmament Conference with this English sister enterprise. "I am leaving for Geneva. Hope to see you in Berlin, soon." His red face beamed. He likes a good swig of brandy. But he became very grave when he showed me an article François Coty had published in his Paris *Figaro*.

"Coty should be boycotted. He is an anti-Semite and a Fascist."

After a general session, Cordell Hull and the South African General Smuts retired to a corner in the stairway hall. The venerable gray head of the American Secretary of State swayed cautiously from side to side. The South African accompanied his speech with vivid gestures with his suntanned head. He stood there, erect and wiry, his hair and pointed beard a silvery flash.

June 21, 1933—Berlin:

Signora Cerruti, who is able to adapt herself to the demands of the day, gathered a bouquet of many nuances of brown in her salon. As a gesture of independence, however, she has indulged herself in the private joke of weaving anti-Nazi colors into the brown wreath.

There was Rathenau's brilliant sister, Frau Andreae. Present, also, was Secretary of State Theodor Lewald, who holds his post as head of the German Olympic Games Committee because his international connections are too valuable for the Nazis to drop him. The 1936 Olympiad is going to be quite dependent on whether Lewald stays on or not.

Another non-Aryan present was Kaethe Stresemann, widow of our late Foreign Minister; the international set makes quite a fuss over this charming woman whenever she appears in society.

The Japanese Councilor of Embassy, Shigenori Togo was, as usual, reserved and silent, though his tart comments on the wiping out of the Social Democratic party show that he does not entirely share his German-born wife's Fascist inclinations.

June 23, 1933:

The traditional garden party at the Foreign Office was held on a note of Nazi propaganda. Margarete von Hindenburg, sponsor of the reception, introduced the "new society" to diplomatic circles.

Edit von Coler, dramatic director of the *Staatstheater*, was among the new set. The blue-eyed, golden-haired woman aroused vivid curiosity. Which of the "Valhalla Gods" had helped her to this brilliant peak?

The Hungarian Nazi reporter, Egon von Kriegner, quoted "reliable sources" asserting that lovely Edit had been helped to the top by the two latest *Staatstheater* aces, Hans Johst and Dr. Ulbrich. There was, however, another rumor, Kriegner added, naming no less a protector than Goebbels as responsible for Edit's success. I was intrigued by her obvious interest in the French Ambassador.

She was most gracious and charming. "I am well aware of the importance of close collaboration between theater and press. Will you give me the pleasure of your company for a cup of tea at my studio tomorrow? My offices are in the premises of the former *Kronprinzen Palais.*"

Edit von Coler said that she had been married to a Finnish general. Her eighteen-year-old daughter, Jutta, was the offspring of this marriage. She married a second time. There is little known about her second husband. She had to drop him to comply with the rigorous demands of the Nazi creed. It is rumored that the Finnish general never existed and that the non-Aryan father of Jutta was both of her husbands.

June 25, 1933:

The *Staatstheater* offices are in a side wing of the *Kronprinzen Palais*, where the Crown Prince had his bedroom. Charming Edit von Coler now runs the Thespian Department right from that heavily frequented spot.

Edit, pretty, efficient, with her knot of heavy golden-red hair, would not have been a bad thing for the Crown Prince to have opened his eyes on in the morning. Although the presence of Dr. Ulbrich, attending to his business next door in the former Crown Princely bathroom, might have proved a bit of a distraction.

The dramatic director is a pleasant person, versatile, erudite, brimful of energy, and a good musician. The family provided a good artistic background. Her father was the sculptor, Professor Ludwig Manzel.

It's intelligent of the Nazi party to have such a representative. She is smooth, adaptable, and fits into the most exclusive salon. And that, I am convinced, is her real function, for which her theatrical activities form a shield, that of salon espionage. With special attention paid to the salon of François-Poncet. He is, however, more than a match for her, having tendered her a polite but cold shoulder right from the start.

Another of these female informers is Walli von Richthofen. She entertains on a lavish scale in her elegant Potsdam home, paid for by the Gestapo.

"She gets a high salary in return for her confidential information about the diplomatic corps," said Austrian Minister Tauschitz.

The "tea pest," Baroness von der Heyden-Rynsch, belongs to the same profession. She now entertains on a scale to which she would never have been able to aspire under any but the present circumstances.

Edit von Coler is the most attractive of the lot. She invited me to the opening night at the *Schauspielhaus*, telling me that she feels terrible about the current "defamations."

"I'm heart and soul with the National Socialist cause," she said, "but I wish to God I had something to say about that racial business. It's doing us plenty of harm."

June 26, 1933:

"The Berlin women must become the best-dressed women in Europe," said the Fuehrer to Hela Strehl, one of Dr. Goebbels' girls. "No more Paris models."

Consequently, a "Fashion Office" has been set up. The premises, most luxurious, are in the *Columbushaus*. Dr. Hans Horst has been made manager. He wanted me for an interview. I am going to do it, although I am not interested in fashion.

"Publication of the interview is urgent; Mrs. Goebbels is president," he phoned.

That left no safe ground for refusal.

July 3, 1933:

The wind blows east, the wind blows west, and nobody knows which way it will blow next from the office of the Ministry of Propaganda, which has just issued the order: "There is to be no mention made of the 'Fashion Office.' Frau Goebbels is in no way connected with the said office."

Meanwhile, the Ministry for Propaganda has turned the spotlight on the new *Generalinspektor* of German road construction, Fritz Todt. I know this character. He is ruthless, especially with other people's property. Todt has been commissioned to construct several hundred thousand kilometers of highway and *Reichsautobahn*. The New Germany!

July 10, 1933:

The disintegration spreads. All camps and classes change color to brown. Even the *Stahlhelm* has gone over to the Nazis. The disintegration has penetrated beyond the frontiers of our country. People like Lord Rothermere champion their cause.

"Old women of both sexes wail about the so-called atrocities committed in Germany at present," he states in his London paper. "They did the same thing ten years ago because of Italy. Minor transgressions of single National Socialists are of no importance compared to the benefits brought to Germany by the new regime."

What a pity the noble lord has had no opportunity to sample some of the benefits brought to our country, in one of the concentration camps!

It is not alone England who has Nazi champions. They see to it here that the germs spread throughout the United States. They are using the *Karl Schurz Vereinigungen* for their purposes. Founded years ago, the *Karl Schurz Vereinigungen* served to pave the way for a closer relationship between Germany and America. It helped visiting Americans to obtain information about subjects of special interest. The *Verein* is host to American professors, students, and civil servants, groups of whom visit Berlin every year.

Up to 1933, no attempt was made to influence the tourists in any political direction. Most visitors are from small American cities. They have no inkling that they are chosen to be unconscious tools for Nazi propaganda in the States. The Third Reich sees to it that the visitors see only the bright side of the German picture. Back home, they tell of all the wonderful things they were allowed to see. Thus, they spread the lies about the nonexistent improvement, and, what is worse, silence the few voices raised here and there in fair warning against the real face of the new masters of Germany. Most people, of course, don't trouble to think much about the barbarous atrocities committed so many thousands of miles away from democratic American soil.

Dr. Hans Draeger, Doctor *honoris causae* of Jena University, who runs the place, conceals his Nazi adherence whenever it is to his advantage to do so. But I have my strong suspicions, knowing the Karl Schurz house is a hotbed of Nazism.

Tonight, I met Draeger at a *Bierabend* of the foreign press. There was nothing of his usual deference for me. He ushered me into a corner and stormed: "I got into a nice jam because of my friendship for you. You know I have been in the party for a long time. I could land you in a concentration camp for your dangerous gossiping."

"I had no idea you were a party member," I said. "What you said at the Sackett dinner was anything but National Socialist. I forgot all about it since I never wish to harm anybody. Your hint that I have told on you is an insult. I insist on an official explanation. I am sure you talked carelessly all over the place."

Draeger saw I was annoyed. He was not too sure of his ground, apparently. However, he seemed relieved. "Well, perhaps the whole thing is a misunderstanding. But watch out what you say in future."

July 13, 1933:

The new American Ambassador, William E. Dodd, arrived with his family. Consul General George S. Messersmith introduced me at the Lehrter Station. Dodd looks like a scholar. His dry humor attracted me. He is observant and precise. He learned to love Germany when he was a student in Leipzig, he said, and will dedicate his strength to building a sincere friendship between his country and Germany.

I hope he and the President of the United States will not be too disappointed in their efforts. I am afraid the new Ambassador will be very much annoyed by the preposterous theories here.

Dodd denied that he was charged to speak up for the Jews. He seemed upset when he heard that the "horror tales" are innocent fairy tales compared to the actual goings-on.

He is against mass industrialism and explains the crisis in North America with the steady human flow from country to town. "The population should not leave the soil and start anew behind machines. It is an unhealthy state. Also, it is bad economically for immigration to be restricted. Immigrants are the salt of our country. They bring fresh ideas, strength, brilliant minds, money." He thinks Roosevelt's election was the beginning of a new era. "Roosevelt, with the approval of a friendly Congress, plays power politics for the benefit of the country. His executive power is as extensive as the power of a wartime leader."

Mrs. Dodd is a tiny, fragile woman with sympathetic eyes. Their daughter, Martha, is a perfect example of the intelligent young American female. Young William Dodd did not arrive with his family. He is driving the car from Hamburg to Berlin.

July 18, 1933:

I was the only lady at a stag party in honor of my English friend, Arthur Henderson. Gonny took pictures.

He seemed optimistic and was looking forward to the main disarmament conference, beginning on October 16. It really is wonderful of him to keep his spirits so high after all the disappointments of the last months.

He becomes gloomy only when his stomach troubles him. The heat in Rome and the pouring rain here did not bother him. His only complaint was the constant night traveling of the last weeks.

Secretary of State Milch tried to convert him to flying, but he wouldn't hear of it. "I only put foot into an airplane once in my life, together with Lloyd George. But we had first made sure that it had no fuel and that no pilot was around."

I thought it a good thing to make the best of Henderson's high spirits. After dinner, I sat in the corner of the sofa by his side and had a drink with him. I had a Scotch, very much to the surprise of Minister von Blomberg.

"Since when whisky, Bella?" he asked.

"Well, we just consolidate our friendship."

Henderson was most animated and did not hide his concern about Czechoslovakia's fate. "For eighteen months, we have fussed with that disarmament conference. During this period, most of the involved countries have been busy abolishing old and appointing new governments. There's been nothing but dismissals, resignations, elections and reelections. That's why we haven't been able to get anywhere."

July 19, 1933:

Frau von Papen, recently appointed honorary president of the "Society for German Nationals in Foreign Countries," invited me to come to a meeting at which Nazis spoke about the "gallant efforts of our German brothers in Austria to keep their German soil and German nationality." I think Austria is to be the first target.

All this is just part of a greater world picture, a canvas that takes in practically every country in the world. Clubs, societies, unions. All of them acquire the National Socialist point of view and meddle in politics wherever they find the soil fertile. The Welcome Club, a woman's group of the *Bund der Auslandsdeutschen*, now has set up sister groups for ten countries. The club was already *Voelkisch* in pre-Hitler times. It is now crawling with "March casualties." This, by the way, is the name given to those Germans who, alarmed by the notice that March, 1933, would be the deadline for entering the party, scrambled to political safety, without any regard for their real convictions.

Other organizations are the "Society of Colonial Germans," headed by Doctor Heinrich Schnee, and the so-called "Foreign Countries Club," which is in close collaboration with the "German Academic Exchange Service."

Their branches in foreign countries do subtle preparatory work through the medium of hundreds of German exchange students who are sent abroad each year. No student is sent out without thorough training administered by the Ministry of Propaganda, and no one goes who is not a member of the Party.

An American friend of mine, Bess Gould, has a boy who is at Princeton. This is in a letter: "Allan met two boys from Berlin. He brought them home for the weekend. There was no way of getting the talk off politics. They tried ever so hard to convince us of the blessings of National Socialism. A bad influence. My husband and

I dislike it exceedingly. We shall send Allan to another university next term."

On the other hand, the exchange students from abroad who are in Germany receive a thorough introduction to the new German *Weltanschauung*. Their point of view is expertly directed.

July 20, 1933:

The Karl Schurz Society gave a reception for the annual visit of the American Seminar led by Sherwood Eddy. Boston's mayor, James Curley, also was there.

The Germans used the occasion to praise Hitler's last pronouncement of foreign politics, the important *Reichstag* speech.

"Any possible concern in foreign countries as to the aggressive intentions of Germany should disappear. After all, the Fuehrer principle is also represented in America under Roosevelt."

Sherwood Eddy listened politely to all the persuasive arguments then replied in a speech which made the Nazis gasp in consternation.

He opened his address with warm words about his love for this country. He was happy to visit it for the twelfth time with his students. He broached the National Socialist subject most diplomatically:

I noted the unity of enthusiasm and zeal in what you call the "New Germany." I have always approved of enthusiasm and zeal. Besides my love for Germany, I have another, even stronger love in my heart: love for humanity. This love for humanity ties me uncompromisingly to three principles: impartial justice; freedom of speech, press, and assembly; fundamental moral and economic principles. These freedoms have to be accepted by all nations who claim cultural integrity.

I spoke my mind when I was in Russia. And I am going to speak my mind here. In Russia, I appreciated the people's achievements. I criticized their breach of the three fundamental principles of humanity.

As a friend of Germany, I state that you are acting against the principles of justice. There is no room for a twofold justice, one for "Aryans" and "Nordics," and another one for Social Democrats, Communists, Liberals, Jews, and Pacifists. Don't say it's your affair. It concerns the whole world when we in the United States conduct a lynching. It concerns the whole world that Sacco and Vanzetti were, as I believe, innocently executed. When we condemned the Scottsboro Negroes. When we confined the innocent Mooney in jail. The world is also concerned when you commit similar injustice. Didn't your Supreme Justice, president of the Reich's Court, Simon, refuse to lecture in our country when we executed the Italians?

In your country, injustice is committed every day, every hour. What are you doing to Catholics, Communists, Social Democrats, Jews? What atrocities are committed behind the wall of your horrible concentration camps? I see your papers.

With those words, Eddy held up the *Voelkischer Beobachter* of that day. It bore the huge headline, 70,000 JEWS IMMIGRATED INTO GERMANY WITHIN THE LAST 15 YEARS.

"This is not only a wrong statement. It is an instigation of youth, a kindling of race-hatred, a signal for cruel and wanton destruction. This must lead to massacre. With my own ears I have heard the Jew-baiting hurled out in your meetings. I am deeply worried about this country, which I love. Even Russia is better. There, at least, a certain amount of criticism is admitted."

The foreign guests broke into torrents of applause. The Nazis, pale with rage, sat immobile, in cold silence.

July 21, 1933:

Late at night, I went to the office with my report of the Eddy speech. Some editors grinned; some pretended indignation. All of them asserted it could not be released.

I gasped when I read the piece by double-tongued Thea von Puttkamer. A patchwork of Eddy's introductory part which ended in Eddy's solemn pledge to advocate friendly understanding for the new Germany in his home country!

Thea von Puttkamer is to be handled with extreme caution. She has a little trick of provoking anti-Nazi remarks and informing the Gestapo. She is said to report international antagonists, and many an expulsion can be traced to her. She has also helped send people to concentration camps....

Our editor-in-chief thinks I am tactful in precarious situations. He asked my advice today when he had to reply to a complaint of Goebbels' about a story. He handed me the already signed letter to read before he put it into the mail. I read it through. "Doctor, the letter is all right. I would, however, advise you to change the complimentary phrase."

The flustered secretary was lucky that I detected what had slipped her and the editor's attention. The letter ended "*Heilt Hitler!*" By the addition of a single "t," the obligatory "*heil*" had been changed into an imperative warning to "heal" Hitler. A mistake, but it would probably have been considered a malicious one.

July 25, 1933:

A stag dinner in honor of T.V. Soong, Chinese Vice-Chancellor and Minister of Finance. I was the only woman except Gonny, who hovered in the background taking pictures. This was the Chinese visitor's first trip to Europe. He has a good Western varnish from prolonged sojourns in the United States, being an honorary doctor of Harvard University.

Soong was obviously pleased when I asked him about his three eminent sisters, especially about Mme. Chiang Kai-Shek. I told him that I had received much information about China from the Councilor of the Chinese Legation Beue Tann and his Russian wife, who are dear friends of mine. I spoke about stimulating evenings I spent in their company and our talks about Chinese art, history, and politics. I tried to evoke the atmosphere in Tann's house, the fragrance of the green tea which we sipped from fragile cups.

We had an interested listener, Dr. Gottfried Feder, Secretary of State. He is the originator of the department store boycott and a Jew-baiter par excellence, and the author of the double insult, "The Jews are Negroid."

He now cut in with obvious flattery: "Heavens, Frau Bella, you certainly are versatile!"

"In spite of the fact that I am a Negro, Dr. Feder?" I inquired innocently.

Stepping out into the mild summer night, Gonny and I were stopped by two young S.A. men. They clattered their money boxes in front of us. I declined, explaining my feelings.

"Nobody'd know you are anti-Nazi from the color of your money, and we don't mind," they commented. But I assured them that I did mind.

August 7, 1933:

Spain has sent her former Foreign Minister, Louis de Zulueta, as ambassador to Berlin. He has the ascetic, shrewd, subtle and pious appearance of a Jesuit priest. He is a critical and observing person.

The Nazis appear highly interested in representatives of the Spanish republic. The first reception brought quite a few party officials to the embassy.

August 9, 1933:

I would say that Nazi propaganda is much too transparent to work were it not for the fact that it very often does work. I don't know why, unless it is because people are deceived by its obvious bluntness and are caught unaware.

This reflection is brought on by my visit to the Ibero-American Institute. The Latin Americans have been lavishly entertained and fulsomely flattered. It does things to their self-esteem. While at their exhibition, my eye fell on fifteen enormous volumes of German school material, arranged for South American consumption. A completely doctored education from kindergarten through the university.

"Why German schoolbooks for South America?" I asked in my naïve and unknowing innocence.

"Don't be so curious, Bella," the secretary, Dr. Henrich Panhorst, said firmly.

August 15, 1933:

I receive a great many urgent requests to obtain foreign visas through my friends of the corps. I have helped several hundred emigrants to reach the security of a free country. I have even managed to get some prisoners out of concentration camps. The weak point of the Nazis is that they are sensitive to foreign opinion, and it is through this weakness that I get most of my results in these cases.

The American Consul General, George Messersmith, always acts in a truly magnificent fashion. He is full of sympathetic understanding for the victims of oppression who come to him for advice and assistance. His help in removing obstacles, in getting around difficulties, has been invaluable. I have also received considerable help for my numerous protégés from the Czechs, the Spaniards, and many of my South American friends.

August 18, 1933:

English Military Attaché's party. The Emperior Wilhelm II's son-in-law, the Duke of Brunswick, appeared in brown S.A. uniform. His son, the Prince of Hanover, wore the black and silver S.S. uniform. It's remarkable how much in the way of insult the Hohenzollerns can assimilate, if they think it is in their interest to do so. They never resent an insult except from those who are weaker than they. The Nazis have never spared invective against the Hohenzollerns, and yet they enthusiastically raise their arms in the Nazi salute and their voices in the Nazi *heil*. Frederick the Great must revolve rapidly in his grave, these days....

August 20, 1933:

Had a big lump in my throat tonight at the farewell party for Dr. Adalberto Guerra Duval, who is transferred as Brazilian Ambassador, to Lisbon. We have been friends since 1921. His after-dinner speech made it very hard for me not to cry.

"I want to say good-bye to my friends. You are one of them, dear Frau Bella. You are living through a critical time. All of us are deeply shocked at the injustice and infamy done to you and your fellow believers. Let me thank you for your helpful assistance in my diplomatic endeavors. Your understanding and enlightening advice and information were of invaluable help. I know I speak for the entire diplomatic corps of Berlin when I tell you that we consider and will always consider you as a dear friend and as the Germany Ambassadress to the diplomatic corps in Berlin." I could not say a thing, the lump was too big.

August 21, 1933:

At the press conference, Richard heard that Edgar Ansel Mowrer, president of the *Auslands Presse*—foreign press—will have to leave Germany sooner or later.

"Mowrer is much too smart to be used by them. His integrity is unimpeachable. They watch him and his reports closely, just to find a pretext for his expulsion."

Reich Chief of Press Dietrich summoned Mowrer to the Ministry of Propaganda.

"You'll have to leave Germany."

"Why?"

"The Fuehrer read your book. He can't stand it."

Mowrer shook his head slowly. "That's funny. I read his book, and I can't stand *it*, either."

August 25, 1933:

Dinner in honor of Major von Stuelpnagel, "*Stahlhelm* district leader of North America and Canada."

An altogether ghastly affair! It cannot be denied that these veterans who gallantly fought for their country during the World War are in a state of complete disintegration. They are easy prey for the Nazis.

Stuelpnagel's speech sickened me. From the dais, I watched the revolting sight of black, white, and red flags obediently adorned with the swastika. Several battalions of the Stahlhelm were assembled. Commands were shouted. The military band struck up.

Stuelpnagel had been making disrespectful remarks about the National Socialists in private at the dais table where I had a privileged position with the *Stahlhelm* heads and their ladies.

The picture changed when Stuelpnagel rose. He praised the Third Reich with tears of emotion in his voice:

"We German-Americans were deeply moved and elated when for the first time we saw the flag of the New Germany raised by our New York Consulate General."

The entire crowd of upright veterans joined enthusiastically in his "*Heil* Hitler." I could see that hope for anything better was futile. Poulette once quoted: "Every nation has the government it deserves." It was not original with her, but it certainly seems to be a shattering and disturbing truth.

It's not curious that all this is beginning to make me feel like a stranger in my own country, that I am beginning to be aware of a feeling of hostility to my fellow countrymen. My roots are beginning to be loosened. I know it and can do nothing about it.

It is awful to hate where one has loved, to condemn where one has approved. It's terrible to look around you in the world and see no place that is yours.

September 9, 1933:

The Dodds have moved into the *Tiergartenstrasse.*

The Ambassador did not hand his credentials to Hindenburg until August 30, as the President had been on his estate and everyone had gone to attend the Nuremberg Party Day. Therefore, the *ricevimento* was postponed until today.

At the reception, there was a mixture of morningcoats and S.S. uniforms. Domestic and international society attended. The "new" elite was represented by people like Prince Hereditary Hosias Waldeck Pyrmont, an early party member. His official role was that of escort to the "diplomatic train" on the "Party Day." That is, he had to spy on the foreigners. He is a rather saturnine individual, thin, dark, with cruel eyes and mouth.

Dodd had a contemptuous grin for the S.S.-uniformed guests who were introduced to him.

September 12, 1933—Kitzingen:

I visited our family tomb. Many generations of our family are buried in that cemetery, an hour's ride from the station through old Franconian villages. A melancholy pilgrimage! Each landmark, each curve, is familiar to me. On the road leading to the cemetery stands the factory of an old family friend, producer of the world-famous *Lebkuchen*. At the entrance to this street, I read a poster: ONE-WAY STREET TO PALESTINE!

The steeple of a lovely little baroque church I loved is disfigured by a swastika. The cross has been removed by sacrilegious hands.

The family tomb has been robbed of its two heavy bronze chains. The marble headstones are smeared with swastikas. It was a bitter relief to realize that those who rested there would not suffer.

September 17, 1933:

Leni Riefenstahl came to my racetrack fashion show. I have known her for a considerable time.

Right after the World War, it became fashionable to give big house balls. People had been through some nightmare years. They wanted to forget. At one of these parties, I met Leni, who had been brought by a wealthy silk manufacturer, obviously her lover. Dressed in a tight-fitting black velvet gown, her dark hair combed back from her delicate face, she gazed around her, a dreamy look in her large dark eyes, clinging timidly to the arm of her escort.

We chatted for a while, Leni asking me about the various people with whom she had seen me talking. She talked to me of her narrow-minded parents. Her father's business was selling bathtubs, sinks, and W.C.'s. An exceedingly profitable business, though Leni admitted to a youthful prejudice against the prosaic and inartistic w.c.'s.

Leni was ambitious and wished to become a dancer. When the w.c. dealer discovered that she was secretly taking lessons, he ejected her from his respectable house. She rented a modest furnished room and tried to obtain a foothold in the proper circles.

Her first attempts at dancing were disastrous. The critics coldly tore her to pieces. A young Dutchman had written the music for her dance creations, and she rewarded him, it was said, by becoming his mistress. He was only the first of a long succession.

The silk manufacturer disappeared from the picture and was succeeded by a film star known for his Alpine pictures. Malice had it that Leni's daring mountain-climbing scenes were faked in the studio.

In her early film career, she wanted to precede her pictures with a stage appearance in which she performed a dance of her own invention. There were plenty of people to give her good advice about this. But she would not listen, and when the curtain rose, she tramped, barefoot and with enraptured eyes, across the stage. The barefoot dance was a "must" in the middle twenties. The reviews were uniformly wicked and vicious. Fate helped her out, however; she tore a ligament climbing some mountain or other. Her leg remained noticeably scarred, and her career as a barefoot dancer came to an end.

While she wavered between dance and film, she met the tennis star, Otto Froitzheim, at my house. He was then Vice-President of Police in Berlin. A remarkably eligible man. He lost his heart to her and would have liked to marry her, but at the time, any high official would have ruined his career by marrying an actress. Leni decided to stick to her art, and that was that.

Then the producer, Arnold Fanck, appeared in her life. He made her the star both of a snow movie and of his private life. Traveling all through Europe with him, she had a brief period of happiness, which lasted until the painter Jaeckl happened along. He, in turn, was replaced by the ski champion, Hannes Schneider. Ski champions were, apparently, to her liking, because she exchanged Schneider for Guzzi Lantschner.

She lived in a whirlpool of traveling, dancing, cinema work and love affairs. Shortly before the outbreak of the Nazi revolution, she returned to Berlin for a prolonged stay with her current heartthrob, the Jewish producer, Franz Sokall, who featured her in a picture named *Storms on Mont Blanc*. They took a duplex in the west section and entertained lavishly. I met many people at their parties, among them Max Schmeling, Ernst Lubitsch, Ernst Udet, and Bruno Loerzer.

Leni never got a great deal of credit for her work in the pictures, most of it being chalked up to her directors. She is supposed to be a favorite of Adolf Hitler's, but it is difficult to say just how successful she has been in obtaining his favors. It is true, however, that she climbed high and fast after January, 1933. The official films of the Nuremberg rally this year are to bear her signature, but it is pretty well understood that they were entirely done by competent collaborators who will, nevertheless, stay conveniently out of sight.

* * *

She was looking her prettiest at the racetrack. "Beautiful and lifelike advertisement for the party, aren't you?" I said.

She took my arm. "Bella, dear, introduce me to some of the foreign diplomats and to Minister of War von Blomberg. I have been dying to meet him. Hitler promised to present him to me, but so far he hasn't kept his promise.

That accounted for the affection. "I thought you could get anything you wanted from Hitler."

Leni blushed, which she has learned how to do with good effect. "Oh, it isn't what you think. He asks me to dinner a couple of times a week but always sends me away at a quarter to eleven because he is tired."

"I wonder how some of your old friends and admirers who did have the good taste to select the correct race while being born would feel about it," I suggested dreamily.

Leni has carefully preserved her enraptured, dreamy look. She has built herself up a good role, that of the shy, overworked, timidly aloof being who shrinks from the rough touch of reality. Plenty of people fall for the part. Some malicious tongues say, however, that Leni squints.

I let her chatter on. But she did not get very far in her desire to meet all my diplomatic friends. All she got out of me was an introduction to my secretary.

October 8, 1933:

Ambassador Dodd has been observing the Nazis too keenly for their comfort.

"The Nazis are cruel," he said, "but not original! Most of their decent economic ideas they have stolen from the assassinated Foreign Minister, Walther Rathenau. They stole the 'First of May' from the guilds; last week's 'Harvest Day' from the United States, where it is called Thanksgiving Day; 'Strength through joy' from the Russians, the 'Labor Front' from the Italians, and their cruelty from the Huns.

"They did not invent anti-Semitism. They simply were the first to organize it so it could be used as an effective weapon of the state."

October 12, 1933:

The American Chamber of Commerce gave a luncheon for the new Ambassador, William E. Dodd. The Ambassador discussed "Economy and Nationalism." He went back to the time of Julius Caesar. He spoke of the chaotic period after the discovery of America.

"England applied autocratic methods to establish a kind of economic nationalism. Export of gold was prohibited." Here the Ambassador turned to Hjalmar Schacht, president of the *Reichsbank*, and said mockingly: "Well, such measures are kept up even in our progressive era.

"The English experiment ended in 1688 with the Glorious Revolution, which cost hardly more than twenty human lives. The corresponding experiment in France lasted somewhat longer. Countless families were impoverished, thousands of the opponents sentenced to death. France had been 'excellently organized from above' but went to pieces during the revolution." Dodd mentioned the big American crisis a hundred years ago. Henry Clay, an eloquent speaker, attempted to isolate America from the rest of the world. After a spurt of initial success, the endeavor met with failure.

Later on, I complimented Dodd: "I enjoyed all these nicely disguised hints against Hitler and Hitlerism." He grinned sardonically.

"I had no delusions about Hitler when I was appointed to my post in Berlin. But I had at least hoped to find some decent people around Hitler. I am horrified to discover that the whole gang is nothing but a horde of criminals and cowards."

October 20, 1933:

Got an invitation to Lord Mayor Dr. Heinrich Sahm's. He does not entertain newspaper people as a rule. He had the Dodds, Minister of War von Blomberg, President of Police von Levetzov, and others from the cream of Berlin society.

"What courage!" I thought, "to ask me to a formal dinner!"

After dinner, a slim bald gentleman in a tailcoat accosted me. I did not get the name he murmured. He did not look too Aryan, and I was surprised to see a miniature party badge on his lapel.

I found out that I was talking to the Vice-Mayor of Berlin. I know the Nazis set Oskar Maretzky to watch the "tall cod" whom they don't trust.

I took the first opportunity to remind Maretzky of the fact that he was talking to a "Negress." Maretzky seemed amused and protested: "I am only against Jews, not against Jewish women. Especially not against charming Jewesses." He tried to convince me that he was against this part of the program.

Maretzky inquired whether it was really true that more than 12,000 Jews had died for Germany during the World War. Tomorrow I am going to bring him the *Gefallenenbuch*—the book of the Jewish soldiers who were killed in the war—which has a foreword by President von Hindenburg.

October 21, 1933:

Took the *Gefallenenbuch* to Maretzky. He was in S.A. uniform and most affable. After a while, he imparted this remarkable information: "I checked on that book. The Ministry of Propaganda has informed me that these 12,000 Jews in question just died naturally between 1914 and 1918."

"How can a man of any culture believe and repeat such outrageous rot!" I snapped.

October 25, 1933:

I have wasted many hours of my life by being punctual, but in the main, punctuality is demanded at formal diplomatic entertainments.

The Guatemalans, however, are different. I was invited to dinner by the Minister of Guatemala. Seven-thirty!

I appeared on the dot. So did the other German guests. The rest were almost exclusively South Americans. There was little sign of them. The servants ran around in dismayed confusion. The host showed up, muttered an apology, and dashed out. When he had been absent quite a while, he sent his secretary to replace him. The hostess had not yet appeared. The clatter of dishes indicated the hasty setting of a table.

With all the household excitement, time passed rapidly. The South American guests arrived leisurely, one by one. At nine-thirty, the hosts appeared, and dinner was served. The evening was a success. The whole atmosphere was so pleasantly far remote from the stiff formality and eternal etiquette of diplomatic entertainment that I found it charming.

October 30, 1933:

General Kemalettin Sami Pasha is a well-known figure in the diplomatic set. He has been here since 1925 as Turkish Ambassador. He is a striking-looking man, slender and vigorous, with a chiseled swarthy face illuminated by fiery intelligent eyes. Although his right arm is paralyzed, an aftermath of the fourteenth bullet that wounded him during the World War, he has managed to train his left to do everything. With the paralyzed right arm pressed to his body, he has complete mastery over horse and tennis racket. He even writes with his left.

Great ceremony for the tenth anniversary of the Turkish republic! The Germans were particularly eager to share in the holiday.

Formal soirée. Outside, the Tiergarten was wrapped in fog. The old Renaissance Palace glowed in dazzling light. The mighty gates were flung open. An endless stream of cars rolled in. A cordon of perfectly trained servants in green uniforms, the golden half-moon on red background adorning their collars, took care of the wraps and coats of the arriving guests. The General, in full regalia, the highest order of the Turkish republic pinned to his uniform, stood side by side with Princess Emineh, beautiful daughter of the former Turkish Minister, Abas Halim Pasha. The Princess was exquisite in a silver-gray gown coiling around her feet in a long train and glittered in the thousandfold fire of her gorgeous diamonds.

The assembly was a scene of overwhelming splendor. Military uniforms, elaborate gowns, sparkling jewels. An almost arrogant display of elegance and of names. The officials remained in animated groups in the reception rooms. The younger set drifted upstairs, attracted by the rhythms of dance music.

Many Brown officials, although not necessarily belonging to the dance-eager set, climbed the marble stairs to the first floor, too, heading for the bar. Torrents of champagne bubbled down their greedy throats.

"That seems to be the big attraction," said Dagnino contemptuously. "Most of the new gang did not know before January, 1933, that things like champagne, caviar, and the like would ever be within their reach. They knew them only from window displays in expensive shops. Come on, child, let's have a look at the spectacle."

Chief of Staff Ernst Roehm and Group Leaders Gehrt, Ernst, Sanders, and Kirschbaumer had gulped down such quantities of champagne that they were drunk an hour after the start of the reception. It was only eleven-thirty when General Hans von Seeckt asked a young attaché from the Foreign Office to remove the staggering S.A. men from the scene of their disgrace.

The "gentlemen" protested. With their loot of several dozen bottles of the sparkling liquid, they had settled down in a little boudoir. Group Leader Karl Ernst, comfortably stretched on a pink silk sofa, had planted his boots on a damask stool. He roared for more champagne. Suddenly, Alfred Rosenberg, the "Party Pope," entered upon the scene. *Staatsrat* and Group Leader Ernst was busy rocking a Brown Shirt on his knees. Rosenberg was cold with rage at the sight.

I could not hear what the "Party Pope," as usual in formal tails, hissed through his clenched teeth. I did hear, however, what Roehm had to say. He slapped his thigh and shouted:

"Look at that Baltic pig. The sissy hasn't even got the guts to drink!"

Rolf joined us. "It's true. Drunken people often speak the truth. Rosenberg is known in the party as a coward. Just like Hitler and Hess, he leaves decisive steps to others."

Our whispered conversation was drowned in Roehm's hoarse voice.

"Too snooty to wear the Brown outfit, that upstart Baltic Baron! Tailcoats won't do him any good. Say, Baron, who the hell do you think you are? Goering said years ago he'd find out what business you had in Russia from 1917 to 1919. Surely, the Russians didn't allow any *anti*-Bolshevist to study in Moscow!"

None of the international diplomats missed the show. Rosenberg, shaking with fury, disappeared.

"Pity Hess isn't here. That spy wouldn't wait for the night to end before giving his report to Hitler," said Robert Ley.

I was amazed to see Ley quite sober. It was most unusual.

November 8, 1933:

Quite by chance, I changed my mind and went to hear Schacht's speech on Martin Luther. My secretary had obtained the script of the address over the phone from the secretary of the *Reichsbank* director. My report on Dr. Schacht's address was ready to go to press before the *Reichsbank* president delivered it. My secretary had given me the latter's best regards. "Knowing how busy you are, he thinks there is no reason why you should attend the lecture. And anyway, you will meet afterward at the Italian Embassy."

I headed my car for the Italian soirée. However, my hands followed the command of some subconscious bidding. Hardly realizing how it happened, I found myself in Schacht's audience. What I heard had nothing in common with the address phoned from secretary to secretary!

This intimate friend of the Berlin Jewish society, this man who had been honored by the friendship of Foreign Minister Stresemann and his wife, did not skip a single one of Martin Luther's manifold anti-Semitic remarks. Martin Luther, as he was quoted now, had certainly been a Jew-baiter.

Certainly, Jew-baiting is a legal affair since February 1, 1933. But there is no excuse for Schacht's infamy. Schacht has not always been prosperous. Everything he has he owes to friends who are no National Socialists.

When he discovered me, he said: "Frau Bella, I meant to save you the trouble. Didn't my secretary phone?"

"Yes, he did, Doctor. Just the same, I am glad I came. Your lecture was really enlightening."

November 13, 1933:

Poulette used to be on friendly terms with the Direktor Niemanns of the Mannesmann factories. I kept telling her they were Nazis, but she was too stubborn to believe me.

Now she is cured. The Niemanns celebrated the foundation of the anti-Dollfuss "League of Austrian Fighters in Germany." It is a substitute for the "Austro-German National League," which has been disbanded by Dollfuss.

After the party, Poulette was in a terrible state. I picked her up, and we drove aimlessly across the Grunewald. Doing this, you can speak your mind without being overheard. The louder the motor, the more I feel at ease.

"The League is not supposed to be known to the general public, especially not outside Germany," said Poulette. "From here the Austrian Nazis are directed. Prime Minister Goering's brother-in-law, Dr. Riegele, who escaped from Linz to Germany, and Secretary Theodor Habicht, who was expelled from Austria in June, are both in it," said Poulette.

"What else is there, Poulette? You seem terribly upset."

My motherly friend unburdened herself desperately: From January 1 on, press members will have to give evidence of their Aryan descent."

"Why should *you* worry?"

"I have reason, Bella darling. I wrote for my papers, chased all over the place getting them. Finally, I found out that my grandmother was Jewish. Nobody knew anything about it. Now I lose my living."

I tried to cheer her. "We'll find something else, both of us."

November 25, 1933:

Poulette doesn't want to come along to the Foreign Press Ball. Today is the anniversary of her husband's death. I hate the idea of leaving her alone now that she has found out about her grandmother. I felt uneasy. Poulette haunted my mind. Tomorrow morning, I'll pick her up and take her out to my house. She loves running around with the dog.

The "Little Press Ball" was great fun. It is "little" compared to the ball of the domestic press, intimate and extremely elegant. Berlin international society comes privately, without any display of orders or official rank. The three long dais tables were headed by Norman Ebbutt, the "silent man" of the London *Times*. Louis P. Lochner of the Associated Press, who was a necessary part of the Berlin merry-go-round, which knew him as "Louis P.," and Sigrid Schultz—blonde, vivacious, charming and ever ready for a heated oral skirmish with some Nazi youth. The Dutch couple, Max Blokzyl and his wife, were also there, amiable and gay, but suspected of being Nazi sympathizers. I would handle them with care.

Prince August Wilhelm, tall, with piercing eyes that remind you of the eyes of his ancestor Frederick the Great, and Duke Eduard von Koburg, leader of the S.A. Motorized Forces, a striking contrast to the Prince, with his stooped, dwarflike figure. Both were in S.A. uniforms. After dinner, the unprepossessing Duke Eduard strutted around with his Fascist dagger, an honor bestowed upon him by Mussolini.

"That Koburg walks as though he were on stilts," said General of Police, *Staatsrat* Daluege. "It might leak out that his grandmother deceived the Grand Duke with that Jewish court banker."

November 26, 1933:

My dear Poulette is dead. Why did I leave her alone that night! Why didn't I act on my instinct!

I phoned her house at ten o'clock this morning, frightening her servant by such an early call. I was told that "the Baroness has left a note in the kitchen that she is not to be disturbed."

Suddenly, I understood. I rushed to the garage and drove to Poulette's rapidly.

"The Baroness is still asleep," I was told. I walked past the little old maid into the bedroom and flung open the shutters and windows. On the bedtable were two empty tubes that had contained veronal and a note for me.

A nervous few moments, with servants flying about, the doctor summoned and giving orders which were only half heard and scarcely comprehended, even by me.

During the agony of waiting, I read the letter, blinded by tears.

> I can't live any more because I know I will be forced to give up my work. You have been my best friend, Bella. Please take all my files and use them. I thank you for all the love you gave me. I know you are brave, braver than I am, and you must live because you have a child to think of, and I am sure that you will bear the struggle far better than I could.
>
> Yours,
> Poulette

Four doctors tried their best. She did not come back to life.

"She did not suffer any pain," they said, in an attempt to comfort me.

November 27, 1933:

The first morning without my telephone chat with Poulette. How I am going to miss her! I went over to her house. The Emperor and the Empress had sent a wreath. I put it at her feet. She would have been proud to know it.

The telephone bell cut the solemn silence. "Foreign Office—Protocol." "Ru's" well-known voice: "Frau Bella, I am deeply shocked. I know how terrible your loss is. Frau von Huhn died of pneumonia."

"Nonsense! Who told you that? She committed—"

"Frau Bella, please understand, our friend had pneumonia. Further explanations are undesirable. In your interest, as well."

I understood.

November 28, 1933:

The funeral was heartrending. Mammi von Carnap saw me home. Something was on her mind. "Bellachen, we are all so shocked that the new regulations should have this effect!"

"But, Mammi, don't you realize? This is only the beginning. This thing will turn against all of you who helped to create it."

"Frau von Neurath advises you to hurry up and get baptized. They are very anxious at the Foreign Office to avoid a second *casus*, Poulette."

Poor old fool! Doesn't she yet understand that this has nothing to do with creed or religion?

November 29, 1933:

I accepted the invitation for an intimate dinner at the house of my friends, Captain Lueder and wife, because I was sure to find Lueder's old friend, Minister of the *Reichswehr* von Blomberg, among their guests.

I wanted an opportunity to talk to him about the inhuman cruelty of the decree which had caused the death of my dear friend Poulette. Von Blomberg sat next to me at table. Our conversation continued long after dinner. The Minister told me that he, Foreign Minister von Neurath, and Secretary of State Bernhard had held long conferences these last days.

"We are very anxious, Frau Bella, to have you keep your job. The diplomatic corps feels exactly the same way about it. The Nuncio spoke to us in the name of all the foreign diplomats. Secretary of State Dr. Heinrich Lammers, chief of Hitler's office, is on your side. He and Vice-Chancellor von Papen, together with us, have submitted a petition to Goebbels. My adjutant is going to forward the correspondence to you."

I told him how grateful and touched I was. "Frankly, *Herr Reichswehrminister*," I said, "I know this trouble is not for my sake. You are afraid of the adverse opinions of the foreign diplomats."

Blomberg tried to defend the Nazi measures. He placed the usual blame on journalists of the Second Reich who agitated against the Nazis from their foreign havens.

I knew it was useless to try to make him understand the emotions of those escaped journaliasts. I tried to explain my own position to him.

"It is not fear of the outside world that keeps me here but the greater field of activity. Inside Germany, helped by my international friends, I can be of greater help to my unfortunate fellow-believers."

Blomberg, a reasonable man, except for his blind adoration of Hitler, apparently grasped what I wanted to make clear about myself. A Prussian soldier all his life, he is nevertheless amazingly well-bred. He has a good critical sense and mental agility. Yet now he started in to praise Hitler. His eyes shone with genuine rapture. "He is one of the greatest men of all time."

It flashed through my mind that this was an opportunity to get hold of the latest anti-Nazi literature. Just as Blomberg would not admit any weakness in his hero, I would not admit that there was such a thing as anti-Hitler literature written by emigrants. He fell for my ruse.

At nine o'clock this morning, his orderly brought a load of the entire output of last week's exile literature. I was pleased to find some publications which I had not yet seen, although, of course, my international friends furnish me with almost everything printed in that field.

December 10, 1933:

I have resigned from the various voluntary charity offices I held for many years. I now concentrate on welfare work for the suppressed only. All welfare organizations, including the Red Cross and the *Winterhilfe*, which we handled for many years, are now under Nazi control.

Eva von Schroeder asked me to be present at Frau von Neurath's for further discussion. She did not refer in so many words to my resignation. She handed me, instead, an announcement lately released:

The *Winterhilfe* of the German people is for the benefit of the people of all races, creeds, and nations living in this country.

I, therefore, attended. Frau von Neurath was knitting, and around her sat twenty-one ladies. She was chatting in her pleasant Swabian dialect.

At her request, I sat next to her. She welcomed me warmly. She would not consider giving up my valuable help and thanked me for all that I had done in the past. Then she employed a bit of typical Nazi parliamentarianism. Without giving me the chance to say a word in reply, she rose.

"Bella Fromm has just pledged her further collaboration in our charity work," she announced to the assembled company.

I did attempt to make some sort of protest, but Eva von Schroeder cut in, "Bella, you can't refuse. We are taking care of everybody."

December 13, 1933:

The Neuraths gave a party in honor of Fulvio Suvich. As Suvich is Mussolini's Secretary of State and Mussolini is Hitler's current idol, the affair was turned into a command courtship of the Italian guest. Germany was represented by its top aces: Franz von Papen with his affable grin and Prime Minister Hermann Goering with his jovial boisterousness. He had donned the uniform of an army general and clattered around under a full load of decorations.

Later on, and very much to the surprise of the guests, Minister Rudolf Hess, Hitler's "understudy," appeared without Frau Hess, who does not like to go in society. He is not a sociable sort either. His appearances in public gatherings of this kind are very infrequent.

I met Hess for the first time, a gloomy morose individual with an air of intimidating people. He hardly spoke. The guests stood around with their coffees and brandies, chatting and gossiping after dinner. Hess sat in a deep armchair removed from everyone, his eyes fluttering from group to group.

Goering's Secretary of State, Paul Koerner, accosted me. "Minister Hess wants to be introduced to you."

"Black Grete," as Hess is dubbed by his comrades, came over

and clicked his heels, avoiding the handclasp. I gave him a quick, penetrating glance. Tall, slender, well-built, somewhat effeminate looking. Not much poise. Unsteady, vague, sly eyes, bushy brows that meet in an almost straight line at the ridge of his nose. His nose is certainly not his best feature. It is fleshy, ill-shaped and ends in a knob. His large, almost lipless mouth gives him the look of something cruel and obstinate. I wondered whether the rumor was true that he paints his toenails red.

Standing there in his S.A. uniform, he made an effort to start a conversation. Without apology, fat Goering joined us. His pudgy hand, adorned by an enormous ring, held a big cigar. He said: "Oh, I'm glad I found you. I want your photographer-daughter to take a decent picture. Not one of those awfully realistic ones that show every inch of my waistline." Then, turning to Gonny: "Get going, shoot from an angle that emphasizes my medals. It's quality I want, not volume."

While Gonny set to work, Hess watched without saying a word. As soon as Hermann, content and jovial, had left us, the "watchdog" turned to me:

"Mind you. No picture is to be published without my approval. If, by chance, I am included in a group picture, I forbid you to print it." All this he hurled at me hastily, in a rude and bullying manner. Then he withdrew abruptly to return to his eavesdropping.

One of the Black group leaders, Rolf Rainer, had witnessed "Black Grete's" eruption. "Hess is always so rude," he said. "He was polite to you, compared to his shouting and bellowing when dealing with us. We know it's his inferiority complex."

It was rather amusing to watch the Nazi leaders spying on each other. Himmler, from Munich, was there and Gestapo chief Diels. There were more. None of them can trust the others. There's a constant race on to be the first to inform on the other fellow and get his job.

Frau Meissner complimented me on the charity tea held yesterday, which was something of a success.

I was sweetly appreciative. "Well, you do that sort of thing very well yourself," I said. "I still remember the great tea you gave about a year ago, to introduce your friends to Ernst Lubitsch. The diplomats were crazy about him."

Frau Meissner made a hasty "Jewish Round-Survey," as we call it, of the room. "Lord, what a mess that was!" she said. "I was so worried that they might not like my making such a fuss about him."

I was pleased to see her so upset.

Most of the ladies displayed lovely and colorful new gowns, but Frau von Papen remained faithful to her threadbare black silk garment with its green patina of venerability.

We had something of a time with Goering's pictures this morning. Hess, who does not seem to be altogether fond of Hermann, confiscated most of them. We got his approval only on those that displayed the full weight and volume of the Prime Minister. None of those that gave a fair view of the decorations could be used.

December 15, 1933:

Traffic jam at the Martin Luther Strasse. Only passengers and cars bound for the "Scala" and provided with tickets were allowed to pass. Gigli is singing for the *Winterhilfe.*

Everything was elaborately staged with full Nazi pageantry. The S.A. hordes outside the Scala gave Hitler the reception his divinity entitles him to. Goebbels and his wife were received with similar pomp and ceremony.

I was seated near Hitler's box, No. 7. The house was so jammed that tailcoats and brocades even crowded the stage.

When, after Gigli's first song, the applause had died down in expectation of the next aria, applause set in from Box No. 7. Violent applause! Hitler is a good actor. Gigli was forgotten. The entire audience, so well-behaved and composed as a rule, broke into a frenzy of ovation. Little bunches of violets were flung into Box No. 7. People climbed on chairs and bannisters to get a better glimpse of their Fuehrer. It made my blood curdle to think that the hysterical man with the face of a wild tomcat was the subject of this passion. There he sat, in his ugly brown garments, flanked by Magda Goebbels and the Italian Ambassadress—Beauty and the Beast. The adjoining box, very much to his annoyance, was taken by Victoria von Dirksen. Hitler is said to be sick and tired of finding himself so frequently next to "that old hag." He has given orders for better future arrangements in this regard. The "old hag," separated from glory and honor by the much too sordid partition between the two boxes, seemed raging with jealousy and envy.

December 17, 1933:

Blomberg sent me the correspondence between him and Dr. Goebbels about me. The way these gentlemen sign their letters is mildly amusing. Blomberg ends his epistles with an obedient "*Heil* Hitler." Goebbels seems to consider Blomberg unworthy of such sacred words. He deems "Best regards" good enough for him.

The advice of the Minister of Propaganda on how to handle the case of Bella Fromm consists in enmeshing it hopelessly in a tangle of red tape until all chance of getting it straightened out is lost.

1934

Contemporary Events

145

August	26	Hitler asks the recovery of the Saar.
October	9	Fascist agents murder King Alexander of Yugoslavia and French Foreign Minister Barthou at Marseilles.
October	17	New law requiring all ministers to take oath of loyalty to Hitler as leader and chancellor.

January 2, 1934:

Presidential New Year's reception as usual. Since 1923, the reception has been of a very formal nature. If somewhat less glamorous than under the monarchy, it is at least as ceremonial and rigorous, to accord with the Old Gentleman's preference.

After the preliminary ceremony came to an end, the Papal Nuncio presented the congratulations of the diplomats and their countries to the Field Marshal.

Hindenburg, as a specially gracious gesture of response, set out for the famous *Rundgang*, stopping to talk to every diplomat for a moment and ending the conversation by a handshake. This part of the ceremony is especially important as a symbol of age-old tradition. I was, therefore, interested when the Swedish Minister told me that Hitler had had the bad taste to ape the *Rundgang*, to assume equal standing with the venerable President.

January 3, 1934:

Some nice new regulations have come in along with the New Year, a rather charming portent for the future.

"Beginning January 1, the sterilization law becomes valid. Its aim is the prevention of unfit progeny." As inhuman a law as ever the minds of savages gave birth to.

The new law regulating writers has now been extended to the working press. It will probably knock the last solid ground out from under my feet.

January 4, 1934:

All the Ullstein papers carried my reports about the New Year's reception in full. "Not a blunder in your entire report, Bellachen," said the Chief of Protocol approvingly.

The editor-in-chief, Dr. Erich Welter, called me to his office this morning. "Chin up, Bella," he began, "we need you and we will fight for the right to keep you here." A pause. "The Ullstein press has received a verbal veto against articles *signed* by you."

What a devilish blow! The latest regulation requires the signature of the author to every article. No editor in Berlin would dare to print anything without my signature. Just where does that leave me?

January 5, 1934:

I got a telephone call late at night asking me to come to the office at once. Something important must have happened.

Something had. Weeks ago, one of my colleagues, Franz Gubler, had shown me a satire he had written, lampooning the army. Dr. Welter had refused to publish it. "He's right," I had told Gubler. "You must be crazy to expect him to take such a chance at this time."

Now, Gubler had replaced Dr. Welter for a day and had taken the chance himself.

For a little while, nothing happened. Nobody seemed to take notice of it. Then the lightning struck. The Minister of War had read it. Dr. Welter was in despair. Blomberg had called him at his home, thoroughly enraged. He said he would see Hitler, have the whole place closed up tight, and send everybody to a concentration camp.

"Bella, dear," said Dr. Welter, "as usual, you're the only one who might be able to help, or else it means ten thousand employees thrown into the street."

I thought that I was a pretty frail reed to lean on, with my own job about to be snatched away from me. "I'll try, Dr. Welter," I said. "But we'll probably have to make some concession."

"Tell him Gubler will be fired."

I jumped into my car, trying to think out a plan of action. Blomberg, I knew, was having a stag dinner party. Sybille, his daughter, came into the hall to see me.

"Not now, if you want to have any luck," she cautioned me. "Come tomorrow morning, for breakfast."

It was good advice, I thought. I passed an uneasy night and returned at eight the next morning.

"Well, what the hell do you want?" Blomberg greeted me excitedly.

"I'm going to shut up your damned pack of scribblers!" A stream of angry invective flowed around me, and I used the only weapon that might be effective in such a situation. I broke into tears. Blomberg faltered, lost his place, and his anger leaked away. "What do you want me to do?" he barked, now somewhat tamer.

"We want your help, *Herr Wehrminister*," I sniffled.

"That *verdammte* Gubler will have to be fired, that Bolshevik...."

"Swiss citizen," I cut in through my sniffles.

"I don't care what he is. Either he is back on his Swiss mountain in forty-eight hours, or I'll blow your publishing house off the map."

I was relieved but tried not to show it too readily. I went on pleading through my tears, deliberate tears, this time. "All right," I sobbed, "I'll take the bad news to the office. The poor devil will get thrown out immediately."

The General was appeased. "How is your own affair working out, Frau Bella?" he asked.

"I imagine I'm going to get fired, too," I said. "There seems to be no other way. Minister Goering spoke to Goebbels about it. He said afterward it was about the worst blunder he could have made, because Goebbels would never help anyone for whom he had intervened."

January 15, 1934:

Housewarming at the new Italian Embassy. The building, in the most elegant and exclusive part of Berlin, was bought from a Jewish banker and restored from top to bottom. One architect was not sufficient for the Cerrutis. They hired the services of Berlin's two most famous architects, by the purest chance, non-Aryans.

The ramp is awe-inspiring, flanked by columns with lanterns, adorned with Italy's golden crest. The portals are protected by exquisitely beautiful heavy bronze trelliswork.

The miserable drizzle of January rain was forgotten as soon as one entered the hall. The rough northern climate seemed unreal. This was sunny Italy. It was like being in Venice, in one of the magnificent *palazzi* of the doges.

Marble steps lead to a vast marble hall. Flowers are everywhere. The fragrance of a tropical garden; lilacs, almond trees, lilies of the valley in graceful bowls, bushes of orchids; carnations and roses in tall, slender vases. The entire luxuriance set against a background of palm trees.

Footmen in blue silk tailcoats and *escarpins* serve the guests. Part of the fashionable, stylish crowd in the reception hall was seated in Renaissance pews from Italian churches. The spacious library leads to several salons. Indirect light; antique wood paneling, castle portals, dungeon gates shipped to the embassy from Italy. Priceless paintings of the old Italian masters. The stately dining room can be converted into a music salon. The curtains of its high French windows are woven in pure gold threads. A flood of electric light gives warmth to the rooms. It glitters in countless facets over the vessels, the Venetian chandeliers and mirrors.

The guests were guided around in groups, as on a sight-seeing tour of a castle. The private quarters are on the next floor; followed by a suite for illustrious guests—truly regal quarters!

The Cerrutis serve dinner on gold plates. Their servants walk noiselessly, passing the dishes, their expressions blank under the white wigs. Soft music accompanies the dinner.

The afterdinner coffee broke the spell of the enchanted castle a bit. It was amusing to watch the groups gossiping and flirting. Blonde Susanne Renzetti had turned the head of Herbert Scholz, the handsome Referent for Foreign Affairs at the *Aussenpolitische Amt.* Society had been watching the amorous game for weeks with benevolent irony.

Hermann Goering and the Crown Prince, arms linked, stood at one of the marble fireplaces, telling each other jokes. The slenderness of the former heir of the German throne emphasized the enormous fatness of Hermann.

January 16, 1934:

At the reception given by Giuseppe Renzetti, president of the Italian chamber of commerce, the party lions appeared in luxurious number. "The order of the day is 'good neighbor politics with Italy.' The homage paid to the host, with his Jewish wife, was indirect tribute paid to Mussolini, whose friend he is," said von Bose, Papen's right-hand man. One after the other, the Nazi guests bent devotedly and politely over the well-groomed little hand of the hostess. Schacht, especially, adores her. Goering, a friend of the host, brought the actress, Emmy Sonnemann.

Roughneck Hans Kerrl showed his unpleasant face. A new feather in his cap is the beginning of a feud with the Protestant church. He wants to establish the church under Nazi control, with a puppet state bishop.

Robert Ley, leader of the Labor Front, as usual could not take his liquor. He was drunk within ten minutes. I had trouble with him. His attentions were embarrassing.

Goering's chief of press, Martin Sommerfeldt, used the opportunity to discuss my professional worries with me. "The Prime Minister appreciates your importance as a mediator with the diplomats. Maybe something can be done. Right now, Goering is trying to persuade Hitler to take authority over the press from the dwarf's clutches and put it back into Goering's hands. If he manages to talk Hitler into such an arrangement, you are safe and under our full protection."

Sommerfeldt, in necessary precaution, had ushered me into a remote little boudoir for this conversation. Looking around, I discovered a small card, half hidden in a gorgeous basket of orchids. "With the compliments of Joseph Goebbels."

January 20, 1934:

The political management of the Ullstein papers submitted a petition to Goebbels today in my behalf.

I have very little hope. Some of the Nazi press is being very vicious about it. The *Weekly Survey* published an article against me under the flaring headline: MOLES AT WORK, CRAWLING WITH INVECTIVE AND FALSEHOOD. ULLSTEIN AND THE 'DESTRUCTIVE BELLA FROMM.' It makes me feel hopelessly important. I don't wish to be a *cause célèbre*.

January 24, 1934;

I think I know why they're trying so hard to save my job at Ullstein's. Karl Jundt is behind it. He's our former Munich correspondent. Secretly, he's been on the side of the National Socialists for quite a time. When the proper moment came and "unreliable" members of the old staff were discharged by the score, it was made clear, by the party as well as by the cells, that Jundt's presence was "desirable."

Shortly after he became manager of all the morning papers, he sent for me. He wished to "protect" me. In return, I was expected to help him worm his way into the diplomatic set. But I had no desire to repay my friends in the diplomatic corps by introducing a practicing Nazi among them. By way of hiding my real intention,

I went with him on a tour of Berlin's smartest nightclubs, together with a friend of mine who is a high official. I learned one thing about Jundt that night; he is no convinced Nazi but simply an opportunist.

Soon after that, he told me that during a long conference at the Ministry of Propaganda, the "Bella Fromm problem" had been taken up in detail. "It seemed that a compromise was desirable" because certain diplomats had requested that I be kept on. "Let's consult the Ullstein cell. Right now, people like that may have more influence than the higher-ups," Jundt suggested.

The *Zellenobmann*—the head of the cell—came in then. A skinny, gloomy fellow, sparse black hair, modish but vulgar in appearance, with a lace handkerchief dangling from his breast pocket. I had never seen him around the Ullstein offices before, and I did not think he was the *Zellenobmann* at all but a spy from the Gestapo.

He questioned me, and to my surprise his questions kept centering on the French Ambassador, François-Poncet, the entertainment, the guests, the Ambassador's remarks and views. Seeing what he was driving at, I launched on a complete exposition of the social events at the embassy. I spoke about the artistic interests of the Ambassador, most of which were, to my inquisitor, completely uninteresting. I told him about the charming manner that François-Poncet has when he wishes to snub anyone, and about the German lady who bragged to him about her exhaustive acquaintance with the works of Goethe. At a dinner party at the embassy, she began to quote from a comparatively minor and not too well-known poem of the Weimar poet's, one that you might imagine to be unfamiliar even to the most erudite Frenchman:

> *Und so lang du das nicht hast*
> *Dieses Stirb und Werde*
> *Bist du nur ein fremder Gast*
> *Auf dieser dunklen Erde.*

The Ambassador, who had been listening politely, cut in on her. "May I take the liberty of correcting a slight inaccuracy?" he inquired. "It is *'trueber Gast'* not *'fremder Gast'!*"

The Nazi was at a complete loss. When the lace handkerchief had gone, Jundt beamed on me. "You win," he said. "Let's go to the Kempinski for lunch." I was extremely doubtful that I had won.

January 25, 1934:

Well, it seems as if I am beaten! For weeks and weeks, I have put up a stiff resistance, always carried along by the idea that my duty is here, that my mission is to stick to it. To use my influence, social and professional, to help the oppressed escape the hell that awaits them.

This idea alone drove me through these weeks of humiliating and agonizing parleys and negotiations. There have been endless hours of waiting, of cooling my heels in unheated reception rooms for the official in the well-heated office to admit me, only to dismiss me after a minute's evasive and unsatisfactory talk. Sometimes, I thought I could not take it any more. But I struggled on in grim determination, groping my way through the tangle of red tape and malice.

I have always been a lover of peace, with a horror of the useless bloodshed of war and violence, but now I am not so sure. The people of Germany need some sort of liberation. Perhaps a war of liberation...a war against Hitler. I hesitate to put this down, since war is against every instinct I possess. But it's beginning to look more and more as if there were no other way out.

January 26, 1934:

I'm still getting a salary from Ullstein, so I go there occasionally. I saw Brecht the last time I was there and got some uncensored political views. They are second hand, by way of his friend Goebbels, whom he calls "Jupp."

The German-Polish pact having just been consummated, Brecht said that would not prevent Poland from "getting a swift kick in the pants just as soon as the Poles aren't of any use to us any longer. We're palling up with Poland because we're not ready for Austria yet, and the *Reich* can't afford to have enemies on two sides. There's a lot of undercover work going on in the Balkans, too. Germany needs agricultural products and oil. Rumania and Bulgaria have 'em. We'll run 'em ragged with our surplus of finished products. They're all falling for the 'Red' danger that Goebbels is plugging."

Himmler, according to Brecht, had said that a deal with Russia would be about the final straw to cling to.

"Himmler has turned his anger on one of Hess's best friends, Martin Bormann, an important guy, tied up with the *Feme-Moerder*," Brecht said.

Martin Ludwig Bormann was a member of the *Rossbachorganization*, one of the Free Corps of postwar Germany. These organizations have been responsible for the so-called *Feme-Morde* (named after the illegal secret tribunal of medieval days) which liquidated politicians such as Rathenau, Erzberger and Kurt Eisner and spread terror in Germany. Most of the members of those corps later on joined the Hitler party, and the S.S. practically was built out of the former Free Corps Escherich, a competitor of the Free Corps Rossbach.

I have seen Bormann. He is one of those blond Nordic types that Nazis like, with a slit of a mouth, cruel eyes, and an overbearing manner. His hobby is persecuting churches, and he reads stories of Christian martyrs with relish.

January 30, 1934:

The old aristocratic families who swarm to Berlin after New Year's find pleasure in the parties and balls of the *Adelsgenossenschaft*, at which the court atmosphere is revived. The generals bring their prewar uniforms and helmets. The ladies bring slightly obsolete evening gowns. Etiquette is rigid.

This year, the S.A. felt moved by a nostalgic desire to get a glimpse of court etiquette at one of these balls.

If the gentlemen of the old school had not shown so much regard for the ladies, if the detachment of protective police, who were stationed below the scene at the "Zoo" as a precautionary measure, had not been ordered to refrain from action against the S.A., things might have turned out differently.

At ten o'clock, a horde of Brown rowdies broke into the ballroom. Doors were bolted, and the noisy troopers swarmed all over the place. Old gentlemen were tripped. Helmets were grabbed and used for a roughhouse football game. The ladies were kept quiet by revolvers poked under their noses.

And all this in spite of the fact that there were quite a few party badges in evidence. Recently, members of the old court have taken out the badges from beneath their lapels and pinned them on where all could see them. A proper and opportunistic display of sentiment which did not save the present party from insult and disorder.

Luckily, one of the cloakroom attendants had enough presence of mind to go and get some older S.A. men from the street. They ushered the Brown youngsters out of the place.

February 1, 1934:

"*L'Ambassadeur de France et Madame André François-Poncet prient de leur faire l'honneur de venir passer la soirée chez eux le 30 janvier...pour rencontrer l'équipe française du concours hippique.*"

The evening was a brilliant affair. The scene magnificent. The atmosphere was one of pleasant friendliness. This was the first occasion to bring high-ranking French officers to Berlin since the end of the war. The forty-eight dinner guests were seated around a symphony in pale-pink tablecloth, roses, and almond blossoms which were all of the same color. The multicolored gold-braided uniforms of the international army officers who had arrived for the horse show and tournament from all over Europe were set off by the somber black tailcoats of the civilians and the predominating white of the ladies' gowns. The black sheep, or rather, the greenish fleece, again, was Martha von Papen's eternally shabby Sunday best.

It was amusing to watch Phipps, the English Ambassador. Sir Eric kept a masklike poker face through the most exciting and heated discussion. His eyelids never fluttered. His monocle seemed glued to its place. When he uttered a few words, his voice was completely indifferent, dispassionate.

February 2, 1934:

Foreign Minister Baron von Neurath's ball on the eve of the Minister's sixty-first anniversary. A very formal affair. Uniforms of all shades and designs were predominant. The Nazi officials felt uneasy in the crowd of nobility. They function best when braced by quantities of alcohol. It is not very becoming. They lost control over their heads and feet and were soon unable to conduct any kind of lucid conversation. Impressively towering Frau von Neurath was escorted by one of the younger members of her husband's staff, who introduced "that crowd," as she called them, to her.

Strange that, in spite of their behavior, they gain social ground steadily. I think the reason is the curiosity, the thrill, which the foreigners find in associating with the Brown hordes. Also, perhaps their naïve pleasure in gathering uniforms at their parties, if only brown uniforms. The Nazis misinterpret their minor vanity. They put it down to admiration of themselves and their actions.

A new regulation was the admission on special cards only! Each invitation had been accompanied by a brown card. Upon arrival, each guest had to hand it to someone at the door. This was a precaution against undesirable guests, since the Nazis have fallen into the habit of bringing along two or three bodyguards, chauffeurs, or orderlies whenever they are invited anywhere.

The face and the form of social entertaining in German life has changed considerably during the last twelve months, Rolf and I concluded as we sat in a corner of the ballroom. The contrast between what was before us and what we had known all our lives was so strong that we could not help commenting on it.

"The old elegance is gone," said Rolf sadly.

There was a new attempt at elegance, however. "They leer at Jacqueline François-Poncet. They do their best to ape Elisabeth Cerruti." The result was something less than successful.

A foreign ambassador, bowing to the wife of Secretary of State Walter Funk, turned and saw us.

"Tell me, Frau Bella," he asked, looking back at Mrs. Funk, "what has happened to the German ladies?"

"Extinct," I laughed. "No animal in nature ever became extinct so quickly. There are a few ladies still around, I guess, but they're remainders from olden times, and it won't be long before they disappear, too. The climate around here isn't good for ladies. More conducive to kitchen work and to that greatest function of all for women in the Third Reich—breeding. Women are made into ladies by the attitude shown toward them by men and the state. This attitude has become rather rough. The old elegance has been trampled underfoot by Black and Brown hordes. There isn't much point being a lady in such circumstances, where no man feels under obligation to be chivalrous."

"Hard on the women of the Reich, aren't you?" the Ambassador asked.

"No harder than on anybody else," I said. "We reflect our times, I suppose. German cultural and spiritual inheritance has been swept away. Our new literature describes the heroic deeds of tiny men. They assault minorities, destroy works of art, soil and pollute temples and cemeteries, glorify killers in the textbooks of children...what would you expect from a people that approves the destruction of all that the centuries have built up? And why should the women be any better than the men?"

Rolf was quiet, but I could see that he agreed with what had been said.

February 9, 1934:

The newly appointed Councilor at the American Embassy, John Campbell White, and his wife found a warm welcome here. They are charming people, cultured and distinguished. The fact that Vice-Chancellor von Papen showed up at their very first afternoon reception is a sign that the Berlin elite is willing to open its arms to the newcomers.

Also on the American Embassy staff is Orme Wilson, a relative of the Whites. The Wilsons, too, are cultured and broad-minded and thoroughly hostile to the Nazis.

My particular favorite at the Embassy is Douglas Miller, the Commercial Attaché. He is the best-informed foreigner in Berlin. "His monthly reports are unique," Messersmith once told me.

The picture of the American Embassy staff would not be complete without the Joseph Flacks. Flack is the First Secretary of the Embassy. During a former appointment in Vienna, he married Luise, a charming Viennese with gold-red curls and an irresistible Viennese gaiety.

February 12, 1934:

Mme. François-Poncet has just returned from France. She was upset at conditions there, what with continuing street fights in Paris and the ugly sight of steel helmets and emergency guards riding through the streets of her beloved country. The picture was gloomy. Edouard Daladier's cabinet had resigned. The Stavisky affair was stirring up clouds of dirt and scandal.

February 14, 1934:

Much to the pleasure of the National Socialists here, Paris seems to be in a pretty bad state. Omer Wilhelm talked about the general strike, which had brought everything to a standstill.

"The Communists," he said, "are gaining ground. There seems to be a wave of insanity going around the world. It was either insane or criminal for the Austrian Chancellor, Dollfuss, to order the Social Democrats massacred. Or is it really an idea of Mussolini's? Austria without the Social Democrats! Just made to order for Hitler and his gang!"

February 16, 1934:

Werner von Siemens and his wife Nora had six hundred little golden chairs in their vast music hall ready for the guests who would come to hear the Philharmonic Orchestra or to watch the host conduct, for the benefit of the *Winterhilfe*.

The music hall is impressive and arrogant. A full-sized organ and the huge portrait of Nora each cover almost an entire wall. There is an arrogance, too, in hiring the entire Philharmonic Orchestra and shipping it f.o.b. to one's own house, just for the purpose of swinging the baton, even though it is done in the name of charity.

The guest list was abundantly sprinkled with Nazi officials. The concert was exquisite. Needless to say, the eminent musicians, who have been conducted by Arthur Nikisch, Bruno Walter, Arturo Toscanini, and Otto Klemperer, took little notice of the Siemens baton.

"With money, everything can be bought, even a conductor's baton," I heard Goering's sister, Mrs. Riegele, say.

"Even a conductor," I added mentally.

February 18, 1934:

Hans Thomsen, representative of the *Wilhelmstrasse* to the Chancellor of the Reich, invited me to a reception. I appreciate that courage. Hitler's Secretary of State and chief of his office, Dr. Heinrich Lammers, and Frau Lammers, old members of the party, were among the guests. "Tommy" is a real person. He comes from a wealthy, cultured family and has had a broad education. He speaks seven languages, having been all over the world. He is quiet, reserved, and well liked by the diplomatic set.

"Baby," his wife, is a merry, vivacious brunette with a passion for animals. I remember once when I was visiting the Thomsens, I started to enter her dressing room. Suddenly "Tommy" shouted, "Don't go in there! You'll get bitten!" When I asked what would bite me, he explained that "Baby" had a monkey that had been biting everyone. "In fact, he bit me this morning," said "Tommy" in a resigned voice.

February 27, 1934:

Collecting day for the *Winterhilfe*. Prince August Wilhelm, in his brown uniform, was rattling his collection box underneath the monument to his great-granduncle, Frederick the Great. The strong face above the Prince scowled at the degradation.

"They say *Winterhilfe*, and they mean tanks," said Rolf. "Very little of this money ever gets to the needy."

I watched the way it worked, watched people unwilling to contribute being awed and scared into it. No wonder the Nazis felt it necessary to send all their great out to peddle in the streets.

The S.A. leaders waited in the middle of the driveways, stopping the cars to squeeze a mite from the drivers. They pestered the elevator boys, the charwomen, the waiters, the taxi drivers at their street corners.

"Where do they think we get it from?" grumbled a taxi driver who has been stationed for years in front of the Kaiserhof. "Sweat it through our ribs?" He was the typical old-fashioned Berlin driver, the kind artists use as models.

"Forty to forty-five percent of our wages go each month to the S.A., Labor Front, Strength through Joy, Motherhood, People's Welfare, and every other racket they can think of. My wife has to rack her brains at home figuring out how to keep the pot boiling for us and the kids. There are days when I don't make three marks. Today, I'm skipping it. I'll put the old wreck in the garage. That's cheaper than waiting here in the cold for clients and then giving the money to those robbers."

March 5, 1934:

Seven hundred guests at Franz von Papen's party. I had the honor of being one of them, and to feel my stomach slowly turning sour in me at the sight of Fritz Thyssen and other big industrial figures dancing eagerly in a stately and humiliating minuet around their Nazi masters.

Among the guests was Professor Wilhelm Furtwaengler. He has been thoroughly cowed after his gallant attempt to break a lance for his oppressed Jewish colleagues. The correspondence on that subject between him and the Minister of Propaganda, duly edited by Goebbels, has been published. His feelings have been smoothed over by a title which was tossed into his lap, *Herr Staatsrat.* Some artists would have turned their backs on the scene of such baseness and continued their work in the free air of some other country. Herr Furtwaengler is safe and comfortable, however.

My dear friends, George and Marion Messersmith, may leave Berlin soon. The Consul General is to be transferred. It's going to be a great loss to me and to plenty of others.

March 20, 1934:

Nachat Pasha entertained me at an intimate luncheon. He was in top spirits, the result of a late adventure that had, apparently, pleased him. His German is almost a comic-opera language. He loves blondes.

"Was with beautiful blonde lady," he said. "Met three Brown Shirts. Brown Shirts regard beautiful lady and holler: 'For shame, such beautiful blonde girl with such kinky nigger!' Naturally, I flew quick in temper and hit first dirty Brown Shirt immediately into nose with great quantity of Nazi blood. The other two made hasty getaway but left first hero of Brown revolution lying flat on pavement. I shouted after them: 'How you like kinky nigger, now?'

"I have heard too much 'kinky nigger' business and so made request of interview with Hitler, because I thought to see Neurath will not help. He is coward. Hitler said: 'That must be misunderstanding.'

"I said: 'But no. Your Brown men are instigated to be in hate with other race!'

"Hitler became annoyed. He claimed: 'Your people was first for persecute Jews. You are Egyptian. It is all written with beauty in Bible book.'

"I claimed: 'That was accident took place many thousand years back. Besides, you charge often Bible not truthful, is it not so? Even if true, we Egyptians civilized now. Do you start your new civilization all over now? Go back six thousand years?'"

March 26, 1934:

Hassan Nachat Pasha celebrated his King's birthday with a gala dinner and dance. A versatile man, Nachat. Young, sporty, elegant, yet he occupied the chair for criminal law at the University of Cairo. For formal parties, Nachat likes me to check on the sitting order; to see that the numerous German and foreign servants have taken care of every detail and, most important, to select the wines. Because of his lovable manners, I once nicknamed Nachat "Sunny Boy," and the whole diplomatic corps has adopted that word.

My two neighbors at table, the Persian Minister and the Egyptian Minister to Berne, looked extremely Semitic. An S.A. group leader across the table continually drank my health. I pretended a chronic blindness throughout all ten courses of the dinner. After dinner, Secretary of State von Buelow brought him over and introduced him to me. *Legionstrat* Mayr. I was unresponsive, ignoring his outstretched paw.

He tried to flirt, but I continued unresponsive. "Didn't you notice, *gnädige Frau*, that I drank your health all the time?"

"No, I did not," I said. "Among decent people, one does not drink a lady's health before a proper introduction."

He was apologetic. "Sorry, I was upset to see the fair German woman flanked by these semisavages."

I laughed. "You should have drunk to the gentlemen. I was the only semisavage in the group."

He was taken aback but continued his attentions, asking me to dance. I told him I wouldn't be seen dancing with anyone in an S.A. uniform. He tried to persuade me that "the Old Guard of the party" condemns all excuses.

Secretary of State Otto Meissner sailed up to us. When he bent over my hand, I said: "Congratulations for the award of the golden party badge. Too bad our friend Ebert could not have lived to witness your success."

The somewhat asthmatic chameleon cast a frightened side glance, but no one seemed to have noted the remark. Relieved, he laughed. "Thanks. Do you mind my saying that sometimes you are much too courageous for comfort or peace of mind?"

He dashed off to the champagne bar. The returning Mayr now said:

"That's the reason I'm sick of the whole cheap game. Filthy characterless pigs like Meissner and Schacht are allowed to display the highest distinction of the party. We, who risked our lives for the party, are no longer proud to wear the badge."

I never admit anything to a Nazi, if I can help it, but it seems to me there is some justice in what he says. But why should a Brown savage be concerned about justice?

April 15, 1934:

The Bulgarian Prime Minister, Mushanoff, spent a few days in Berlin falling for the usual Nazi tricks. He looks like a high-ranking officer of the Guards in mufti. An elegant, dapper, old-time cavalier.

He was received by Hindenburg and Hitler. Schacht gave a dinner in his honor. Chalk up another gain for German foreign policy, much to the pleasure of King Boris, who has been casting sheep's eyes at Germany for some time.

A little Fascist branch in the Balkans would be very much appreciated by King Boris and his father, ex-King Ferdinand.

April 16, 1934:

Bredow told me today that at the *Wilhelmstrasse* they are hopeful for the speedy finish of the National Socialist government. The bosses of the party are continually knifing each other. When that has gone far enough, they think, the whole structure will topple. Even the Secretary of State, von Buelow, is optimistic.

I wish I could share their optimism, but it seems to me that the structure is being too solidly constructed to topple so easily. They begin with the children, cramming their little brains with ideas that confuse and dope them. From six to ten years of age, little boys are drilled in the *Pimpf* sections. Afterward, they "advance" to the "Young Folk." When they are fourteen, they become members of the "Hitler Youth."

A similar schedule is laid out for the girls. Between the ages of six and fourteen, they are fed with Nazi ideas in the "Young Maidens" organization. From fourteen on, they become "Hitler Maidens." After which the Camp, or Household-Work Year for girls parallels the Labor Year for boys.

The Hitler Youth is trained along military lines. The "Young Folks Leaders' School" has its departments for press, propaganda, culture, sanitary and hygienic knowledge. They are equipped with information service and aeronautic bureaus. Grounds for gliding machines, training of expert glide pilots, pilots' prep schools, all are included. The pilot schools furnish the "German Aviation Union" with a steady flow of new growth.

The peak of the so-called Military Prep Schools are the Schools for Leaders. They are the hotbeds of education for the "master race" and its leaders.

With these tremendous preparations for the upbringing of a Spartan generation, the children are dragged away from the loving custody of their parents at a tender age. They are brought up in a regimental spirit which is fatal to their minds and characters.

Yesterday, my daughter Gonny came to me in tears. She loves Germany but sees no future here. She wants to leave. I cannot say I blame her.

"I went to see Uncle Messersmith," she said. "He told me wonderful things about the United States. The freedom, the equal chances, President Roosevelt's program. He promised to help me get to America."

The girl is right. The countless humiliations mount up until the human spirit can no longer take it.

April 17, 1934:

Dinner at the Ibero-American Institute, to celebrate the appointment of Heinrich Faupel, a retired general, as chief of the institute. Nobody at the institute bothers any longer to camouflage the Nazi propaganda with which the organization is heavy-laden.

After the World War, General Faupel served as army instructor to the Argentine government. He returned to Germany recently. "Part of my job was to weaken French influence there and strengthen German ideology," he told me during a conversation.

An old World War general whom I have known for many years was my neighbor at table. "Why did you exchange the 'General' for the S.S. *Standartenfuehrer*, General?" I asked. "Somehow, it doesn't quite seem to fit?"

The General explained wistfully. "I'm afraid it doesn't. Lots of us think so now, although we supported the movement in good faith, thinking it would help save Germany."

"It is never too late to rectify a mistake, General."

He looked around for an instant. "Would you jump off a train going a hundred and twenty miles an hour?" he asked with a trace of resignation.

April 28, 1934:

The *Vossische Zeitung* has at last had to close its doors and call it a career. Dr. Welter wrote me a touching letter in full appreciation of my services. I was sentimentally fond of the *Vossische*. To see it crumple away like a toy balloon made me feel, more than ever, that another period had come to an end.

May 6, 1934:

Gonny left today. Now the Nazi ideology has left me without a child, although there is some consolation in the thought that she will have a happier life in a free land. The last blow she received before leaving was the notice that she had been dropped from the Olympic swimming team for not being a party member.

May 12, 1934:

Ran into Putzi Hanfstaengl at the ramp of the American Embassy. The Dodds were giving a farewell party for the Messersmiths.

"I wonder why we were asked today," he ruminated. "All this excitement about Jews. Messersmith is one. So is Roosevelt. The party detests them."

"Dr. Hanfstaengl, we've discussed this before. You don't have to put on that kind of an act with me."

"All right," he said. "Even if they are Aryan, you'd never know it from their actions."

"Of course," I put in, "if you're going to do away with right and wrong, and make it Aryan and non-Aryan, it leaves people who happen to have rather old-fashioned notions about what is right and wrong, what is decent and what is obscene, without much ground to stand on."

I suggested that he could always refrain from attending a party. "I have to be there, being chief of press of the *Auslandsorganization*," he said.

I told him that Consul General Messersmith was held in such high esteem by his colleages that he is practically regarded as having ambassadorial rank.

"All right, all right," he said, a little more softly now. "I have lots of friends in the United States, and all of them side with the Jews, too. But since it is insisted on in the party program...."

He took a paper bag from his pocket and offered me a fruit drop. "Have one," he said, "they are made especially for the Fuehrer." As a child, I used to love these *Lutschbonbons*, so I took one. Before I put it in my mouth, I noticed that it bore a swastika. Try as I would to make the hideous mark disappear, it remained leering at me until I had finished the drop.

May 18, 1934:

Von der Heydt was rather moody last night at the farewell dinner the American Chamber of Commerce gave for the Messersmiths.

"The industrialists are beginning to feel that perhaps everything isn't as it should be after all," he said. "I tried to open

Thyssen's eyes for years. But he kept handing out money and support. Goering sees that it keeps up. I'm upset every time an invitation to one of Hitler's musicales shows up."

"Why?" I asked.

"Because it costs a juicy sum. A list entitled 'For the Party' is kept at the door of the reception room. Goering hangs around to see that no one overlooks it. The other night, the industrialists had a plan. No one was to sign for more than twenty thousand marks. Thyssen was first. He wrote down that amount. Goering appeared from nowhere and slapped him on the shoulder good humoredly. 'What's all this, Herr Thyssen? You know everybody expected you to write down a hundred thousand marks tonight.' Thyssen smiled jovially and corrected the figure."

"Well, I guess they think it will pay, in the end," I said.

He shrugged his shoulders. "Lots of them are going to have the shock of their lives. Don't think they're not frightened. Even Hindenburg has finally waked up. Von Papen and the great landowners are trying to figure out how to disband the S.A. and get rid of Hitler. It's certain that Goering will stand by Thyssen, by industry and the bankers. Behind him is the police force. You see, big business considers Goering a guarantee against excessive Nazi radicalism. They wouldn't mind having the Crown Prince at the head of the government."

I laughed shortly. "I've heard that story before. Wishful thinking. They'll all stick together in a common fight. As for your friend Thyssen, he is an opportunist, but he's neither clever nor smart. His fear of Communism is wearing pretty thin. It never was anything but a transparent excuse for his views, anyway."

May 20, 1934:

Brecht, the Nazi journalist, came to see me unexpectedly. "It appears that certain people at the Ministry of Propaganda think diplomatic society reports should be written with the cleverness of Bella Fromm," he said. "I have a proposition. You write the column, I sign it. Split fifty-fifty."

"Thanks," I said. "I won't work camouflaged."

He dropped the subject and chattered on in his usual fashion about party gossip.

"Roehm wants to have his S.A. formations incorporated into the army. Blomberg vetoed it. Roehm also has a yen for the air-power command. He has resented the fat Hermann ever since the latter escaped from the 1923 flop. Hermann is in a rage! You can do anything to him except fool around with his *Luftwaffe*, and he could murder Roehm in cold blood. Roehm's also got a private feud on with the *Stahlhelm*, because Seldte refuses to order his men to salute the S.A. first. Do you know Himmler?"

I nodded.

"He was a chicken farmer when he wasn't on duty spying for the *Reichswehr*. He kicked Diels out of the Gestapo. Himmler can't stand anybody, but Roehm least of all. Now they're all ganged up against Roehm: Rosenberg, Goebbels, and the chicken farmer."

There is nobody among the officials of the National Socialist party who would not cheerfully cut the throat of every other official in order to further his own advancement. Hitler likes it that way. Keeps them on their toes. Also, he apparently thinks that a man who has the ability to fight his way through may be of use to him.

May 25, 1934:

Ball at the Austrian Legation. Minister Stefan Tauschitz affirmed solemnly: "We are not Nazis, and we are not going to be Nazis." I don't trust the Styrian boor.

I sat with Omer Wilhelm, who seemed very grave. "Something is in the air," he said. "It is almost tangible at the daily reception. The Nazis especially have the jitters. The constant clashes between Roehm and Franz Seldte will surely end in the abolition of the *Stahlhelm*. Have you noticed how the Nazis are stressing the *Lebensraum* slogan? There are a hundred million Germans populating the world, although quite a few of them may not speak the language. By race and creed they are brothers. In other words, the way is paved for an expansion, a movement to reunite the 'German brothers' who are now scattered over the surface of the earth.

May 26, 1934:

The Belgian Minister and Countess de Kerchove de Denterghem gave a gala soirée in honor of the Special Envoy Baron Holvoet, who announced the death of King Albert and the accession of King Leopold III.

Papen said to Blomberg: "The new King is against rearmament. He intends to sign agreements with his boundary neighbors."

Blomberg chuckled in a pleased fashion but let it pass without further comment.

May 28, 1934:

King Boris of Bulgaria is visiting Berlin. My Viennese paper
wanted a full report. A stag luncheon was given at the legation.
The Bulgarian Minister invited me to interview the King before
the party.

We were talking on several matters of current interest when a
message came in that Minister Goebbels would be fifteen minutes
late for lunch. King Boris compressed his lips for an instant but
did not utter a word.

As I knew that the invitations were for one-thirty, I took my
leave at one-twenty, staying in the legation office to watch the
arrival of the guests. One of the legation staff rushed in agitated.

"How dare they make my King wait!"

"In the Third Reich," I smiled, "everybody who is not a Nazi is
kept waiting. And each Nazi expects to be kept waiting by Nazis of
higher rank."

At one-forty, Goering drove up, preceded and followed by cars
containing bodyguards of six men each. He seemed placid and
entirely unaware of his lateness, for he did not even trouble to
make a formal apology, I understand. Shortly afterwards, Goebbels arrived. Fifteen minutes late, as announced.

Now King Boris and his guests could sit down.

June 1, 1934:

Miles Bouton, of the *Baltimore Sun*, is pretty realistic about the
Nazis.

"They're a tough lot, and you're not going to be able to get rid of
them before they've started a war, a war they can't help losing,
because they only know how to deal with physical factors; all other
considerations, moral, spiritual, and the like, elude them."

He has been on the blacklist of the Ministry of Propaganda. I
spoke to Frau von Papen about it. I told her Miles Bouton was
fond of Germany, had opposed the treaty of Versailles, and had,
on a great number of occasions, shown that his feelings are not
directed against the Germans. What I did not say was that he
abhors the Nazis. She was impressed and said she would speak to
her husband about it.

As a result, Bouton got word this morning that he would have to
leave the country as soon as possible.

So much for the voice of Herr von Papen.

June 10, 1934:

The newly appointed Japanese Military Attaché is an obvious hypocrite. Plump little Colonel Hiroshi Oshima is as slick and smooth as an eel. He is of impeccable Japanese politeness, extremely shrewd, intelligent, and versatile. His delicious little wife is wrapped in costly embroidered silk kimonos. A pretty smile is painted on her lips, a permanent smile.

Hiroshi Oshima has been in Germany before. He repeatedly emphasizes the similarity of National Japan's ideology with that of Nazi Germany. It appears that the Ribbentrops have been trying hard to build up a strong friendship with the Japanese people. The Nazis are doing their best to make the yellow men forget that Hitler's racial theories class them with the Jews and Negroes.

June 16, 1934:

Dinner at the English Embassy. Among the Germans invited were Admiral Dr. Raeder, Lord Mayor Sahm, and Goering. Punctuality is *de rigueur* in diplomatic circles in general and at the English Embassy in particular. Dinner was served at 7:30 sharp. The chair next to the hostess remained empty.

Without having taken the trouble to phone an apology, as I later learned, Hermann Goering strutted into the dining room just when the lackeys were removing the soup plates. Their stern faces and noiseless feet made fat Hermann's boisterous entrance all the more gross. Beginning at the door, as he moved his paunch gaily across the room, medals and decorations tinkling and clattering, he shouted to the hostess, "Person-to-person call from Venice." By this time, he had reached the empty chair: "Had to wait till the Fuehrer was on the wire."

The German guests were embarrassed. Hermann knew no such feelings. He turned to Raeder: "I was all set to follow him to Venice, in case he needed me. You know what he said?" 'For God's sake, stay where you are. I am coming back earlier than I had planned.'"

Raeder cleared his throat and wiped his mouth. The other guests looked into their plates. Phipps' monocle glittered in his frozen mask. François-Poncet clenched his teeth in a broad grin. The servants tiptoed around the table.

Rolf had heard the same afternoon, at the office, that the Venice conference was turning out to be a rather one-sided parley. Mussolini was firm about putting an end to Nazi agitation in

Austria. He gave Hitler a distinct hint that Italy would take to military measures if the Nazis did not stop it.

June 18, 1934:

Klausener told me that Papen's speech at the University of Marburg has caused something of a stir. He had dared to criticze the regime, and it was rumored that Hindenburg approved.

Papen had said that Germany must not leave herself so open to criticism by other nations by suppressing all freedom of internal criticism. She must not take a path that can lead only to vagueness.

"Fraenzchen," said Klausener, "never composed that one himself. He isn't smart enough. Dr. Edgar Jung wrote the script for him, as usual. Let's hope Fraenzchen hasn't stuck his neck out too far this time." I am in hopes that he has.

At the Italian Embassy, I met Parske, publisher of the *Diplomaten Zeitung*. He pretends to be anti-Nazi. That's as may be. Nobody knows where he came from. He is, however, extremely well informed.

"Ribbentrop arranged for Hitler's Italian pilgrimage," he said. "Then he went to Paris to see whether he could smooth the way for military equality. But Foreign Minister Barthou refused to see him. However, with the help of influential friends—perhaps Madame de Portes managed it—he got to see the Foreign Minister at a party. It did him little good, because when he started pleading for a reinforcement of German military strength, Barthou cut him short.

" 'I know more about your S.A. and your *Luftwaffe* than you might imagine, my friend.'"

June 19, 1934:

Richard, my dear old newspaper friend and colleague, came for a little chat this afternoon.

"There are a great many contradictory rumors circulating these days," he said. "They seem pretty upset in government headquarters. Goebbels in his press conferences gave strict orders not to mention Papen's Marburg University speech."

He also told me that *Die Lorelei*, with its beautiful poem by Heinrich Heine, was still being sung in the schools. However, the schoolbook reads: "Writer of the text unknown." An attempt to legislate immortality out of existence.

June 22, 1934:

Had the Schleichers, General von Bredow, and Rolf for dinner on my garden terrace. Schleicher is rested, but he seems worried. Kurt looked sadly changed in mufti. Elisabeth was amiable as ever and pretty to look at.

We were all quite pleased about the blow Papen had struck at Goebbels' suppression of free opinion and criticism. Schleicher was still wondering why Papen had shown this sudden outburst of courage. He said:

"The government wants to come out of its international isolation. It looks, moreover, as if Hitler has suffered a serious setback in Venice. Many people seem to have overlooked the little back door he has kept open for himself, in case of emergency, leading to some kind of Russo-German understanding, although he is strictly opposed to an Eastern Locarno."

Schleicher continued: "I can't understand how the French Chamber could approve the deferment of legislation for a longer army service—especially with Barthou fully aware of the feverish armament speed here."

I used the opportunity to scold Schleicher once more for having resigned last January. "Why didn't you stick to your plan to keep the Ministry of War and to designate Gregor Strasser as head of police and domestic affairs? Appointing Hitler as Chancellor could not have done much harm in such a combination, with the two most powerful ministries in hands which you considered to be reliable."

"Because," Kurt defended himself, "I knew that Goering had declared last summer that they would fight any government opposed to their plans. I knew Georing meant business. I had either to go or to stake everything on one card. Therefore, I took both offices. I was foolish enough to trust in Hindenburg's word of honor as an officer!"

Rolf said: "Goering admitted some time ago that a cabinet with Hitler as Chancellor, Schleicher as Minister of War, and Strasser as Minister of Police and Home Affairs might have led to the irretrievable destruction of the National Socialist party."

Schleicher gasped.

Hitler has gone to Neudeck. Heaven knows what he is trying to extort from the Old Gentleman this time!

June 29, 1934:

Cocktail party at 19a Regenten Street, the Czech Minister's.

One of the guests was Prince Bentheim, in S.A. uniform, accompanied by his wife, who hails from the slums and is a Gestapo salon spy. The Prince was rendered garrulous, as usual, by his too hastily gulped liquor. He had firsthand information about the Venice fiasco from one of his close friends who was with Hitler's staff.

"Hitler was really pitiable," he said. "The Duce had the whip hand all the way through, with 140,000 men at the Austrian border. He insisted that the Austrian business be dropped. Hitler struggled and twisted but had to give in. It was funny to see Hitler's reaction when the spotlight was deflected from him. Mussolini stuck out his chin far more than even the usual distance. He posed for countless attitudes, all of them familiar. The cheering crowds, at least those that were allowed on the streets, hailed their Duce and scowled at Hitler.

The Fuehrer is going to have to let off steam against someone. Perhaps it will be against Dorothy Thompson. They've established a Dorothy Thompson Emergency Squad that rushes translations of every word she writes. It won't be long now. They're just waiting for an excuse to kick her out of the country."

Bentheim took another swig and another tack. "Goebbels has gone to work on the girls at the Ministry of Propaganda. He's worked out a scheme to get rid of them before they get too troublesome. He selects a nice, wholesome young group leader, advances him in rank, and marries him off to his last sweetheart. Then he honors the advanced youngster and the dismissed sweetheart by his presence at their command wedding performance. The last one was his blonde young friend, Maria Stahl, who is being married today to Josef Terboven, district leader in Essen."

July 1, 1934:

Such a hurricane of disaster has come upon us! Rolf phoned yesterday morning. All he said was: "I'll see you at our meeting place." I tore out in my car, breathless with anxiety.

"Your friend Schleicher was shot this morning," whispered Rolf, as he climbed into the seat by my side. "It is known that he came to see you only a short while ago. You'll have to be careful, Bella! There is a wholesale butchery in full swing."

We drove to Mammi von Carnap's house. I don't know how my legs carried me, but somehow I found myself in Mammi's sitting room. Mammi listened to our report, trembling with fear. Rolf returned to his office. I stayed with Mammi, to compose myself and plan what to do.

Kurt and Elisabeth von Schleicher's assassination was such shattering news to me that I sat there, my head spinning, the ground falling away from under my feet. But something had to be done. First of all, I had to try to get out of a gala soirée which had been scheduled for tonight in honor of Prince and Princess Kaya of Japan. I did not feel the strength to undergo such an ordeal of forced gaiety and polite conversation with two of my best friends murdered. The protocol turned down any timid suggestion of my backing out of tonight's party. It would be simply insane if I did, they thought. The slightest thing might arouse suspicion.

Somehow, I managed to get into evening clothes. I pinned my medals to my gown, put on a forced smile which stayed there for the rest of the evening, and drove out to *Tiergartenstrasse 3*.

The checkroom had a funereal atmosphere. Dr. Sahm shook my hand. "Thank goodness, you are here, Bellachen." I knew exactly what he thought, although he was no longer able to speak frankly, for he was watched day and night.

"I was worried about you, too" I admitted. "You have always spoken your mind very frankly." At this point, Admiral Dr. Raeder arrived. He greeted both of us in the same revealing way. He seemed very uneasy.

The party was sheer torture for the German guests; a thrill for the foreigners. We Germans greeted every newcomer with a sigh of relief. Nobody knew who had been lucky enough to escape and who had succumbed.

After dinner, when we were grouped in the orangery, a young gentleman of the *Wilhelmstrasse* appeared. He whispered something into Sahm's ear. Sahm grinned: "Every single one is welcome to me." All sorts of rumors had spread by now. It had leaked out that Hitler had flown from Godesberg to Munich during the previous night. Goebbels, interrupting the Essen wedding festivities, had not left the Fuehrer's heels since. A measure of precaution and self-preservation! Rumors concerning Roehm were heard. Some had him shot, some merely arrested.

Everybody left early. I went with a handful of friends to meet some trustworthy foreigners in a little bar.

July 3, 1934:

"Heads will roll." Well, they've set it into practice with a horrible vengeance. I am staying out here in the country on the Zabern estate. Waiting, reflecting, and wondering which of my friends the fiends caught.

News came this afternoon that Ferdinand von Bredow had perished in the bloody slaughter. A horrible shock to me. The terrible passing of one more of my intimate friends.

The bearer of this particular news, a friend of my host's, had come straight from the Rhineland. He had heard a story from an employee of the famous Nazi meeting place, the Hotel Dreesen at Godesberg. It appears, according to the account, that on the eve of the modern St. Bartholomew's Slaughter, Hitler, Goebbels and Victor Lutze, *Obergruppenfuehrer* of Hanover, spent hours at a table on the hotel terrace. A gorgeous view, which as a rule threw Hitler into fits of ostensible rapture. But this time, the Fuehrer had no eyes for it, nor for the splendid sunset. He was preoccupied and tense. Late at night, there was a telephone call, apparently the alert signal. Hitler clutched the receiver so hard throughout the entire call that his knuckles were white. At its conclusion, pale and shaken, he ordered their immediate departure.

July 4, 1934:

Back in town after two days with my friends in the country. The "Fourth of July" reception at the American Embassy was filled with electric tension. The diplomats seemed jittery. The Germans were on edge.

Slowly more news spread. The massacre had been a general settling of accounts with everybody, in which the opportunity had been used by the various party leaders to wreak vengeance on their enemies. Hitler, for once, had sided with Goering. Hitler had left Munich for Wiessee, where he arrested Roehm. Details about subsequent events were varying. There was general regret that Schleicher was the one to lose his life while Papen only paid with a couple of teeth. He had escaped with a beating, no one knew why or how. Most of the guests would have preferred the reverse.

Dagnino said: "Hitler spared Papen for future dirty work. It is really shocking to find that nobody seems realistic enough to recognize Hitler's base political aims. He is ruthlessly determined to overturn Germany and Europe politically, even at the price of war. He does not mind wading in blood. He is willing to pay any price to satiate his wolfish greed and ambition. If Europe goes to pieces—well, that would be just too bad!"

I joined another group. There the topic was François-Poncet and his growing apprehension concerning his own safety. He considers asking for a prolonged vacation in France and would like to stay away from Berlin with his family for a while. There was a rumor that the Nazis suspected a certain high French diplomat of having been associated with a plot to overthrow the present German government.

July 5, 1934:

Strange, the international diplomats, who should know the worthlessness of words, take at face value whatever certain Germans say against the regime. You'd think they would understand that people like Neurath, Dieckhof, Luther, or Schacht are strong supporters of the Fuehrer in spite of their severe criticism and protest. The German Nationals, with their desire for more power, greater influence, and prewar pomp, are even less trustworthy than genuine Nazis.

Ribbentrop is busy establishing friendly ties with the foreigners. I am convinced he is going to kick Neurath off the scene as soon as he can afford to do so. He won't spare Schacht either, when Hitler's through with his services. Schacht clings desperately to the apron strings of the American Ambassador, as a possible emergency exit.

July 8, 1934:

In my office works a young photographer. He is tall, blond—a perfectly cast "Aryan." After Hitler seized power, this young man was seen only in the black S.S. uniform. After June 30, the day of the purge, he was absent from the office for several days. Finally, this morning, he came in—a changed man. He was jittery and uneasy and was constantly watching the door. When questioned as to his strange behavior, he broke into tears and stammered: "I had to shoot in the Gestapo cellar. Thirty-seven times I shot...Thirty-seven are dead...Thirty-seven are haunting me...I can't escape from those thirty-seven ghosts...."

We were shocked. The "Long One," as we nicknamed him, left the office, without a *"Heil* Hitler." Brecht, who was hanging around, also went out.

July 10, 1934:

Today, when I phoned Mammi von Carnap, I distinctly heard the "click" proving that my wire is tapped. Up till now, I had refused to believe it when people told me about the Gestapo's listening in.

July 15, 1934:

At the American Chamber of Commerce, Hitler's *Reichstag* speech at the Kroll Opera was the main topic of comment. Nobody believes that Hitler's life was endangered or that a counterrevolution was planned.

The Chamber bristled with Nazis today. It looks as though a general Brown courting of the Americans is starting. From now on, it is possible that our words, even in that circle, will have to be picked carefully.

The foreigners broke off their conversations or lowered their voices when a German approached their groups. The latter look rather ashamed of the whole business.

The whole nation had had to listen to Hitler's speech.

Indeed, all Germany has to listen to any big shot of the party who bellows his utter nonsense for a couple of hours over a national network.

Rolf has trustworthy friends almost everywhere. One of these, at the Ministry of Propaganda, gave him more details about the recent events.

"Goebbels has had the new *Roehmische* (Roman) villa searched. He ordered the entire staff of his section to attend to the unsavory task. All documents and papers have been taken to the Ministry of Propaganda. Roehm's place, although not yet entirely finished, was of an almost barbaric lavishness and luxury. Goebbels hunted about in the colorful, yet rather messy house and probably took an erotic delight in doing so. He picked up extravagant items of ladies' underwear, makeup, and other feminine paraphernalia that seemed to lie around everywhere in this homosexual palace. The reactions of the different onlookers were interesting: the genuine contempt of some and the unconcealed lustful awe of the rest.

"The plans for the massacre had been well laid and exhaustively scheduled. In the general turmoil, radicals and other disturbing elements were to be conveniently annihilated. At the same time, it was to be a sort of lesson to the German people. The lesson of total mastery of the knout.

"Goebbels, himself, is utterly corrupt. He draws support from Quandt for the education of his wife's child, Quandt being her first husband. At the same time, it is known that he pockets funds from the 'Aid for Families with Numerous Children,' an institution supposed to assist only the needy.

"His tongue is merciless. He is a limping, vitriolic devil. The other day, he came to the ministry and mocked Meissner. He stripped him to the bare soul for his foibles, especially his veracity. 'Well, but we really should be lenient, since he helped us to power.'

"So did Papen. He did a great deal of the dirty work for the party. They resent his assistance, as people always psychologically resent their benefactors. To show him what a nonentity he was, they slaughtered the people around him on June 30."

July 18, 1934:

We had not seen or heard from our photographer since he made his confession.

This morning Brecht came into the office, with a cat-ate-the-canary look, and said: "Have you heard about the 'Long One'? He passed...He talked too much...." We understood.

July 25, 1934:

The Nazis killed the Austrian Chancellor Engelbert Dollfuss. The Austrian Minister Tauschitz was in Vienna, "by coincidence." I wonder whether there is a connection between the revolt of the Styrian and Corinthian Nazis and Tauschitz, "the Styrian boor"?

When I received the shocking news about the Dollfuss assassination, I went at once to the Austrian Ministry to express my condolence. Councilor of Legation Rudolf Saemann was touched: "You are a courageous person to come here. So far, you are the only one in private German circles who has had the courage."

The same afternoon, Yvonne Wilhelm had given a tea. The diplomats were extremely upset. Count Arco, the *Telefunken* engineering wizard, had the audacity to say: "Of course the Nazis murdered him." He glanced around quickly to make sure that nobody was eavesdropping, especially his ambition-ridden wife. "I am afraid that it is not going to be the only political murder outside Germany.

"The 'Austrian Legion' is nothing but a German Nazi army in

Austria. For the time being, they have been ordered back to Munich. German Minister Kurt Rieth furnished the murderers Planetta and Weber with passports to make good their escape."

On my way home, I dropped in at Secretary of State von Buelow's. He was deeply depressed and humiliated about all the further "disgrace" heaped on Germany's name. He told me that Dr. Sauerbruch has been in Neudeck for days. The President is seriously ill.

July 31, 1934:

Intimate tea at Mammi von Carnap's. Everyone speculated on whether we were in for a war. Conny von Frankenberg, about to return to Switzerland, thought Hitler's attitude positively obscene.

"He sits in Bayreuth, drinking in his beloved *Goetterdaem-merung*, while his hatchet men go forth at his order to assassinate Dollfuss." Papen was also in Bayreuth. He got what he wanted. He is to be appointed Special Envoy, the same title that Ribbentrop has. It remains to be seen whether Hitler will place the same confidence in him. After a month of disgrace, he finally come back into favor. He will be sent to Vienna.

"Fraenzchen" is the typical *schneidige Kavallerie-Officer*. He does not give up easily. His friends used to call him dumb, but it seems they were quite wrong. Papen is really a sly, cunning fox, ambitious and familiar with all the wiles of political intrigue. He wormed his way through politics and society. He is smooth, well-groomed, impeccably suave and polite. A constant smile is frozen on a rather depraved-looking face, and his gray eyes are continually darting around. Quick to take advantage of every turn in the political game, he would not hesitate to flatter someone one day and denounce him the next.

The Italians seemed rather proud of Mussolini's reactions to these doubtful affairs in Austria. "Mussolini's army is on the alert at the frontier. Madame Dollfuss and the children will be his guests for a while," boasted Countess Serra, of the Italian Embassy.

Schuschnigg has become Chancellor of Austria; Prince Starhemberg, leader of the *Heimwehr*, Vice-Chancellor. After the war, the Prince became a member of the German Free Corps Escherich.

"We must keep an eye on Ley, the Commissar of Public Safety," said Tauschitz. It seems rather important to me to keep an eye on Tauschitz, who plays a most cowardly game here.

August 2, 1934:

The President of the Reich has died. I venerated the soldier in the Old Gentleman. Yet it's difficult for me not to feel that it would have been better for Germany, and perhaps for the entire world, if it had happened eighteen months earlier. We may yet come to know that the peace and happiness of the world were destroyed by the senility of one man.

Goebbels' voice announced the death over the radio. Flags were lowered to half-mast. An almost impenetrable silence followed. I reflected on the enormity of Germany's disaster and on the role that unfortunate old man had played in it.

It was Memorial Day, a day of somber reflection anyway. A day on which to think of the heroes who gave their lives for a cause that is no longer considered sacred. The Jews were not allowed to hoist flags in honor of the fallen, though thousands of Jews mourned their own kind who never returned from that holocaust. All these men paid for an idea with their lives. For an ideal of freedom that has been stripped from those of us who remain.

August 3, 1934:

In yesterday's great cabinet session, Hitler appointed himself Fuehrer-President. He is to be called Fuehrer and Chancellor of the Reich.

Blomberg lost no time in having his army take the oath of allegiance to the new President. Hindenburg's frequently mentioned last will has, as yet, not been brought forth.

"Meissner is said to be here from Hindenburg's estate, trying to find the Old Gentleman's last will in his files in Berlin," phoned Mammi von Carnap to me.

August 4, 1934:

Rolf is back from the Bayreuth festival. I had dinner with him, and he told me the gossip.

We could always tell when Hitler was coming to a performance because the S.S. and plainclothesmen would be spread carefully throughout the audience. He arrived, as a rule, when the house lights had gone down. He would be with his staff and Winifred

Wagner. She has a hard time of it with her children, they say.
Especially with "Mausi," as Friedelind is called, who refused to
join the Hitler Maidens, and who has taken something of a
dislike to Hitler. Children see certain things rather clearly.

At the *Festspielhaus*, Hitler never seemed completely at ease.
But he apparently stuck it out as a sort of alibi for the Vienna
terrorism. During one of the performances, he received news of
the Dollfuss assassination. He seemed unmoved. I suppose he
had been expecting the news. During that intermission, the
Fuehrer made it a point to show up in the *Theater Restaurant*. For
half an hour he strutted up and down among the guests, his
flock of bodyguards drifting after him. Hitler's Adjutant,
Brueckner, said Hitler felt that he must put himself on display so
that people would not say he was in Vienna to stage the murder.

Secret orders have been issued. Since July 1, certain places
have been on a "black list" for us, places of public entertainment,
restaurants, clubs, certain aristocratic and diplomatic houses. So
far as our official duties permit, we're supposed to shun foreign
newspapermen. That goes for members of the ministry offices,
military, party members, and *Stahlhelm*.

Rolf met Ribbentrop in the office. The wine merchant bragged
a lot about his excellent international connections. He had met an
American couple; the husband represents a great industrial
combine of the States in Berlin. According to him, the lady was
very ambitious socially. "They never knew," he said, "that they
acted as my doorman to American Ambassador Dodd, who had
refused every overture of mine for an intimate talk. Americans
are fond of uniforms. American women love to have their hands
kissed. You simply have to know the formula."

Ribbentrop, despite his excellent manners, does not always
know the formula. He addresses higher officials in the third
person, a formula left over from monarchistic times. Maybe he
thinks this makes an impression.

August 8, 1934:

Yesterday at noon, Hindenburg was buried with medieval pomp
and ceremony at Tannenberg. A photographer for the Associated
Press told me today: "We foreigners got a raw deal. Each special
shot was reserved for the 'Court Photographer,' Heinrich
Hoffmann. We were hardly permitted to move around. The photo
despot, P. D. Ziegenbein, of the Ministry of Propaganda, seques-

trated the photographic permits without any reason. 'Gentlemen,' he told us at 9:00 A.M., 'you may knock off for today.'"

August 10, 1934:

Next week, Germany goes to the polls. Night after night, the radio screams out the history of the Reich's savior. In between, the bigwigs of the party urge "Blind Obedience in Gratitude," "Loyalty to State and Party," "Loyalty to the Party Above All."

August 15, 1934:

Richard came to see me, all hot and flustered. "Bellachen, Hitler has Jewish blood in his veins. Paul Wiegler, our fiction editor, found out through Viennese friends!

"Hitler had a very beautiful grandmother. She was vain, ambitious, and money-greedy. She had a job as a lady's maid in Vienna, at a wealthy, non-Aryan banker's house. It is known that she brought an illegitimate child into her marriage with Schicklgruber. Well, that offspring of her romance with the Jewish banker was Adolf Hitler's father."

I became very indignant! "That would be the most disgraceful blow of all to the Jews—if it were true! Haven't we enough to bear, without adding a Jewish Hitler to our burden?"

August 24, 1934:

After old Field Marshal Hindenburg was buried, the German people learned that he had designated Adolf Hitler as his successor, thus making him President and Chancellor in one person. How much doubt that may have been felt in the minds of the blindfolded masses is hard to guess. They knew so little about the machinations before and after Hitler's ascent, when the venerated old President became a mere tool in the hands of the ambitious new master class, deceived, confused, and double-crossed by his entourage and closest friends.

"If Sauerbruch would only speak up, we might know more about Hindenburg's death," sighed Rolf. "Sauerbruch is the only one who knows—besides Hindenburg's various watchdogs, together with the forgers of the will, Goebbels and his collaborator Councilor Ernst Brauweiler—exactly when Hindenburg passed away. People are saying that he died the day before his death. So that he was already dead at the time of the hastily convened session of the ministers, during which Hitler's succession was secured.

"Meissner lent a hand in keeping the President as confused and ignorant as possible about domestic affairs. Reports concerning the massacre of June 30 were intercepted. Hindenburg lived virtually confined in Germany's smallest concentration camp—his estate at Neudeck. His Adjutant number two, Count Wedige von der Schulenburg, refused admission to any callers during his last weeks. Not even his old friend and neighbor, Count Oldenburg-Januschau, was admitted, although it was the "old Januschauer" whom Hindenburg wanted to see most desperately. It was Meissner, not Papen, who flew to Berlin to take the testament to Goebbels, who made certain that it was edited before the funeral."

Rolf went on: "The voting results were arranged long before the election. The genuine result would have been completely different. *Regierungstrat* Wilfried Bade, Referent at the Ministry of Propaganda and organizer of the mass parades, is responsible for the overwhelming parade of pro-Hitler ciphers. He disposed of the numerous *No* votes, together with the anti-Hitler cartoons which were found in the ballot boxes."

August 28, 1934:

Went to see Dodd at the embassy. We talked about Dorothy Thompson's expulsion. She had been given twenty-four hours to get out. "You should go away, too," he told me.

"Excellency, a single individual is of no importance. It is still possible to do good work here," I said.

He told me that Hess has promulgated further measures against church and Jews. "As his decrees are secret orders, it is, of course, difficult to put a finger on any of his outrageous tricks."

Dodd is fully aware of the impending catastrophe. He promised to keep my name carefully out of any counter measures. "We are both trying hard to help mankind," he said when he saw me out.

September 8, 1934:

Schacht made a speech criticizing the Third Reich! The press was not allowed to print it. Schacht got it into circulation anyway. He had the *Reichsbank* distribute his sermon in leaflets, at a price of twenty pfennigs!

"That fellow is shrewd enough to make money even with his prohibited speech," said Ribbentrop at his office.

September 11, 1934:

The impudent and deceitful exaggeration that reigns at the Nuremberg Party Day celebration, the bragging, the propaganda, are a perpetual amazement to foreigners. The mass gathering is a powerful drug, however. Not even all the foreigners manage to keep their heads clear in the face of the overwhelming pageantry. Hitler hurled his usual dramatic speech, acquitting the S.A. of any guilt in "Roehm's attempted treachery." A calculated, carefully rehearsed show, its psychological results on the mass mind are really shattering. Those who were not affected by the general insanity found especially interesting, in fact, especially revolting, the fits of hysterical rapture among the women.

Pappi von Carnap said; "It becomes only too clear that Hitler has been chosen by the opportunists and elected by the women. It is only a question of time before he starts military conscription."

September 12, 1934:

Had a luncheon date with Dagnino. He told me about Hitler's "enthronement."

"It was really funny, if you care for that type of humor. We had to turn up in tailcoats, early in the morning. Then we had to listen to his usual lies about peace, so naïve that it was difficult not to laugh in his face. The Papal Nuncio expressed the congratulations of the diplomatic corps, but that's customary, of course. Foreign Minister von Neurath was so self-conscious, so servile, as he always is when Hitler is around, that you could almost see him wag his tail. Secretary of State von Buelow hid his feelings, but not too well, if you knew anything about his real opinions."

Dagnino, who had been in Rome at the time, said the whole setup reminds him of the way Mussolini carried out his coordination. The government machine has worked swiftly. Schools, civil servants, everybody down to the last street sweeper has had to take the oath of allegiance. It is a pleasure to listen to his wonderful French and to be flattered by his thoughtful, chivalrous manners.

He gave me a copy of the *Schwarze Korps*, the Himmler weekly. Each S.S. man has to be a subscriber to the paper. The foreign diplomats get a great deal of fun out of its columns:

> "We announce the birth of our fourth child, our third boy. His name will be Reinhardt Stelling, after an ancestor of his, twelve

generations back, who was born in 1515. Karl Fritz Stelling and spouse Isolde, born Kleiner."

All notifications of birth are composed after a similar pattern. Emphasis is put on the quantity of offspring.

There was another advertisement which was not unamusing:

> Buxom Bavarian woman, P. G.,* deep-chested blonde Nordic appearance, 25 years of age, 1.75 m. tall, of obvious inherited health, actively interested in political and cultural affairs, wants to meet congenial man for the purpose of mutual procreation.

September 15, 1934:

My lifelong friends, the Riecks, came to see me today. Rieck lost his leg as an officer in the World War. They have three boys: Guenther, twelve years of age; Horst, nine, and Juergen, seven. The boys used to come and see me almost every day. Their visits stopped a couple of weeks ago.

Margarete Rieck was pale, and her husband seemed upset: "Frau Bella, we are dreadfully worried. The boys won't listen to us any more. Guenther had to join the Hitler Youth. The other two, the Young Folk. Margarete wanted Guenther to take a bunch of roses from our garden to you. He refused. When Margarete insisted that he obey, he drew his dagger from its sheath and assaulted her, his own mother! He shouted: 'I belong to the Fuehrer first! The family comes second. If you want to continue your friendship with Aunt Bella, I shall have to report you to the party!'"

The usually reserved man burst into tears. "How is it all going to end!" exclaimed Margarete, starting to sob. "They steal our children's hearts and confidence. They are trying to train them into Spartans, into cannon fodder for their next war."

September 20, 1934—Bad Brambach:

Came to this idyllic little village near the Czech border to take a short rest. Driving out was no fun. The German highways are a mess of repair and construction work. Detours everywhere. Everything for Hitler's army roads.

To divert the eye from the torn and uneven roads, there were

---

*Party comrade.

numerous and effectively painted posters and banners, crossing
and bordering the highway:

"Hitler—Work—Bread!"

"Thanks to our Fuehrer!"

"Thanks to our Fuerher for 415,673 hours' work!"

Anti-Jewish posters adorned entrances and exits of villages and
hamlets. Shopkeepers display warnings in their windows: "We
don't deal with Jews." Jewish shops have to announce the fact.

I talked to shopkeepers and people at gas stations and inns. In
many cases, their strictly National Socialist attitude was obviously
a measure of precaution. Many Jewish people told me: "Although
we can't enter their shops, Aryan shopkeepers give us whatever we
need after business hours."

I wonder how long it will be before these simple souls become
actually infected with the poison of hatred.

A man at a gas station, after my attitude had convinced him we
were safe, said: "The Nazis are frightening in their thoroughness.
My children made a trip with Hitler youth. They were taken to
East Prussia. They were given endless sermons on how difficult it
is to travel around in East Prussia, because of the Polish Corridor.
The propaganda went on, telling the children that the western
part of their country, too, was threatened with amputation. 'The
Rhine will be snatched from our hands. Your task is to live for
Germany and to be prepared to give your lives for your country if
need be.'"

October 1, 1934—Berlin:

Ambassador Dodd has helped me obtain a weekly column in
the English newspaper published in Berlin, and I am grateful for
the opportunity to do some more writing.

October 6, 1934:

Had a talk with Frau von Neurath. She was in a state: "It's a
shame how the Goebbels behave! The last dinner at the Italian
Embassy was scheduled for seven-thirty. He cancelled his invitation at seven o'clock! She was to come alone. The entire seating
order had to be changed. At seven-forty, she had not shown up.
Cerruti had somebody phone her house. The maid reported:
'Madam has gone to bed with a headache.' Such rudeness from
people who are supposed to have equal rank with my husband!"

I asked the only logical question: "Why doesn't the Minister resign? You are well off, you have your estate, and there is no reason why you should have to stand this constant friction with the Nazi people."

She blew up: "I would never let him do that. He has to keep his ground."

On my way home, I dropped in to say hello to Rolf. He knew about the incident: "Goebbels and Magda had a row because of a 'new secretary.'"

October 9, 1934:

"King Alexander of Yugoslavia, French Minister of Foreign Affairs Louis Barthou, two French generals, and one Yugoslav general have been shot dead in Marseilles," Richard told me on the phone. I dashed over to the Yugoslavian Legation to see Balugdzic. The old man was shaking with rage and sorrow: "These dirty dogs, the Nazi-Fascists, have done it. They did not want us to live in peace with France. Our King wanted to sign a friendly alliance in Paris, a so-called Eastern Locarno. He also wanted to improve Russian relations and to persuade them to join in an agreement that would assure collective security."

November 14, 1934:

At the Cerrutis', where I found a large crowd and some exquisite music. Joseph Lipsky, the Pole, made his first appearance in the front row with the ambassadors. He was in obvious good spirits. Maybe due to his promotion from Minister to Ambassador, or perhaps to the new Polish pact. Or a little of both, *qui sait?*

Heard that Putzi Hanfstaengl has been bragging about what he considers his latest achievements. He had arranged to have William Randolph Hearst, the American newspaper owner, received at Berchtesgaden, where Hitler turned on all his charm to impress the great man.

Dagnino, never an optimist, seemed more pessimistic than ever about the general situation. "Europe is going to pieces. You can see it all around you. Everything points to another war. That's just what Hitler wants. The others are not prepared, so they have to accept at face value everything the Schicklgruber says about peace. His best bet is the French people. They are completely opposed to war."

Russian ambassador Chintschuk has been replaced by Jacob Suritz. Their first reception was November 7, anniversary of the Russian Revolution. The etiquette was unfamiliar: diplomatic personages, from 4:00 to 6:00 P.M.; ordinary people, from 6:00 to 8:00 P.M.

The diplomats, however, did not arrive until 5:30 and after. Is it possible that they find it more amusing not to be too exclusive?

December 4, 1934:

Saturday was the Foreign Press Ball.

Ambassador Dodd introduced me to William Shirer and his wife.

"You should see more of them," he told me. Well, it wouldn't be tedious. They are pleasant and attractive people. He seems to have a realistic outlook and a brilliant mind; I doubt that Goebbels will succeed in clouding his point of view. William Shirer has represented Universal Service here since August.

December 15, 1934:

Bierabend at the Russian Embassy, on the occasion of the departure of their First Secretary, handsome blond Boris Winogradoff. Lots of gossip, mostly about the Nazi attempts to see which of the foreigners they can buy. Everything in the Third Reich has its price. Beginning with "opinion."

Two of my Aryan friends were caught in the dragnet of mass arrests. I got them out of the dungeon of the Gestapo, with the help of Rolf.

"We expected every minute to be our last," said one of the unfortunates. "For eight solid hours, they kept us facing the wall, with our arms raised. Afraid to move, because if you do, you may invite a blow that shatters your whole system."

The horrible crime for which they were apprehended consisted of eating a plate of chicken soup in a restaurant frequented by homosexuals. The Gestapo raided the place and took away everyone they found there.

December 20, 1934:

Went to see the old painter, Professor Max Liebermann, in his lovely little castle on the banks of the Wannsee, a half-hour's ride from Berlin.

"Well, child, who'd ever have thought such goings-on would be possible in the twentieth century. One can't eat as much as one would like to vomit!" Inelegant, but too apt for comfort. Every decent person is disgusted.

"Not even my letters pass the German frontier uncensored," Ambassador Dodd told me at the Spanish Embassy.

1935

CONTEMPORARY EVENTS

January	*13*	The Saarlanders vote for return to the Reich.
March	*1*	Germany formally occupies the Saar.
March	*5*	British Foreign Minister Sir John Simon and Anthony Eden are snubbed by Hitler, on the pretext of "illness," to postpone their intended visit to Berlin.
March	*16*	Hitler introduces legislation for reorganization of National Defense Forces and proclaims conscription.
March	*25*	Sir John Simon and Anthony Eden visit Hitler in Berlin.
April	*9*	Hermann Goering marries the actress Emmy Sonnemann with regal pomp. Gala celebrations. Ball at the opera and special party for German officials.
April	*11–14*	Stresa Conference by England, France and Italy.
May	*21*	Hitler makes a peace speech at the *Reichstag*.
August	*4*	Increasing oppression of the Catholic church.
September	*14–15*	Hitler announces the Nuremberg Laws at the party meeting at Nuremberg. German Jews lose all political rights.
October	*5*	Mussolini begins his campaign against Abyssinia.

November   18   Economic sanctions against Italy voted by fifty-
two nations.

January 2, 1935:

At a party given by the Douglas Jenkins', Messersmith's successor, there was quite a lot of talk about the Polish tenor, Jan Kiepura, whom the Nazis celebrate as the *Tonfilm* star. "They are very fond of him," remarked one of the sharp-tongued foreigners, "perhaps because he fills their cashboxes, singing for the *Winterhilfe*. They do not tell him that the money is used for rearmament."

February 10, 1935:

Two gala evenings last week. The first was Von Neurath's birthday party, this time in the guise of a country fair and miniature Party Day. My report in the Berlin English newspaper was laconic enough:

"Uniforms were much in evidence among the guests."

The evening was made notable by the black-uniformed appearance of Reinhard Heydrich, known as "the somber ghost behind Himmler."

Heydrich is known as Himmler's bloodiest man. He is six feet tall, lean, trim, yellow-haired. His eyes are blue yet remind one of a frog. His appearance is ascetic, and he rarely, if ever, smiles. They say he is the brains of the Gestapo, merciless, brutal, despotic, and has more power than his master, Himmler. He is hated by the army even more than by his superior. He is supposed to have a Jewish father, a music teacher in Halle, or thereabouts, said the publisher Parske, but you'd never think so from his non-Jewish aspect. He was one of the executioners during the June purge and is also known as the hangman of Gregor Strasser.

I shivered when he clicked his heels politely in front of me. Not for the gold in all the world would I have touched the hand of that murderer-in-chief.

The other gala was a dinner and ball at the French Embassy. Full of glamour. The world-famous surgeon, Professor Ferdinand Sauerbruch, and his wife were among the guests. The professor is a gentle soul, a grumbler. He told with touching tenderness about a starling with a broken leg he found in his garden and which he nursed. Then he grumbled about the extremely low mental standard of the latest medical faculty crop. "Their intellectual state," he claimed, "is appalling. They are picked because of their low membership card numbers, and preference is given to those with fathers in the party and mothers in the National Socialist Womanhood. Five times weekly, they have to attend marching and combat exercises and lectures on the theory of race. Next morning, they sleep through class, if they show up at all." He could have found a field of activity in any country of the world. Why does he stay here? Rumors have it that it is partly because of the surgeon's mistress, Erna Hanfstaengl, a sister of "Putzi." The surgeon couldn't take her out of the country together with his wife and four children. Hitler is said to have courted Erna assiduously back in the 1920s, when Sauerbruch was teaching at the University of Munich. Erna wouldn't give up the surgeon—he seemed to her to be the better risk.

February 12, 1935:

Paid my annual visit to the Nuncio on the anniversary of the papal coronation. My eyes popped almost out of my head when scanning the already laid dinner table I read the place card of table cover Number 26: "His Excellency, the Chancellor of the Reich, Adolf Hitler."

"What is that murderer of Catholics doing here?" I wondered.

February 27, 1935:

Reception at Ellinor von Schwabach's, née Von Schroeder from Hamburg. A real atmosphere of "good olden times." Frau von Schwabach raved about the happiness of her married life. "I would not hesitate to marry my husband all over again. No pure Aryan could have made me happier. He couldn't possibly have become a brute by legislation."

March 3, 1935:

Met the new Japanese Ambassador. Viscount and Viscountess Mushakofi have Western polish and elegance, but they are obviously pro-Nazi.

March 6, 1935:

Went to see Pappi von Carnap. He is ailing a lot and almost always alone. Mammi, an ambitious old woman with a good social memory, just cannot forget that during the Emperor's regime she was high in court circles. Therefore, she is nicknamed *Resident Governess*. When I came, Pappi was telling her once again that she and her crowd were responsible for the Brown Shirts.

"Papen was here from Vienna. He came to see me," Pappi said when we were alone. "He says the North Sea islands are bristling with fortifications. There are new airports above and below the ground. A foreigner was shot near Dessau a few days ago because he had, unwittingly, walked too close to an underground airport. The country is becoming an arsenal. Papen is working hard for Austrian *Anschluss*. According to him, the Austrians are looking forward to it eagerly. I have my doubts. By Austrians, he means a few cabinet members."

Papen is playing a clever game. As far as I can see, he is posing as a victim of Nazi persecution, with Hitler's knowledge, and trying to convince the Catholic church of his anti-Nazism by professing sincere piety. To Pappi, he has said that he hates the Nazis and considers National Socialism nothing but Bolshevism. Yet on another occasion, to please his Nazi masters, he had said that the Center party's main principle was to have no principles.

March 8, 1935:

"Hermann is furious with envy," said his Secretary of State Erhard Milch, "because Admiral Raeder was granted more funds for submarines."

March 17, 1935:

Hitler has done it. He ordered the "re-creation of National Defense Forces and the proclamation of conscription."

Although nobody was taken by surprise, the shock was bad. If only the foreigners don't let themselves be lulled by Hitler's phony peace talk!

Karl von Wiegand is here. His flair for catastrophic events is uncanny. I asked him whether he thought it likely that foreign countries would take any energetic measures. "I don't think so," he sighed. "Even France, the grumbling sick man, will sit down at the table and negotiate peace with a man who means war."

March 20, 1935:

Went to dinner at the Café Josty with a few friends from the corps. The manager, recognizing good clients when he saw us, was very anxious to please. Our party of eight ordered an exquisite meal.

Meanwhile, I noticed a young couple who had seated themselves at the next table. The husband, well-behaved, and in a low tone of voice, placed his order. Three waiters, waving their napkins, rushing madly to give us good service, started setting our food before us.

I couldn't help glancing at the couple. A page boy had just placed a teacup with a slip of paper in it before the young man. The young couple read the slip of paper and blushed. They seemed about to rise from their seats. At our table, the first champagne was opened with a loud pop.

"May I take the liberty?" I said to them in French, and removed the slip of paper from their table and translated it to my party.

"We do not serve Jews," read the notice.

As one body, the other seven at my table rose to their feet. Councilor of Legation Marlin spoke in a purposely loud tone.

"Sorry, but this lady feels that this also affects her." He gave me his arm. Another gentleman from our table gave his arm to the young woman. We left the place, a group of ten, leaving the manager and waiters standing in silence around the iced caviar platters, the hors d'oeuvres, and the uncorked bottles of champagne.

March 28, 1935:

The English Minister of Foreign Affairs, Sir John Simon, and Anthony Eden "were allowed" to pay their delayed visit to Berlin. What is more, they were allowed to break bread with Hitler as guests of the Minister of Foreign Affairs. The next day, they were even Hitler's own dinner guests. They were also allowed to sit through a concert in the Reich's Chancellery. One thing they were not allowed: to talk. Talking was Hitler's privilege. Paul Schmidt, the official interpreter, had an easy job. The English guests understand German. If they only understand, too, the kind of wind that blows here! I have heard Frau Ribbentrop say: "Sir John is all out for Germany's friendship."

At a reception given in their honor at the English Embassy, I found Simon and Eden looking very surly! Eden was on the point of leaving for parleys in Russia; Simon was returning to London. Eden told us about the dinner partners at Hitler's table.

"It was interesting to meet Winifred Wagner, the *Hueterin von Bayreuth.* Never could figure out, though, how it was that out of so many millions of Germans it had to be Richard Wagner's daughter-in-law who was drawn into that political circle."

One of the English Secretaries laughed. "Hitler was anxious to have a few people around who could talk to you in your language."

Other passing visitors are the Messersmiths, on their way from Vienna to the United States.

"Hitler's certainly headed for war. I wouldn't mind joining the army in a war against the Nazis," said Messersmith.

He believes an acute crisis is impending in Vienna.

April 1, 1935:

Farewell reception for the American Naval Attaché, Chester H. Keppler. He has been promoted to the rank of commander and ordered to his country's west coast. The entire crowd of international military attachés attended. All spoke of the same matter: "Are we heading straight for another war?"

"You could avoid a war by rearming at the same speed," I said to a French general. "You know what is going on here. You, yourself, told me recently that Goering has reinforced the antiaircraft force and that it is now under his personal command."

"It is impossible to arouse the French people to the idea of another war," replied the general. "We would be easy prey for your armed forces."

"Why don't you strengthen yourselves, then?" I asked, in the height of my naïveté. "Democracies play at war as though it were a sporting event, and you must never strike another fellow until he has you down and helpless."

April 2, 1935:

Went to see American Consul General Jenkins to get a visitor's visa for the United States. He despises and abominates the Nazis.

I want to see Gonny. Also, I'd like to get a firsthand impression of how outsiders feel about us. Surely they cannot all be as blind as they seem.

"You really have a mission," said Rolf. "A mission to warn them against what's going on. It is a duty to mankind. And mankind is bigger than a political party. I've told you confidentially much of what is going on. How we are rearming at sea and especially in the air. All that is needed to head aggression off is equal strength. It might prevent the whole world from going to pieces. Maybe the new pact between France, Russia, and Czechoslovakia is the first bulwark. Who knows? If a firm hand is not put out now, next year Hitler will march into the Rhineland. Pledges mean nothing to him.

You know that. Everybody knows it. Warn them also about the flood of Nazi agents in North and South America, in every embassy, in every consolate, in every branch German business office. They get their orders daily and hourly from Goebbels over the air.

I feel hopeless about it. Who is going to heed these warnings? Dodd remarked to me only this week on the complacency with which his warnings are received over there. Smart man, Dodd. Yet, it's interesting to see how he's taken in by Schacht. He doesn't understand that Schacht's lukewarm opposition to extreme elements in the party has nothing to do with decency or compassion. Schacht is a practical man. He's interested in German overseas trade, not in the humanities. It's hard for a man as humane and as just as Dodd to understand that type.

April 5, 1935:

Dr. Mastny, the Czech Minister, sent for me. "What are your plans for the future?" he asked me kindly. "We've pledged a sum in the corps so that you might build up a new career. François-Poncet and I thought perhaps you could furnish all of us with wine. That's quite an item in the life we have to lead. You are an expert, and your family's firm has a recognized name."

I was so touched that I got all choked up and, for a moment, couldn't speak at all. "I don't need capital," I managed to say at last. "Just clients."

"You have those already," said Dr. Mastny. "You can start as soon as you return from America."

We talked politics for a while. "We have to get along with Hitler, somehow. It's too dangerous not to. We're awfully small, and he's awfully powerful."

"At least, you're a democracy," I began.

"That's true," said the doctor. "But you need more than that. You can't stop airplanes with epigrams."

April 6, 1935:

I thanked François-Poncet for his help.

"It's going to be hard for me to call upon you as a salesman after having had these exceptionally confidential years with all of you."

"Think nothing of it," he said. "Beginning as a wine merchant, you never know where you'll end up. Think of Ribbentrop!"

"I'd rather not think of him," I said.

April 7, 1935:

At the Swiss Legation. Good music, delicious cold buffet, exceedingly low spirits. His Excellency Paul Dinichert was greatly perturbed because the Nazis had kidnaped the refugee journalist, Berthold-Jacob. He had made a *démarche* in the name of his government.

"We demand extradition," he said in indignant fury.

It was remarkable how suddenly he was able to change from uncontrolled fury to pleasant suavity when he welcomed the new arrivals, Nazi Minister of Domestic Affairs Frick and his wife.

They lead a quiet life, the Fricks. Hardly ever entertain, are rarely seen at parties. He is an early party member, having marched with Hitler in 1923. He was a police official at Munich police headquarters and is one of those left over from the old "informer" days. Frick issued faked passports for *Feme* killers who found it necessary to flee. He is one of the instigators of race-baiting, but he must be credited with protest against Himmler's ruthless methods "which so much resemble those of the Russian *Tcheka.*"

Frau Frick, who is much younger than her husband, is quite attractive. They were married only recently—after she had got a divorce from the well-known architect, Schultze-Naumburg. She appears completely in love with her new spouse.

Schmidt-Pauly was present, too. He said that Neurath is very irritated at Goering because of the latter's constant interference in foreign political matters. "As though Ribbentrop weren't enough of a headache for us!"

It seems that Rib and the new Japanese Military Attaché, Oshima, are pretty thick these days. Something's brewing...some poison cup is being prepared.

April 8, 1935:

People are puzzled at the failure of the Simon-Eden sentimental pilgrimage. The English Councilor of Commerce told me that it did not surprise Eden, who expected just what happened. He wanted, however, to put an end to England's policy of "Wait and see." He is afraid the English Labour party expects too much in the way of opposition from their German comrades. This is the reason they oppose rearmament. He is disappointed in Laval, who is so engrossed in his flirtation with Italy that he has had no time to turn his attention to Germany.

German workmen are so hopelessly in the clutches of the cell watchdogs that they cannot make a move. To say nothing of the fact that a good portion of German labor has voluntarily sided with Hitler. A trip through South Germany confirmed my views. There, the old familiar *Gruess Gott* has entirely vanished. Its place as salutation has been taken by the assumed name of an Austrian corporal, the modern Teutonic equivalent of God.

Rolf has seen a new secret order.

"Jews are to be eliminated as far as possible from clubs, resorts, trade schools, and other schools."

In this connection, it might be noticeable to point out that genealogists are doing a grand business. There are advertisements in all daily papers: "We provide you with every kind of document and evidence."

Pedigrees are for sale in the Reich, as is almost everything else. For a reasonable sum, you can be made into an Aryan practically instantaneously. Nature and God used to require more time.

April 11, 1935:

Saw fat von Brandenstein for the first time in a long while. He talked about the "Crown Princely wedding," as François-Poncet called Goering's nuptials.

The night before last, Emmy Sonnemann appeared at the opera in full regalia, a fifty-thousand-mark tiara glittering on her head—a gift from the bridegroom. Probably not paid for, as Goering is a tough man to collect from. Even the *Spindlewerke* have to dry-clean the white silk liveries for Hermann's servants on terms that stretch into eternity. A timid suggestion concerning the advisability of paying last year's bill, made at the "private office of Goering," was harshly rejected with the advice that they should consider it an honor and a privilege "to work for the Prime Minister."

A pretty public wedding yesterday, with Hermann leading Emmy to the *Dom* through a lane of old generals who stood at attention with sabers drawn. He had arranged for princely honors and for princely gifts, which he "ordered" from cities, unions, factories, business concerns, and private individuals of means. Everybody was advised about the Prime Minister's wishes and where to get the things. Little gifts from museums were obtained by the Prime Minister's personal requisition. From several big cities, he received twenty-eight bomber planes. There was a car from Mercedes, a yacht from a shipping firm...I cannot remember everything that Brandenstein told me.

The wedding party at the Kaiserhof comprised three-hundred-thirty persons high in government and army circles, with Hitler, of course, the focal point of most eyes. The dinner was fabulous. Wines at ten dollars a bottle. As the courses followed one another, each more sumptuous than the last, Hitler grew ever more silent and morose. The barbaric splendor seemed to outrage him. After dinner, he rose to deliver a little speech. By that time, he had worked himself into such a temper that he could hardly conceal his rage. When he got to his feet, his chair slid from under him with such violence that it knocked down a crystal floor lamp, which fell with a loud crash. The whole scene operated like clockwork. Crash! Bang! At the same time, four doors, cleverly camouflaged in the wall panels, were flung open, revealing S. S. men, guns drawn, ready to leap. At Himmler's wink, the invisible doors closed. The S.S. men vanished. Hitler cleared his throat for the wedding toast.

Emmy can thank Hitler. The fat boy very likely would never have thought of marrying her. She played the hostess in his house. She was always to be seen in his car, with a bodyguard of the *Feldpolizei*. Somebody must have whispered into Hilter's ear that these goings-on were shocking. Instead of separating the couple, he gave orders to legalize the relationship.

April 12, 1935:

"Emmy Sonnemann must feel like a dream come true," said Yvonne. "The First Lady of the Reich. Hitler will probably never marry, so Emmy will remain in her high niche."

It may be a dream come true, but somehow I have a feeling that Emmy deserved a better lot. When she came from Weimar in 1933 for her first engagement at the *Staatstheater* in Berlin, she certainly did not expect to become the wife of the Third Reich's killer number two.

Goering had met her shortly after the death of his first wife, Baroness Karin von Focke. Emmy's warmhearted nature attracted him. Whenever he had a free evening, he flew or drove to Weimar. When Emmy was appointed to the Berlin *Staatstheater*, she found old friends, among them Edit von Coler. Not that all this would have been particularly pleasing to Edit von Coler, the intriguing little dramatic director, who dreaded a competitor. Edit is smart, however. Smart enough to conceal her feelings and her claws.

Emmy is no feminine intriguer. The witty Berliners already call her *Landesmutter*. She is a sympathetic, motherly woman. The Valkyrie type. Tall and heavy, but with a gentle grace. Her lovely blonde hair frames her brow in a large braid. Her big blue eyes are soft and serene. She loves to wear floating gowns which make her look even plumper and rounder. "Hermann likes low-cut dresses," she said. The Reich's First Lady is the exact opposite of skinny, sour-tempered, mean Magda Goebbels.

Emmy is a nice person, but a poor actress. She had little hold on the public up to 1933. After that time, however, she was gold in the box office, because the fat boy might show up during any perfor-mance. A stage box was always reserved for him, and there was a ticket rush whenever her name was announced on the playbill. Party opportunists who wished to attract Goering's attention sat through numerous performances of *Faust, Wilhelm Tell* or *Egmont.*

Emmy has been wonderful in her loyalty to non-Aryan friends and colleagues. She intercedes for them with Goering whenever she can. It's interesting to speculate on how long she can keep it up. Goering, too, is watched and shadowed. All the top men spy on each other.

At her wedding, Emmy insisted that her Viennese friend, Herma Clemt, be bridesmaid. They had been through dramatic school together in Berlin. During vacations, Herma shared Emmy's room in the little flat behind the candy shop which Emmy's parents ran in Hamburg. Together, they signed their contracts for the Berlin *Schauspielhaus.* Herma is a fine actress. Goering arranged it, and any racial flaws that existed in Herma were forgotten. The Berlin *Staatstheater,* which gave her a contract in 1933, was very glad to get an actress of her talent and ability.

Large masses of our people are fooled by the obvious joviality of the fat Goering and have a not-too-discerning liking for him. His joviality is a rather thin camouflage for a barbarous cruelty that led even Ernst Roehm to call him a brutal sadist. Goering is not particularly brilliant, and that has helped in his popularity, as too-great brilliance is apt to make the bulk of the population uneasy and supicious.

April 16, 1935:

Tea with Balugdzic. He is an amusing old man. "Yugoslavia, of all places, had to be selected for Goering's honeymoon! God forbid that he suffer any harm. My entire staff worked overtime for Goering's pleasure and security. A battalion of plainclothesmen was sent ahead. Another battalion followed in his trail. We had countless meetings with Himmler's people. Our authorities had to promise every assistance. The German refugees in Yugoslavia have to report daily at police headquarters."

"It has cost Schacht fifty thousand gold marks in foreign exchange to give Hermann a honeymoon...a major operation to get that much out of Schacht," said Rolf. "The Mercedes Company gave him a new car without running boards. That's to prevent anyone getting a free ride, especially if he has a gun, a bomb, or a demand for justice."

Goebbels has wisecracked continuously about the wedding and the trip at his press conferences. He got little response, though, Lord knows, there was humor enough in the situation. But he is hardly the one to point it out.

May 14, 1935—At sea:

Went by car to Bremen. Never saw so many airplanes. Sentries everywhere. The dockyards hummed with activity. Work on submarines proceeding at a terrific pace. The headwaiter at the hotel said: "You ought to see the goings-on in Wilhelmshaven!"

I have a nice stateroom with private bath. At meals, I am seated at the captain's table, between retired Captain Zuckschwerdt and the captain of the vessel. Zuckschwerdt was captain of the *Cormoran* during the World War. His trip seems rather mysterious. He has a silver fox farm at the Alaskan border...he says.

May 20, 1935—New York:

I am with my child! Everything else was forgotten when I discovered her wet little face in the crowd down below on the dock.

The last night at sea, I did not sleep a wink. I was out on deck at six in the morning. Overwhelmed by the sight of the New York skyline bathed in the bright light of day. It has been described to me countless times. But it was so new and awe-inspiring nevertheless. The gigantic silhouette stood sharp against the pale blue sky. A myth of modern achievement come true!

Gonny wanted to spread all of New York at my feet within the first twenty-four hours. She dragged me through the medley of streets around Wall Street. She was pleased how impressed I was by the tiny Trinity Chruch and the old cemetery among the tall buildings. Progress and tradition side by side.

The first night at Times Square made my head spin. The dazzling display of flickering advertisements, figures and names, flashing and disappearing in uninterrupted glitter, was bewildering—like a mirage, a fairy tale of plenty. Poor old Europe—fortunate America! The difference between the Old and the New World seems symbolized in this mélange of color and light.

May 22, 1935—New York:

Hitler's "peace message" has restored confidence in many a credulous soul here. The majority, however, reacted with utter apathy.

Is Hitler going to sign a pact with the Russians? Is he really rearming at the speed the newspapers say? These questions I hear every day.

I had a letter of introduction to Governor Lehman. Since he is on a vacation, his brother Arthur received me downtown in the awe-inspiring building in Hanover Square.

Scrupulously mindful of Rolf's warning, I tried to arouse Arthur Lehman to the danger. He seemed keenly interested. Not sufficiently so, however, to jot down notes.

"I understand and sympathize with your state of mind, Mrs. Fromm. It is only logical that you should be very upset. But it can't happen here. We are a free country," he said to me.

June 10, 1935—Washington, D. C.:

What an enchanting place this city must be to live in! It is beautiful and dignified, open-spaced, and, though pulsing with activity, of an almost rustic serenity.

Foreign Minister von Neurath had advised me to pay my first Washington call on the German Embassy. Today, I visited German Ambassador Hans Luther at the old-fashioned German Embassy building on Massachusetts Avenue. Luther seemed to have become smaller since I saw him last. His head is definitely bald now, he has gained in weight but not in appearance. He could not frankly meet my eyes. The little man seemed uneasy and frightened. He pretended to be very pleased to see me and was "very eager to hear about all the friends back home."

I felt most uncomfortable among the hodgepodge of things and furniture which fill the rooms at the embassy and which were more than dissonant. He complained of the generally frozen attitude of Americans toward the Third Reich.

"It couldn't be otherwise, with all the horror tales they're spreading around. Back home, everything is tranquil. No harm comes to anyone. Here the press bristles with hair-raising atrocity reports."

I let him talk this familiar line. When he was through, I answered him: "Doctor Luther, there is no reason why we two should pretend. You will remember that we used to see each other mostly at the homes of respected non-Aryans in Berlin. I am sure your feelings toward these old friends are very different from what you think it your duty to pretend now. But don't worry, I have no intention of reporting our conversations in Berlin. But you ought to know that it is much more important for you to be popular in American circles than to play for the approval of that infamous gang back in the Third Reich."

Luckily, we weren't talking in that vein when Dr. Herbert Scholz sneaked in to join us. For years, I had had to bear him hanging around at every tea and cocktail party in Berlin. He complained: "We have a pretty hard job on our shoulders as German diplomats in Washington. People back home don't realize how their foolishness reacts on us here. I was shocked to read this week that some rowdy youngsters smashed the windows at Bernheimer's antique shop in Munich. The man is internationally renowned and respected. I, myself, used to be a client of his. Such excesses outrage the feelings of people here. I heard many indignant remarks about this particular case."

The tenor of the blond Herbert's remarks seemed to surprise Luther. I thought it was amusing, as I don't judge these Nazis by what they say but by what they do.

He went on: "I wrote a letter this afternoon and made it very clear to friends in the party how embarrassing such incidents are. They should be prevented by all means."

I happen to know that Scholz is on very good terms with Heinrich Himmler. In June, 1934, the latter seems to have saved Sholz's skin from the general purge. Scholz's protest, therefore, should reach the right channels. His father-in-law, Dr. Max von Schnitzler, director of the I. G. Farben concern, joined the S. A. for business reasons. Frau Scholz and her mother display themselves as ardent Nazis. Scholz's protest would be a valuable one, if ever delivered.

I had a most stimulating luncheon with the Rumanian Councilor, Radu Florescu. We have been friends since his Berlin days. We went to a charming country club. Florescu asked: "What does Hitler really want, the Corridor, Austria, or Czechoslovakia?"

"The three of them, and something more," I said. "He wants to be the master of the world."

Radu talked freely. "We have the impression that the Polish

Foreign Minister, Beck, is rather easy pickings for the Nazis. Even François-Poncet seems at times to be taken in by them."

I tried to explain the "phenomenon François-Poncet" to Radu: "I have talked with him many times lately. The French Ambassador certainly considers the welfare of his own country above all else. He is very thorough and has studied the Nazis carefully. Still, there are some features about the Third Reich which seem to impress him. These technical or adminstrative achievements almost obscure for him the fact that all the propagandistic 'thousand-year' programs do not prevent them from breaking any ten-year pact between cigarette puffs without the slightest compunction. I am sure that François-Poncet keeps his government *au courant* as to the growing strength of Nazi Germany. The question is, does Foreign Minister Laval wish to see the danger! Laval's tolerance of the *Croix de Feu* is proof that he is, to put it mildly, pro-Fascist. It only remains to be seen which of the two dictators he will eventually join."

I was eager to see German Councilor of Embassy Leitner. He lives only a block from the Florescus.

"You won't have any luck with that coward," I was warned. "Leitner is one of the Nazi camp followers. The possibility of a report from Scholz to Himmler scares the daylights out of him. He is much too cautious to show you the slightest friendly gesture."

June 12, 1935—Washington, D.C.:

The sweltering heat is hard to bear, with five or more various invitations a day! Everybody is eager to know about the Third Reich. I am in demand to quench this thirst for knowledge. They are very interested in Ribbentrop and want to know more about him. They believe here that in the near future he will replace Neurath.

Danish Minister Watstedt, who appreciates a good glass of wine, said: "Ribbentrop is not only an expert wine salesman; he is also an aggressive and efficient salesman of the National Socialist idea. He sold it to 'important firms' in England. Lord Rothermere and Lord Lothian bought it wholesale and made Hitler their favorite brand. Ribbentrop is on an intimate footing with the Clivedon set."

I know the name is taken from Lady Astor's country place. It was easy for him to get on good terms with the English nobility. In Germany, however, he was turned down for membership in the *Adelsclub*. Although he may not have been a genuine "von," he was certainly a genuine snob, Herbert Scholz had said.

Another English group which Ribbentrop cultivates is that of Sir

Oswald Mosley. A train of satellites sparkles in his wake. Foremost, and much in evidence, is Mosley's sister-in-law, Unity Freeman-Mitford, who is enamored of Hitler. She was seen at a Nuremberg Party Day in hysterical rapture. Her youngest brother injured her Nazified sensibilities by having been husband number one to non-Aryan "Baby" Friedlaender-Fuld, the coal heiress.

Another satellite of Ribbentrop in London is the Austrian-born Jewess, Steffie Richter, now Princess Hohenlohe-Schillingsfuerst by marriage. She and her family are born informers. Steffie managed, as far back as 1923, to be expelled from France for that reason. Her sister, in the "same business," screens her activities behind the sign of a tiny fashion shop in the western section of Berlin. "Madame Subskin," known in England as "Mrs. White," and the Princess are a notorious "sister team."

June 15, 1935:

Vera Florescu and I went for a party to Representative Sol Bloom's fairyland place, a kind of Italian *palazzo* on Columbia Road. The huge terrace, supported by massive columns, is filled with exotic plants and flowers. A glamorous background for the glittering international crowd. Sol Bloom's salons contain priceless antiques. The portraits of countless illustrious men, with autographed dedications including that of the Pope, adorn the rooms. The pictures are displayed in heavy gold frames made by Mrs. Bloom, an expert goldsmith.

"The German Ambassador is no longer invited to this house," I was pleased to hear an official from the Department of State say.

June 19, 1935:

High tide of excitement today at the garden party of the Swiss Minister, because of Ribbentrop's success with the London naval treaty.

The humidity and heat were killing, but the excitement did not subside. The discussion grew sizzling when a young lady just arrived from Berlin spoke her mind about the Scholzes. "Don't trust them too much! Whatever their line may be in Washington, it remains a fact that they are passionate Nazis. Scholz always wears the S. S. uniform in Berlin. Their task here is not just that of diplomats. They are present as Nazi agents."

Many of the guests appeared to find this difficult to credit. The tall blond couple are "so smooth, so likeable." I knew it to be the truth, however. People can be so blind.

July 4, 1935—New York:

Went to the dock this morning to say good-bye to Captain Krone, who is in command of the *S. S. Berlin.* It was hard to believe my eyes. Neatly drawn up on the pier in military formation was a battalion of storm troopers. Black trousers, the loathsome high boots, the swastika band around the right sleeve of the brown shirt. Arms were raised. Heels clicked. The Nazi flag, coupled with the Stars and Stripes, flapping insolently in the free air.

There was a great deal of protest by American passersby. But the "*Heil* Hitler!" salute went on without interruption, and the *Horst Wessel* song of glorification to a pimp rang out lustily on this American dock.

The occasion, I learned, was the departure for Europe, as guests of the Third Reich, of eighty members of the Steuben Society. Most of them American-born of German descent. Each newly arrived guest was received with a hearty "*Heil* Hitler!" Most of them raised their arms in response to the salute. It was depressing.

Well, they say it's a free country.

July 20, 1935— Berlin:

Everything seemed small and out of proportion after the big adventure of America. I had to get accustomed, very quickly, to the "Round Survey" all over again.

The ride from Bremen to Berlin was full of surprises. The preparations for war have increased to the proportions of an all-out effort, and vast strides have been made. A little frightening, I thought, when you consider the complacency and optimism in the United States.

On the last evening at sea, I became acquainted with a HAPAG official who said he was on his annual trip to report to his firm. His uncle is in the office of a German ministry. He tried to convince me that he is cured of what he called "the Nazi disease." But this is hard to believe of the man who, with Spanknoebel, Dr. Griebl, and Fritz Kuhn, founded the "Friends of New Germany" organization. He says it was this very thing that cured him, however.

"The *Auslands* Organization kept sending speakers from Germany who appeared in uniform roaring "*Heil* Hitler!" and raging openly against the Jews. We had quite a few German-American Jews in the

Friends of New Germany, and the German representatives made many embarrassing situations. After a while, the Jews left." That's his story.

July 28, 1935:

Bierabend at the Argentine Legation. A crowd of Spaniards, Latin Americans and Nazis. Upon the arrival of Dr. Ritter, *Ministerialdirektor* for National Economy at the Foreign Office, I heard Secretary of State Funk say: "Look, there's another one of those deceptive hamburgers, Nazi brown on the outside and Moscow red on the inside."

Rolf commented: "The money raised July 4 for his New York Steuben Society hasn't been wasted. They raise their arms and *heil* Hitler with all the enthusiasm of veteran Nazis, payment which the Third Reich expects in return for the expenditure."

August 2, 1935:

The Cerrutis are transferred to Paris. Signora Elisabeth invited me for a farewell luncheon. We sat in her boudoir. I pointed, in loathing, at the portraits of Hitler and Magda Goebbels with her children.

Mrs. Cerruti whispered: "Diplomatic window dressing." Just the same, I cannot help feeling she has a slight leaning in their direction, though she is sorry for the oppressed.

I became quite outspoken about conditions in general. Signora Cerruti sprang to her feet, a look of alarm swept over her attractive face. She stopped my mouth with her tiny hand, dragged me from my comfortable armchair and ushered me hastily into the adjoining bathroom. "Bella, for God's sake, there is a telephone in the boudoir. How can you be so thoughtless! You know that diplomats' telephone wires are also tapped. The Netherlands Minister had workmen from Holland. For three days, they were busy isolating every wire inside the house." Considering that the receiver on the telephone was down, I failed to see how the Gestapo could overhear our conversation.

Coincidence brought me that same afternoon to the study of the Polish Ambassador. His telephone is carefully embedded in a well-padded, dark green coffeepot warmer! Perhaps there is something to it after all.

August 4, 1935:

I hear from Pappi von Carnap that the Papal Nuncio is outraged by the Nazi slanders against the church.

"They bring fake lawsuits against monks just to bring discredit upon them. It doesn't matter whether a charge is proved or not. The important thing is that it's made.

"They threaten children and frighten them into testifying that the religious brothers have committed sexual offenses. They arrest nuns and charge them with attempting to smuggle money and valuables out of the country. The trials drag on for weeks and weeks, confusing everybody and smearing the church with their dirt."

September 14, 1935:

During the summer season, the François-Poncets are "at home" each Saturday in their lovely villa, half an hour's ride from Berlin, at the idyllic Little Wannsee. Tea is served on the terrace, tennis is played. The host joins the tennis fans for a game mostly to lose weight because of the little paunch he has acquired since he arrived here. The guests walk around, float in rowboats, or just relax and talk politics.

The host and Ambassador Dodd questioned Rudolf Kircher of the *Frankfurter Zeitung* concerning the "revelations" Hitler would make in tomorrow's speech at the Party Day. Kircher had no idea, he said. He pretends to be anti-Nazi with the foreigners. "Nevertheless, I am sure he is just as bad as his colleague, Freidrich Sieburg, correspondent of the *Frankfurter Zeitung* in Paris, or Paul Scheffer of the *Tageblatt*," said Dodd.

September 15, 1935:

Had tea at the Uruguayan Minister's, Virgilio Sampognaro. He is a lovable gentleman, cultured and charming.

The broadcast of Hitler's hymn of hate shook both of us badly. Brandenstein foretold the coming of the Nuremberg laws three years ago, it flashed through my mind.

Secretary of State von Buelow, whom I met at the hotel entrance, greeted me. "One feels ashamed to be a German," he said.

October 12, 1935:

Another new Spanish Ambassador: Francesco Agramonte y Cortijo. This time, I believe, one much more to Nazi liking. And vice versa. In appreciation of his obvious ideological tolerance, he was honored by the attendance of Hitler's Special Ambassador, Joachim ("von" since 1925) Ribbentrop at the embassy reception. When he entered the room in S. S. uniform, an English attaché scoffed, not too softly, "Here come Ribbensnob."

Walking over with his notorious visitor, the host inroduced us. They say that when people have been together long they even begin to look alike. I don't know about that, but I will say that Rib attempts to act like his beloved Fuehrer. He gave me the same long, hearty, meaningful handclasp, the same intense, deliberately overacted soulful look, the same prolonged kiss on the still-clasped hand.

"Oh, Herr von Ribbentrop!" I said quietly. "The hand is a non-Aryan one."

He was embarrassed. Pressing his left arm across his stomach, he raised the right arm, clicked to attention, and spluttered: "*Heil Hitler!*" Onlookers suppressed their giggles. Giggling at the S. S. uniform is not considered safe. I must say he is better looking than most Nazis. His figure is excellent. The grayish hair gives him that distinguished touch that he seems to fancy. His manner is blasé, but his eyes are the eyes of a fish.

The "traveling salesman" despises the English for taking him and his agents so wholeheartedly to their bosoms in London. He scorns the English aristocrats for providing such a fine market, whether it be for his liquors or for the political crimes and lies of his country. He is an expert salesman. Right now his commodities are wine and treachery.

Of course, Ribbentrop has excellent manners. His home sets one of the best tables in Berlin. Remarkable food and wine are served. When Hitler came to his house, however, there was only a modest vegetarian meal.

His wife, Anneliese Henkell, wanting a title as badly as Rib himself, coaxed the sales price for the "von" from her father. A bargain for Ribbentrop: a title, a rich wife, a career.

"I stand solidly on my two legs," he boasts. "Each leg is worth a million marks."

For all his sneers at the British, his villa at Lenze-Allee in Dahlem, the most fashionable part of Berlin, is run in a strictly English fashion. Even the menu is issued in English, and the butler does not understand a word of German.

A sandy-haired S. A. man, his collar adorned with several stars, was introduced by Ribbentrop: "The office chief of the Nazi party in

Spain, Group Leader Burbach." Group leaders in foreign countries! What do you have to do to the nationals of foreign countries before they grow suspicious of you? Is it possible, perhaps, that they welcome the introduction of Nazi principles? They cannot all be just merely dumb. The numerous German "Foreign Offices" which have sprung into life since 1933 should have aroused the suspicion of the world, too.

Our dear old "A. A.," the Foreign Office, with its red tape, its ancient corridors with the threadbare red carpets, its antique furniture and standing desks, its chairs, which have been tottering since Bismarck first imposed an enormous strain upon them, has had competition for a couple of years. A powerful competitor is the *Aussenpolitische Amt* of the party. It is in charge of Alfred Rosenberg—the "Baltic swine." A close second is the *Auslandsorganisation*, also of the party. Formerly stationed in Hamburg, it has now been made a part of the old Foreign Office. When the Fuehrer put Ernst Wilhelm Bohle, with his special Foreign Espionage Department, under the venerable roof of the Foreign Office, von Neurath waxed indignant, but his rage got him precisely nowhere.

The most powerful rival organization, openly spoken of as "Foreign Office Number Two," is the office of Special Ambassador von Ribbentrop. "Office Ribbentrop" has more absolute power than the real Foreign Office. It has considerable funds and spends extravagantly. It has a staff of several hundred employees. The office manager has the title of minister. The gang of "Bureau R" collaborate closely with the Gestapo. Positions are given to the nobility, mostly to those who do society espionage for Ribbentrop. The international diplomats receive them with open arms. These gentlemen hold secondary jobs as group or *Standarten* leaders in the private armies of the party.

Military Attaché General Oshima is persona grata at the "Bureau R" which insists on friendly relations with Japan. At the same time, they are trying to knit closer ties with the Soviet Union. Minister von Raumer, office chief, is in personal charge of this precarious task.

October 20, 1935:

It will be generations before the Germans can find their way back to an ethical code of life. The evil Nazi doctrine with its abject conceptions is deeply planted in the minds of adults, youths, and children. To root out these ideas, which endanger the whole world, and to reeducate Germans to a regard for man's most sacred heritage of liberty, is something that cannot be done in one generation. It will take more than the short period of a single human lifetime to clear away the effect of these noxious times. A vile, poisonous fruit the present-day education of the German is bearing!

Today, I had dinner with my old friends, Ilse and Otto Kapp. Otto has reentered the army, with the rank of colonel. With no children of their own, they have lavished all their affection upon the two little daughters of Ilse's brother.

Inge and Lolo, the two little girls, sat at table with us. Inge had not come to see me for weeks. I asked her why, though I had a feeling that I knew the answer.

Inge looked at me as though trying to visualize me all over again. "Aunt Bella," she said, "you don't really seem so—so fiendish."

Her father reprimanded her with a stern glance. "Don't blame the child," I interceded for her. "I know what they teach her in school."

Relieved, the little one chatted on without inhibition. "I told Herr Runge, that's our teacher, that you weren't like that, Aunt Bella. So he said we didn't understand how wicked you really were. Then, for the rest of the lesson, he read to us out of a book about Jews…that they are evil…they look like devils…they should all be killed. He said we should spit at them whenever we see them."

Blonde, delicate, sweet Inge! The words, though not her own, came strangely from her lips.

"On our way home," Inge continued, "Ursel and I saw an old woman. She looked very poor, and we thought she might be Jewish. Ursel said we should spit at her. So she ran up to her and spat on her coat…it was an old coat…torn…I didn't spit, Aunt Bella. I thought it was disgusting. Ursel yelled at her: 'Old Jew witch!' She says that tomorrow she will tell the teacher I wouldn't spit, too."

We sat there in silence for a moment or two, eight of us. Then I said: "Inge, darling, you are intelligent enough to know that evil has nothing to do with the race a person is born into. It is God who decides whether you are to be a Jew or a Christian. There are nasty people everywhere, but most people are the same whether they are Catholic, Protestant, or Jewish. All worship the same God…the God of Love."

"I won't do it," said Inge quietly. "I won't do it. Even if they punish me."

"That's right," said her father. "I wouldn't want you to. If you felt that you could do it, I would never want to see you again."

That's today. Later, with her education continuing in the same strain, I wonder whether even Inge will be able to stand against it.

October 25, 1935:

Ilse Kapp came, pale and disturbed. "I did not come before everything was settled. The day after our talk with Inge, Herr Runge discussed the Jewish question again. 'Inge,' he asked, 'do you admit that all Jews are damnable and vile?' 'No,' insisted Inge.

"That same night, the Gestapo came to take my brother away. We did everything in our power. He escaped with a severe warning and some horrible scars on his body. I have just been to his house to see him."

October 28, 1935:

Rolf and I walked through the Tiergarten. "The Jewish children will have to leave the schools after Easter," he told me.

The Franconian *Gauleiter*, Julius Streicher, has for years distributed a filthy anti-Semitic weekly. "The only paper Hitler reads from A to Z," he boasts. Which makes it obligatory for the other *Volksgenossen*. His eight pages must be prominently displayed under glass in swastika-decorated brown cases which stand in halls, offices, and at street corners. Now the Olympic Committee has advised Hitler to remove these cases before the influx of visitors for the games. Hitler will put them into cold storage for the duration.

Rolf spoke about the occupation of the demilitarized zone in the Rhineland, which is expected to come before long. March is the latest month named. Hitler always favors the third month of the year to stage his surprises.

November 18, 1935:

Heard some very interesting news at the L. P. Lochners' reception. It seems that Schacht, wanting to find out where all the expense money the high officials get, beside their considerable salaries, was disappearing to, marked all bank notes that went to Goebbels, Goering, Himmler, and Rosenberg. When they returned in payments from foreign countries, the story leaked out.

"This time the fox has launched a boomerang that may break his neck," said Rolf, when I spoke to him about that news. There is, in his opinion, only a short respite left for Schacht. Positions like his are too much in demand by party members.

November 25, 1935:

Germany honors her poetic dead! Germany's "Blubo," the "Blood
and Soil" poet Herman Loens, who died as a voluntary soldier in
France, has been rediscovered by the propoganda machine, dug out
of obscurity and his grave, and his body transported to Germany.
Under the management of the Ministry of Propaganda, his home
town bristled with preparations for a state funeral.

But something went wrong. Loens, though a poet in the true Nazi
sense, had been injudicious enough to have an "irregular" grandmother! When the story got around, Goebbels developed a severe
case of cold feet in his literary enthusiasm. He lost interest in the
"Blubo" poet, and the state funeral was postponed *sine die.*

So the poor poet's body was held in cold storage for a week. Back
home, the wreaths faded. The preparations stopped. The relatives
were at a loss as to the next move. Luckily, however, von Blomberg
heard of the matter. He sent for the war hero's coffin and arranged
for a decent military funeral.

November 28, 1935:

Pappi is ailing a lot these days. His illness has not softened his
implacability toward the new masters of Germany, however, and he
lectures Mammi constantly on her shameless way of running after
them. "You should have more pride," he tells her. "Bella has to attend
all these affairs for her newspaper. But there's no reason why you
should."

They are training the "Hitler Youth" the "new pagan" way, filling
them with brutality and megalomania. The leader, Baldur von
Schirach, whose nobility is as artificial as Ribbentrop's, addresses
speeches to his disciples that might fall strangely upon sensitive ears.

"Family life," he remarks, "is an old-fashioned conception. We
have no need for it in our new life, which puts the state above all.
Don't trust anybody. Watch your wife. Watch your children. Watch
everybody. And report their activities to the government." If this
type of new ethics doesn't lead to the complete breakdown of human
society, then there is nothing to be learned from all the history of
civilization.

For girls, half a year's labor service has become obligatory. My
friend, Margarete, has tried to keep her daughter Hilda out of it as
long as possible. All mothers dread this labor service and the
excursions of the "Hitler Maidens," for most of them are no longer
maidens when they return and at least fifty percent come home

pregnant. Birth control is prohibited in the Third Reich. When Hilda finally had to join the labor services, she came back expecting a baby. Margarete was desperate. Hilda, however, said, "I am proud to be able to give HIM (Hitler) a baby. I hope it will be a boy to die for HIM." Turning to me, she said: "Please do not call me Hilda any more, and refrain from using the familiar *Du* when talking to me. I am one of the Fuehrer's brides and do not care to talk to anti-National Socialists."

Hess says: "Germany needs strong, healthy offspring. A German girl is honored by bearing illegitimate children." Himmler's propaganda on the subject, as expressed in his article in the *Schwarze Korps*, is similar. "Try out the future spouse," he urges. "How else can you tell if the choice is a good one?" Unlimited free love! There should be a great deal of protest from professional love circles it seems to me. It practically puts professionals out of business.

Foreigners who are acquainted with well-known Jewish artists or scientists are frequently shocked by the sudden and inexplicable disappearance of these friends. It is difficult for them to understand why Aryan friends or colleagues do not dare to inquire about the whereabouts of those who have disappeared. They generally vanish just before dawn, dragged from their beds.

There is a Dutch joke going the rounds here. A Dutchman, who had been listening to the bragging of a Nazi concerning the excellence of the National Socialist state for about as long as he could stand, said: "Yes, all that is true, I suppose. We're rather backward, in Holland, compared with you. But we have one thing to be said for us: When we hear a knock on our doors before dawn, we know it's the milkman."

December 6, 1935:

"Empress" Hermine, during one of her stopovers in Berlin, invited, once again, some hundred and fifty guests to the *Niederlaendische Palais*. There is always the same routine. In the vast entrance hall, two tottering old castellans with snow-white hair sit behind huge antique desks. They give the pen, with shaking hands, to each guest, who has to enter his name, address, and telephone number in one of the two guest lists. Another ancient castellan ushers the properly listed guest inside. The chamberlain on duty introduces each newcomer. Then follows the serving of refreshments, the gossip, the tepid piano recital. Last night, everything went according to schedule—inside. A little surprise upset the routine in the hall when the Gestapo appeared and confiscated the guest lists. The castellans were frightened and bullied into silence.

The "imperial" receptions don't last late into the night. I was back home and asleep when the doorbell rang: The chamberlain on duty had found out what had happened. Hurriedly, he gathered five young noblemen. Furnishing them with names and addresses of tonight's guests, he sent them on a round of warning. I went downstairs to unlock the door. Young von Troelsch, after a hasty side glance, slipped in and reported what had happened. "You'll know how to act, *gnäudige Frau.*"

Did I know! The ever-ready emergency suitcase in my hand, I jumped into my car and drove out into the country. There I propose to stay until I get a hint that the danger is over.

1936

Contemporary Events

January	20	King George V of England dies.
February		Air raid shelters become obligatory in all buildings in Berlin. Air raid and blackout tests are ordered.
February	2	Lord Londonderry visits Hitler.
March	7	30,000 Hitler troops march into the Rhineland.
March	25	United States, England and France sign new naval pact.
April	15	Unrest in Madrid.
June	4	Leon Blum forms Popular Front government in France.
July	17	Start of revolt and civil war in Spain.
July	23	Charles A. Lindbergh arrives in Germany. Is guest of German government. Visits war production and airplane plants.
August	1-17	Olympic games in Berlin.
August	5	Germany sends the Condor regiment of "volunteers" under command of Colonel von Richthofen to Spain to assist General Franco.
August	11	Joachim von Ribbentrop is appointed German Ambassador to England.
September	9	Hitler at the party meeting at Nuremberg announces a four-year plan to make Germany self-sufficient in raw materials.
October	25	Germany introduces butter cards.

January 5, 1936:

A perfect example of German propaganda in foreign countries was the experience of my old friend, Rosso! A frail man of forty-five, he had spent twenty years in Brazil. His wife was a native. She and the three children spoke only Portuguese.

In 1933, Rosso had lost his good job on a plantation in Brazil. Soon he received a visit from a "party member," a Brazilian subject in German pay. The agent asked the unemployed Rosso: "Would you consider returning to Germany?" Señor Rosso, formerly Herr Ross, did *not* want to. He had no money for the trip. No job waiting in Germany. His family would feel lost in a country where they couldn't even speak the language.

The Brazilian party member coaxed: "People like you, Mr. Rosso, are needed in Germany now. The Reich defrays all expenses. The Ibero-American Institute in Berlin awaits you eagerly." He persuaded Rosso, after two further visits.

"Ibero-America" has a job for Rosso, certainly. Only, of course, he had to become a party member first. He was deeply shocked by the New Germany.

"As a devout Catholic, I cannot lower myself to their level." But five people had to be provided for. He set his teeth and bowed his head.

Yesterday, he came to see me, after a four-weeks' absence. The Ministry of Propaganda had given him a couple of thousand-mark notes to take a South American newspaperman on a trip through Germany. He had for years assailed the Third Reich in his paper. Through the mediation of German diplomats, he had been invited on a four-weeks' round trip to Germany to see things for himself.

Theodore reported:

At first, the South American was on the alert, suspicious and critical. I had strict orders not to leave him for a minute and to make sure that the sight-seeing remained limited to the bright side of the picture. Inspections were made only by previous appointments. Nothing was ever shown that had not been carefully planned beforehand. From day to day, his enthusiasm grew. He was insatiable in his desire to see more. He repeated again and again that we would be delighted to read his reports, and he meant it. Finally, the last day came. The ship was to leave next morning. We went on a strenuous farewell binge and drank like fish. When we got back to our hotel room at 3:00 A.M., we were dead drunk. I dropped on my bed and without undressing fell sound asleep. One hour later, a noise aroused me. My protégé was carried into the room! He had only pretended to be drunk in order to have a last, unwatched look at Hamburg's night life. He had hardly stepped into the street when three S. A. men, slightly drunk, had barred his way, shouted "Damn Jew!" and knocked him down. Three front teeth were the price the newspaperman had to pay for his attempted independence. He was in a red-hot rage:

"I am going to show you. Now you will really be delighted with my articles, you damn Nazi dogs. I did not trust you right from the start," he threw at me.

January 14, 1936:

Musicale at the home of Councilor of French Embassy Pierre Arnal and Madame Arnal.

Very chichi. I was interested only in the Walther Funks. Fat Walther has never been very popular, and he has never been quite sober. I remember him when he was intimate with non-Aryan Emil Faktor of the *Boersenkurier*. They were inseparable.

It is a matter of prestige that the Secretary of State to the Ministry of Propaganda resides in a luxurious palace. Heaven knows whom he chased out to obtain his quarters at Sven Hedin Strasse. The former owner has probably found shelter in a concentration camp.

Mrs. Funk, née Sofie Urbschad, was interesting to watch. She was dressed to the teeth. With brick-colored cheeks and flickering little pig's eyes, she seemed the perfect mate for her constantly inebriated husband. Her sparse hair dyed titian red, her coarse fingers glittering with cheap stones in grossly mounted rings, she sat there buried under an ermine cape and had the time of her life. She talked profusely and very audibly, giving a vivacious description of "Waltherchen climbing the cherry trees, picking cherries."

February 8, 1936:

Saw quite a bit of the Dodds in the last fortnight. I love going there because of Dodd's brilliant mind, his sharp gift of observation and trenchantly sarcastic tongue. I like it also because there is no rigid ceremonial as observed in other diplomatic houses.

Among the guests was Duke Adolf Friedrich of Mecklenburg. His sleek courtesy always gives me the creeps. He said he planned a South American trip in the near future. Just another one of the harmless "tourists" sponsored by Ernst Wilhelm Bohle, chief of the *Auslandsorganisation.*

Dodd told me that Lord Londonderry had been to see Hitler this week. He thinks that the former English Air Minister has a strong feeling of friendship for Germany. "Which does not improve the general alertness in England."

"If only we had more diplomats of your brand, Excellency," I sighed.

"Are you talking wine again?" he chaffed.

Febraury 10, 1936:

For a long time, I have had an agreement with the Foreign Office to inform them of any invitations from the Russian Embassy and obtain their advice whether to accept or not, according to the prevailing breeze. "As a rule, it is not considered discreet to accept for other than official duty calls," I had been told.

So, once again, I called for their approval on a Soviet soirée I had been invited to attend. Bassewitz, the Chief of Protocol, was "not competent" to decide. "Better get in touch with the office of the Foreign Minister."

Obediently, I called the office. Von Kotze, Neurath's right-hand man, advised, "Call Ashmann, chief of press of the Foreign Office."

Aschmann made me call Neurath again.

I called Kotze once more. He, meanwhile, had learned that the· Gestapo was to be asked.

I protested. "I'd rather not go at all. I have no desire to phone the Gestapo if I can avoid it."

Kotze grew fidgety. "Please, don't cancel the Soviet invitation."

"Well, then ask the Gestapo yourself," I snapped and hung up.

Kotze called back a couple of minutes later. "No objection to your going. They believe that you are very correct and careful with your speech in foreign circles."

So tonight I went to the soirée. It was one of the most exciting parties I have attended in a long time. After dinner we were shown Russian movies with English titles. I felt my blood curdle when I saw the powerful bombers dropping a stream of parachutists to the ground.

"Is there any other country in the world where such a thing would be possible?" I asked my neighbor, a French officer.

He laughed: "A German, of all people, shouldn't ask such a question. Don't you know what your *Luftwaffe* is doing."

"There, I caught you! You are perfectly aware of what is going on, and you don't move a finger!"

After the show, the host, Ambassador Jacob Suritz, said to me: "Yesterday at the French dinner party, we had a most beautiful Moselle wine. Did you supply the François-Poncets with it?"

"Yes," I said, "it is a Berncasteler-Rosenberg."

"I loved that brand," said Suritz. "Would you be good enough to have three hundred bottles sent to me? But be sure to have them labeled with another name. I wouldn't like to have a Rosenberg at my table."

February 20, 1936:

"Air Raid" is the watchword of the day. Air raid shelters have to be built into every new house. Very frequently there is an air raid alarm tryout. Sirens shriek and fire alarms whistle between 6:00 and 7:00 A.M. The block warden counts his sheep. If one of the flock has not turned up in the shelter, he dashes to the apartment, knocks, rings the bell, and shouts until the missing lamb is roused.

Needless to say, Aryan and non-Aryan shelter seekers are strictly divided, the latter being placed in the least safe space of the shelter.

The shelters are equipped with radio, light, heater, benches, and couches. Cans of food are hoarded. Every possible accommodation for a long stay is provided.

Last week, we all had to be prepared for a night air raid. We had to plaster the inner windows with black paper. We had to cover our lamps, motorcar bulbs included. The air wardens inspected every room in each apartment and in each house. If even a thin streak of light showed through a window, the warden would report the offending tenant to the police for punishment.

March 7, 1936:

Well, Rolf was right again, and thirty thousand of Hitler's troops
have marched into the Rhineland against the advice of his military
chieftains. And there isn't anybody stopping him. Rolf and I went
to the *Reichstag* meeting in the Kroll Opera.

A noisy pageant. With flags, Hitler Maidens, lanes of S.S. and
S.A., crowds of onlookers, radio cars, movie trucks, and, of
course, a multitude of loudspeakers. They multiply everything in
the Third Reich, just as a person with an inferiority complex
magnifies his aggressive mannerisms. A people with a national
inferiority complex.

The Hollywood movie people couldn't have staged it more
impressively. Everybody was there but the French and British
ambassadors, who were sulking. Hitler was, as usual, accusing,
vituperative, cajoling, triumphant, belligerent, pacific, so long as
he got what he wanted.

He raved on while the six hundred yes-men deputies cheered.
Starting off with the inevitable "fourteen years of disgrace," he
worked every stop on the organ. "Locarno pact abolished...New
Locarno...Nonaggression pact with France and Belgium for twenty-
five years... [Quite a comedown from the famous "thousand years"
to twenty-five.]...While we celebrate here, German troops are
marching into the formerly demilitarized Rhineland zone... [They
had, in fact, already occupied the zone.]...Plebiscite about foreign
policies...New elections for the *Reichstag* on March 29."

Upon leaving the Reichstag, Dodd's comment was a dry one:
"The German people have already decided."

"That's right," whispered Rolf. "The results of the voting which
is to take place are already in Goebbels' desk."

We drove out of town afterward. "Austria will go next," said
Rolf.

"Then Czechoslovakia. Maybe, after that, a pact with Russia and
the realization of the famous Nazi daydream, a gigantic block
across the map of the world. Spain, Italy, Germany, Russia, Japan.
We'll get a war, too. It's in the cards. Well, so much the better,
because it'll take a war to get rid of him and his gang."

Rolf was weary and unhappy.

March 8, 1936:

Heroes' Memorial Day at the Opera House Unter den Linden.
In this country, you're either a hero or you're nothing. The Nazi

leaders drove up, cocksure and triumphant. As the masters strutted from their arrogant, heavy black cars into the Opera House, their glance was a boast that the world is shaking in its boots at their deeds.

It is said that the generals waited until far into the night for the allied reaction to the Rhineland march. The allied reaction was silence. Now Hitler knows he can dare anything. He is now master of the German army and of the generals. He has proved the soundness of his intuition, and the generals do not say a word.

March 13, 1936:

The occupation of the demilitarized zone has started a flood of rumors. They're going to build a magnificent series of fortifications facing the Maginot Line. Some say it will be called the "West Wall"; others, the "Siegfried Line." I don't see what difference it makes. The Goebbels office has given strict orders that the topic is to be kept out of the papers at present. Printed information or public conversation of an informative character, with reference to the fortification, is punishable by death.

March 26, 1936:

Martha Dodd's farewell party for Prince "Doctor" Louis Ferdinand, who is leaving for the United States.

Hugo Eckener has fallen from grace. He refused to allow his Zeppelin to be used for electioneering propaganda. So Goebbels gave orders that Eckener's name was to be omitted from the press. Good old gruff, upright, dry-witty bear Hugo Eckener. It isn't his first trouble with the Nazis. When his first five-motor passenger ship was ready to be placed in service, it was proposed that Hitler be godfather.

"I couldn't think of going to the United States with 'Adolf Hitler' painted on the ship. I would like her to be christened 'Field Marshal von Hindenburg.'" Hitler raged. He declared that the name Eckener must never again be mentioned in his presence.

The Czech diplomats were worried because of a possible invasion. Af Wirsén, the Swedish Minister, consoled them with the reminder that, after all, there were still the British and the French.

Madame Mastny said, "By the time they arrive, the Nazis will have marched into Prague."

Which reminded Wirsén of a rather grim joke. Two gentlemen

met in a Carlsbad café. The first one, a Czech, said: "If war breaks out, I have to be back in Prague in two hours."

"Lucky you're so close," replied the other, a German. "I must get to my garrison first. From there, I have to be in Prague in four hours."

Fred Oechsner and his striking brunette wife were among Martha's guests. So was Otto Tolischus, his placid manner concealing a brilliant mind.

A newcomer at the Dodds' party was Baroness Wangenheim, joining eagerly in different groups with her ears flapping. I noticed her familiarity with Paul Scheffer, whom I don't trust either. He stands awfully high with the Propaganda Ministry.

April 10, 1936:

The Norwegian Legation can boast of a genuine Nazi on its own staff. Councilor of Legation Ulrich Stang. He is an intimate friend of the notorious Nazi spy, Walli von Richthofen, and moves almost exclusively in Nazi circles. His daughter is engaged to be marrried to an S. S. man. The foreigners warn that he is to be "handled with care."

Last night I went with a few friends to have dinner at the *Traube*, near the *Zoo*. The place is renowned for its cozy and intimate atmosphere. It is preferred by romantic couples who don't want to be seen. In one of the niches by the veiled light of the table lamp, I detected Stang and Walli. They appeared most embarrassed to be seen together.

April 20, 1936:

For years, I have been in the habit of driving out to a little village to get my supply of flowers and butter from a little old Jewish peasant. Now, however, since the "national elevation"—as Goebbels calls the start of Hitler's regime—I can only get flowers and fruits. The country people have to deliver eggs and butter to wholesale traders.

Today, I found my farmer in low spirits. "What's wrong, Beer?" I asked.

"Can't get my cow to the bull any more."

"What do you mean?"

Scratching his head, he explained: "Like in all small communities, we collect money to buy one breeding bull, you see. Each peasant pays his share. Each can have his cow mated. Now the Nazis forbid the breeding of Jewish cows."

There was not much I could say. I was too overcome to discover that there is such a thing as a non-Aryan cow.

May 20, 1936:

At the musicale in the Swedish Embassy, I sat next to the new Chief of Protocol, Vicco von Buelow Schwante.

"I miss your amusing social columns," he said. "Why don't you work for the *B.Z.* any more?"

"Herr von Buelow," I asked, "haven't you yet read the German press regulations?"

He seemed embarrassed and said hastily: "Your reports had nothing to do with the party."

It's really hard to know whether this is dumbness or whether he's just pretending. Mammi, who overheard the conversation, said that he is a stupid ass and that his wife, Helene, really wears the pants of the Chief of Protocol.

June 7, 1936:

Gala soirée at invitation of Italian Ambassador and Mrs. Bernardo Attolico. He doesn't look much like a diplomat. She's beautiful and exotic, but ice-cold, vain, and inordinately ambitious. Countess Edda Ciano was guest of honor. Mussolini's daughter is in her early thirties, neither pretty nor plain, not too feminine. Looks a lot like her father, with the same features and poses, and falls for nobility. Her hair is violently blonde without any warmth; it doesn't seem natural to me. Also, like her father, she is quite immoderate in her consumption of lovers.

Attolico said that Count Galezzo Ciano is dubbed *Il cervo volante* (the flying stag) in Rome. "Because flying is his passion and horns are his adornment."

She is said to direct her father politically and to settle his private affairs, getting rid of the women for him. Throughout the evening, Edda was surrounded by six or eight dashing flyers in snappy uniforms, specially selected by Goering and under special instructions to please.

Magda Goebbels has been very intimate with Edda ever since they spent vacations together in Switzerland. Edda taught her that there was no reason to be miserable about a faithless husband and that wedlock was only one of the states of a man. Magda was most demonstrative about her friendship with Edda and has carefully maneuvered to keep "those climbers," the Ribbentrops, as far away from her as possible.

There was lots of clamor about the victory of Addis Ababa.

Edda is something to watch, and to listen to, at a party. Seeing Chief of Staff Lutze strutting around wearing white cotton gloves, she asked Prince Philipp of Hessen loudly: "Since when do waiters wear the S.A. uniforms?"

The evening was interesting. Goebbels, the "Mickey Mouse," as Ribbentrop dubbed him, had one of his fits of rage. It appeared that one of the Italian ladies, boasting of how well she was learning German, said that she had read a wonderful book of Erich Maria Remarque.

Goebbels began to foam. "That Communist!" he barked. "He writes about the war and has never been in the trenches."

"I don't see what difference that makes," argued Helene von Buelow, who is a convinced Nazi. "Schiller never participated in the Thirty Years' War."

"Well, who the hell was Schiller?" demanded the dwarf.

Leni Riefenstahl was there, though nobody knew in whose honor she was invited. Goebbels snubbed her. Neither Hitler nor Streicher was present.

"So pale!" I said to Leni. "And no lipstick."

The Fuehrer detests makeup," she shrugged. "You never can tell when he's going to show up, so I've quit using the stuff altogether."

July 16, 1936:

Pappi's suffering has ceased after the ordeal of illness and loneliness. Another friend lost!

Pappi's last words to me, two weeks ago, were: "You'd better leave Germany now, my child. It's going to be terrible here. Soon nobody will be able to protect you any more. Look for a new home while you are still young enough to adjust yourself. Take along the memory of our Germany as a kind of beautiful dream. Everything that is in Germany now will die."

July 18, 1936:

Civil war in Spain! Ambassador Agramonte has been recalled by the republican government of his country. But he stays on, nevertheless, and a company of S.S. has been sent to protect him—from democracy, I suppose.

"I am Franco's representative," he says. Franco, himself, has a slight stain somewhere in his pedigree. But this matter is not mentioned by well-bred Nazis, who decide true Aryanism by decree.

It rather complicates the Spanish diplomatic machinery here. Agramonte clings to an office on the second floor of the embassy where he has his private apartment. The third floor and the offices are in the hands of the representatives of the Spanish republic.

Agramonte asked me to lunch. We did not mention politics. I also saw Satorres and Marrados from the third floor. They do not seem to object to Agramonte's staying on at the embassy. This is the same old liberal tune. Another case of democracy letting itself be trampled on by Fascism.

July 23, 1936:

Talked with an official at the Minsitry of National Economy. "I envy the Jews," he sighed. "They can emigrate. All a German can do is stick around here and be sickened by it, and finally end up a so-called volunteer in Spain with the 'Condor' regiment. You have to 'volunteer,' if they ask you."

There's been a notable improvement in our streets. They've taken away the *Stuermer* showcases so as not to shock the Olympics visitors with the pornographic weekly. Up to now, this has been on exhibition every few blocks for the benefit of those who could not afford the luxury of a private copy.

Hitler has a new hate. Count Henri de Baillet-Latour, president of the Olympic games. Difficulties had arisen during the winter games, when the Count told Hitler that these games must be held free of all racial prejudice. If not, he would cancel the games. Hitler gave in, but it hurt.

While waiting at the dentist, I turned on the radio. I got Goebbels' voice. I listened drowsily, getting an earful of words like "party," "press," "Fatherland," "seizure of power." Suddenly, through my semisomnolence, I heard him say: "Lenin, too, was a national savior."

I saw no mention of it in the papers for three days. No word at all.

I called Richard and asked whether he knew anything about it.

"Yes," he said. "at the press conference, we got orders not to use anything on the subject."

July 26, 1936:

On Friday, Mrs. Dodd gave a cocktail party in honor of the American aviator, Colonel Charles A. Lindbergh. The Lindberghs are here as guests of the government. As a special privilege, they were permitted to land at the military airfield in Staaken.

Lindbergh seems impressed. He appeared pleased when Secretary of State Milch, the unspeakable rat who disgraced his mother's name by inventing the story that he is the son of his Aryan mother by an Aryan lover instead of his Jewish father, patted him on the shoulder. And when a genuine prince, Louis Ferdinand, linked arms with him, his face beamed with happiness. I heard him say to Captain Udet: "German aviation ranks higher than that in any other country. It is invincible."

Mrs. Lindbergh is a gentle woman, one of the most feminine creatures I have ever seen. She appears devoted to her tall, handsome, boyish husband, who is the ideal of the "Nordic" type that the Nazis talk so much about.

Axel von Blomberg, son of the Minister of the *Reichswehr,* and Colonel von Hanesse, Air Attaché at the "Foreign Armies" Department of the Ministry of Defense, told me that they considered Lindbergh a very important personage and that the government here was taking great pains to impress him.

"He's going to be the best promotion campaign we could possibly invest in," said Blomberg.

It was an early hour of the day, but Loerzer, as usual, was already slightly drunk.

"Wonder what the hell is the matter with that American?" he remarked. "He'll scare the wits out of the Yankees with his talk about the invincible *Luftwaffe.* That's exactly what the boys here want him to do. He's been saying that the Russian air force is not worth worrying about, and that the English have very few machines, and those few inferior. Yet they were pretty nice to him in England, I hear."

I heard the same thing at Mammi's. She's in mourning, so her friends drop in on her. Frau von Widkum had been at the gala dinner Duke Adolf Friedrich von Mecklenburg gave in honor of the Lindberghs.

"He seems rather naïve, this North American Colonel," she said, with a trace of asperity in her tone.

Wolfgang von Gronau, president of the Aeroclub, told me: "That was a surprise speech of Lindbergh's at the club's dinner in his honor. First, he mentioned the grave and fearful danger of modern air warfare, and then he praised the powerful German *Luftwaffe*. It was a *most* interesting speech," he concluded.

August 15, 1936:

Olympic games. I attended a couple of times. Everything is colossal. The swastika is everywhere, and so are the black and brown uniforms.

The lack of sportsmanship of Germany's First Man is disgusting and at the same time fascinating. He behaved like a madman, jumping from his seat and roaring when the swastika was hoisted, or when the Japs or Finns won a victory. Other champions left him cold and personally offended at their victories over their Nordic contestants.

The manner in which Hitler applauds German winners is an orgasmic frenzy of shrieks, clappings, and contortions, painful proof that the whole idea of the Olympic games is far too broad for his single-track mind. This is *his* show, and *his* Germans are supermen. That the whole world must admit. He has said some remarkable things.

"The American Negroes are not entitled to compete," he said, for example. "It was unfair of the United States to send these flatfooted specimens to compete with the noble products of Germany. I am going to vote against Negro participation in the future."

He means it, too. Although it is his policy to bid every winner to his box, to congratulate him and shake hands, he has repeatedly snubbed and ignored the colored American representatives. Whenever one of the tall, graceful, perfectly built dark-skinned athletes scored a triumph, Hitler left his seat hurriedly and returned only when the signal for the next event was sounded. "The American team leader should complain," said the Swedish Minister.

Leni Riefenstahl, official photographer, wearing gray flannel slacks and a kind of jockey cap, is obtrusively in evidence everywhere, pretending an untiring and exhaustive efficiency and importance. Meanwhile, her assistants quietly, expertly do the work, which Leni signs.

On and off, she sits down beside her Fuehrer, a magazine-cover grin on her face and a halo of importance fixed firmly above her head. She has priority rights and cannot bear to have anyone else take a shot that she has overlooked. Page boys dash constantly from photographer to photographer, handing them the dreaded slip: "Leni Riefenstahl warns you to stay at your present position while taking pictures. Do not move around. In case of disobedience, press permission will be confiscated."

August 16, 1936:

A glittering swirl of Olympic receptions. The foreigners are spoiled, pampered, flattered, and beguiled. Using the pretext of the Olympics, the propaganda machine has gone to work on the visitors to create a good impression of the Third Reich. The entertainment varies. Warmhearted, friendly gatherings of the international set, showy and spectacular parties at German official houses.

At the Greek reception, I met the good-looking Crown Prince Paul, husband of Emperor Wilhelm II's grandaughter. He seemed vastly impressed by the sight of his royal relatives, Group Leader August Wilhelm and Prince von Hannover, in S. S. uniform.

Ribbentrop and Goering sizzled with activity and gave tremendous public parties in their private parks. It's amusing to watch them trying to keep up with each other. Rib had an ox roasted whole over a roaring fire. Goering presented his guests with the spectacle of Ernst Udet looping the loop over the startled heads of the foreigners. Ambassador Dodd told me they sat there in their overcoats, trying to extract some heat from the round-bellied little stoves that had been distributed here and there in the park. He said it was almost pitiful to see the dancers of the opera ballet doing their pastoral stuff with almost no clothes on, trying to keep the warmth of life in their bodies, which were turning blue with cold.

Goebbels outdid the two of them, running a party for two thousand guests at the Pfauen Island, near Potsdam. For generations, this island has been the scene of royal Prussian hospitality and splendor. Here, the wonderful Barbarina danced for the first time before Frederick the Great.

August 18, 1936:

Gonny's been here on a visit from America. I was a little nervous about her coming back, because I was afraid she might not be able to get away again, so I spoke to a friend high up in the party. He said he would keep an eye on her for me, and that it might not be a bad idea for her to come as it would prove that it was perfectly safe for people to attend the Olympic games. That would be in the nature of a protection for the child. He gave me the name, home and office phones of one of his trusted assistants.

"If you get into trouble, phone him," he said.

However, I am not deluded by this tender concern. Favors from the Nazis were not bestowed upon me for my sake, but for the sake of making the proper impression on the foreign diplomats who, the Nazis knew, took an interest in the treatment accorded to Bella Fromm. I always took pains to see to it that the diplomats did not labor under any illusions in this connection.

It was breathtakingly wonderful to have my girl again. But she has changed. She looks well, and her eye is clear and cynical.

"I could not breathe here anymore," she said. That was all.

Last week, my Nazi friend phoned that it would be advisable for Gonny to leave before the termination of the games, because after the Olympics, there would be no more leniency shown toward people who had left Germany to become citizens of another country.

August 23, 1936:

Argentina and Germany have raised their legations to embassies. The Argentines, at the same time, were *presented* by the Germans with one of the most gorgeous palaces of the *Tiergartenstrasse.*

The palace had been occupied by Consul Wilhelm Staudt's widow. She owns, together with her son, an important export firm. It so happened that mother and son had not been quick enough to enter the party. Therefore, Junior deemed it necessary to demonstrate their devotion to the great cause and donated his mother's house to the government—i.e., Party. Mrs. Staudt raged.

"Here I spent unforgettable hours with the Emperor and Empress. I lived through the most beautiful days of my life. I gave the most wonderful parties in this house. My son donates not his but my house! Just to obtain the good graces of the Nazis!" she complained bitterly some time ago, when I saw her. Today, at the Argentine housewarming, she was compounded of sweetness and honey.

"Imagine, I attended a soirée the Fuehrer gave this week."

"How much did you pledge?" I asked dryly.

"Pledge? Just the palace," she shrugged.

August 28, 1936:

Soirée at the American Embassy. The founder of the *Oberlaendertrust*, from Reading, Pa., and Mrs. Oberlaender were present. The lady seems to like the New Germany. Mr. Oberlaender is less enthusiastic. It is something less than pleasant for him to see his foundation used to fill students and scholars with Nazi doctrines. It was the immortal sciences he was thinking of when he endowed it.

The Papens had stayed on in Berlin for a while after the Olympic games. They were also invited and "very happy to see me."

"You could find a great many more of your old friends," I said to Martha von Papen, "if you cared to make a round of the more exclusive concentration camps."

On the scene also were the Schachts. Frau Schacht wanted to know why my column had vanished from the papers. I told her it had happened two years ago. It seems, according to her story, that she never knows what's going on because her husband always takes the paper to the office with him. After he comes home, she cannot find the time to read it.

Schacht seemed very anxious to please the Ambassador.

"If there is ever a chance to lend Frau Bella a helping hand, Dr. Schacht, please do," said Dodd.

"Any time," said the old fox. "I would be only too happy."

I'll keep it in mind. Talking about it later, I said to Dodd, "Martin Luther said what he believed; Hitler believes what he says; Goebbels does not believe what he says; Schacht does not say what he believes."

Hans Thomsen was there. He's going to Washington as Embassy Councilor.

September 1, 1936:

In the little jewelry shop where I have my things repaired, I was interested in a display of identical cigarette cases. They were adorned with swastika, party badge, and *Luftwaffe* insignia. They differed only in value, ranging from solid gold encrusted with precious stones, through silver and semiprecious trimming, to ordinary trash.

The shopkeeper satisfied my curiosity: "They are made by order of Minister President Goering. He distributes them as rewards or bait. Rank and importance determine the value of the case presented."

September 3, 1936:

Soldiers are going to be needed urgently, as anyone can read in Himmler's *Schwarze Korps,* and in order to supply soldiers for future world domination, the help of the women has to be enlisted. No substitute has been found, it appears, for the bearing of children. This being the case, the women of Germany are being offered every inducement to procreate. Daily, it is being made definitely and unmistakeably clear that the Nazis regard women without children, whether single or married, as creatures with only inferior rights.

September 9, 1936:

Fifteen-year-old Konrad von List came to see me yesterday. He brought flowers from his aunt in Steglitz. It looks as if he were not yet as poisoned as most of the Hitler Youth.

"I went to England with a group of exchange students," he told me. "We had a wonderful time. The only nuisance was that we had to make all those drawings."

"What kind of drawings, Konrad?"

"Oh, you know, before we left for England, our teacher said that he would give an award to the boy who brought back the greatest quantity of sketches and the best. We had to make maps. We drew ground plans of harbors and airfields. Mr. Klepp said we should do it secretly, as it might look rude. Well, we were very careful. Nobody ever saw us sketching."

September 29, 1936:

At the *Bierabend* of the Karl Schurz *Gesellschaft,* Dr. Draeger made another one of his attempts to exchange confidences with me. There was no exchange, but I did get an indiscretion or two out of him in spite of the coldness of the shoulder that I presented to him.

He said that Hitler's Party Day speech, in which he renewed his attacks on Russia, is greatly resented by Ribbentrop, who is at the moment German Ambassador to London. Also by many of Hitler's close circle, who seem, amazingly, to be interested in better Russian relations. The diplomatic wine salesman is also eager for closer relations with Japan. He is still negotiating with the Japanese Military Attaché, General Oshima. Neither of these masterminds has the approval of his respective Foreign Office in these off-the-record negotiations. There is also the slight matter of the "German Legion" for Spain, which has so upset some foreign countries.

"How stupid the French and English are! Why don't they send a few divisions of 'volunteers' of their own to Spain, lick the pants off the Germans, and stop all this futile talk, which gets them nowhere and only accentuates their weakness of decision?"

François-Poncet, however, did intervene at the Foreign Office on the subject of the German "volunteers," Draeger commented. He also saw von Mackensen there, who is Neurath's son-in-law and Secretary of State to the Foreign Office. François-Poncet commented dryly, "I saw the father, I saw the son. I did not, however, see the Holy Ghost."

October 23, 1936:

The Italians never entertain without a musicale.

Count Ciano attempting to be arrogantly condescending, which makes him, with his singular carriage, somewhat ridiculous. His manner was not haughty toward Magda Goebbels, however, who kept her ermine wrap on her shoulders during the entire evening, in complete disregard of good manners. She and her devoted Italian sat in a corner flirting ardently.

I was amused to see him offering a cigarette to Magda out of one of Goering's cigarette cases—solid gold with genuine jewels...the best edition, of course.

It was interesting to watch the departure of Prime Minister Goering. His lanky, tall *Feldjaeger* wrapped him in his wide, sleeveless coat, then stepped behind Hermann and waited patiently until everybody had shaken hands and said good-bye. He kept right at the Prime Minister's heels, shielding him on his way to the car, a living screen against unfriendly bullets. Hermann had not yet taken his seat before the car dashed off with the usual front and rear guard.

Attolico, returning from the gate, said in an aside: "There's nothing like having confidence in one's loving subjects."

Talked to Ernst Udet for a few moments. "We haven't had a chat for a long time."

"What can I do?" he inquired sadly. "Don't think I like it."

"Why do you stay? The world is open to you."

He shook his head. "For me there is no escape. They spy on me, they've tapped my phone, they check on my friends."

"Count Ciano is taking some pretty important pledges home to his father-in-law," Rolf said later. "Goering has told him that we agree with Italy on Spain, Ethiopia, and the Danube Basin." Ciano is going to see Hitler tomorrow at Berchtesgaden.

October 24, 1936:

The French Ambassador had engaged the Calvet Quartet to play for his guests, but the real entertainment took place when the Russian diplomats arrived and the German officials tried to avoid greeting them. Neurath and Dieckhoff were icy cold. Mme. François-Poncet was equal to the situation, however, and ushered the Russian guests to the very first row of seats.

Henry, one of the French staff, was indignant. "This is preposterous. The Nazis snub the Russians in public, but I know that privately they have been in close contact with an extensive clique of Russian army officers. Quite a plot, too. Involves some of Marshal Tukhashevsky's highest staff officers. The clique entered into an agreement to effect the removal of Stalin. Afterward, a pact with Germany against the world. 'Send us a list of your most reliable men,' the generals were told."

The generals returned to Russia and sent the list. It was promptly placed in Stalin's hands. An example of Nazi diplomacy as practiced by Count Werner von der Schulenberg, German Ambassador to Moscow. It accounts, if you believe it, for the torture and execution of so many high civil and military officials in Russia."

October 25, 1936:

We live as though at war. Substitutes for all kinds of goods. Practically no butter. The one-fifth, or, if one is lucky, one-fourth of a pound per head per week is only obtainable on food ration tickets.

As for myself, I have never had such an abundance of butter as just now. The foreigners a long time ago stopped eating the miserable stuff we call butter here. They obtain real, genuine, creamy butter from Denmark and Holland.

With the introduction of butter tickets, a flow of butter from the legations and embassies has been coming to my house. Foreign friends are sending me "fatty regards" now instead of flowers. I accept gladly. The senders know I am sharing it with my sick and needy protégés.

Here is another example of Nazi subterfuge. Walter Quitman had asked me some time ago whether I would like to give him money to take out of Germany for my friends. He had been appointed a government official for economic relations with Poland. He said he would take the money to Warsaw and transfer it to the U. S. A. Now I have discovered that the money never arrived in the U. S. A., but I understand Quitman had bought himself an elegant car and a number of other luxuries.

October 29, 1936:

A notice in today's *Voelkischer Beobachter* that Heinrich Himmler's father has died in Munich and is to be buried with full ceremonial at the Catholic cemetery. Alfred Rosenberg's new religion may save the everlasting souls of his inferiors in rank, but his superiors still appear to find comfort in the old faith, especially when burying their fathers. Old Himmler, of course, never had been a party comrade. I remember him when he was dean of the Wittelsbach high school in Munich. He often complained about his "black sheep Heinrich." "My wife and I are ashamed that our son is involved with those gangsters."

November 10, 1936:

Today, Elsa, a maid who has been helping out in my house whenever we have extra work, arrived in tears. She was married recently. Three months ago, her husband was drafted for "military training." Today, she received notification of his death.

"Your husband died for Germany's honor," read the message.

"Spain," she told me. "I had to sign a promise that I would not talk or wear mourning. They sent me a thousand marks."

Payment for one body delivered. The soul is not valued commercially.

November 16, 1936:

Many of us have dropped behind in our concert-going, not wishing to hear the new music and its Brown master interpreters. But I thought it worth while to hear Sir Thomas Beecham, who had accepted an invitation to conduct the London Philharmonic in Berlin. His program of old masters appealed to me.

There was enormous publicity, as the party considered it quite important. One of the most gala audiences I have ever seen at a concert. I was with some friends. We were struck by the great number of uniformed guards distributed thoughout the house. I knew what that meant and groaned to myself.

"Tough luck," I said to my friend Lizzie when Hitler and Goebbels made their entrance, escorted by a horde of Brown Shirts.

The Fuehrer had the artists' box at the right, just a few feet from my orchestra seat. The slightest turn of my head brought me face to face with him. He looked bored and tired. During the third number, he napped a bit. However, sleeping during a concert is a luxury reserved for common mortals. Goebbels jogged him back to reality with a vicious push of his elbow into the region of the Schicklgruber stomach. Adolf quickly recovered, pretending that he had closed his eyes the better to give himself over to the music. His head began to nod once more. Goebbels grinned scornfully and dug his elbow for a second time into the sacred breadbasket.

During the intermission, Sir Thomas was "ordered" to the box. Hitler clapped him graciously on the shoulder in grateful approval of his artistic achievement. The crowd cheered.

After the last piece, Lizzie nudged my ribs. "Let's run for it," she whispered hastily, "or else you'll have to raise your little hand, or be sent to a concentration camp." We had just reached the exit in our dash when Sir Thomas lifted his baton to start *Deutschland, Deutschland ueber Alles*, which necessarily had to be followed by the *Horst Wessel* song.

November 26, 1936:

The authorities cannot hush up the numerous German casualties in Spain. They are hard put to find explanations, since officially neither we nor Italy ever sent military help to the peninsula. I was at the Ibero-American Institute celebration in honor of its former president, General Faupel, now named Ambassador to Franco's court. We have thus recognized a rebel as head of the Spanish government.

Ribbentrop pays flying visits to Berlin from London almost daily. There is a private plane that waits for him day and night, at Croydon. Rib is Ambassador to Great Britain, acting as though he were Foreign Minister, and, in addition, maintains his "Bureau Ribbentrop." A pact is to be consummated almost any time now, it seems, with Japan. Ribbentrop contrived it, and now he claims the right to sign it, Rolf told me.

"How does Neurath feel about it?" I asked.

"What can he do? He can resign, I suppose. Nobody's going to try to stop him."

All the high party officials, including Hitler, received an anonymous letter today. Rolf showed me the one addressed to his Secretary of State. It was a quotation from an article written by the Leftist scribe, Benito Mussolini, for the *Popolo d'Italia* in 1915:

"This war must go on until Germany is forced to her knees, pleading for peace. Germany must be smashed so thoroughly that she will be unable to do any harm to the world for the next fifty years. The deep-rooted hatred against the Germans throughout the world can never reach the abysmal depths of their own barbarism."

No one knows who sent this nostalgic classic.

Breen, of the English Embassy, said that during a cabinet session, Sir John Simon received word that Ambassador von Ribbentrop had just taken off for Croydon.

"Tell me," Sir John is said to have asked, "what is Ribbentrop really, English Ambassador to Berlin, or German Ambassador to the Court of St. James's?"

I would suggest to Sir John that if he really wishes to know something of the status of Ribbentrop he ask the members of the Clivedon set.

December 17, 1936:

Dinner at the Finnish Legation. The Finns are Nazi Germany's pets, spoiled, caressed, flattered. Goering, Milch, Schacht, Lammers, and many others were there.

I sat with Renée from the French Embassy. Next to our table was Rosenberg, the anti-Christ, with a Finnish lady. I could hear him eulogizing the Nordic appearance of the Finnish race. "They are our kin," said the Baltic swine. "I hope that the day when Germany, Finland, Sweden, Norway, Denmark and the Netherlands will be joined together in one huge Nordic empire is not too far off.

The Finnish lady looked a bit startled. The Apostle of the Third Reich changed the subject.

My stomach turned over when I saw Dr. Hans Frank there. As a lawyer in Munich under the Weimar Republic, he was convicted several times of embezzlement and has an extensive prison career behind him. Not content with such petty crimes, he murdered a lawyer who had prosecuted one of his own thefts. To reward him for these noble deeds, the Nazis, in 1933, appointed him *Reich* Commissar for Justice to Bavaria. His first act was to set his father free from a prison term, also for embezzlement. His next application of justice was to get hold of a rival lawyer and so torture him with cigarette burns that the man died.

1937

CONTEMPORARY EVENTS

January	30	Hitler repudiates war guilt clause of Versailles Treaty. Frees German railways and *Reichsbank* of all international obligations. Forbids Germans to accept Nobel Prizes.
January	30	Ribbentrop in Berlin. Assures the generals and Hitler "England will not dare to wage a war against us."
May	2	Lord Lothian is in Berlin to confer with Hitler.
May	6	The Zeppelin Hindenburg crashes at Lakehurst.
June	15	Arrests of Lutheran clerics.
June	21	Leon Blum resigns in Paris.
July	2	Pastor Niemoeller is arrested.
September	29	Mussolini's first visit to Berlin.
October	14	Duke and Duchess of Windsor are guests of Nazi Labor Front Leader Robert Ley in Germany.

January 1, 1937:

The Russian Ambassador Suritz sent me a huge basket of blue hyacinths with a two-pound tin of caviar buried in its fragrant depth. I was especially touched by his chivalrous gesture in sending it, not by ordinary messenger, but by one of his embassy secretaries.

I asked the young Russian to have a cup of tea with me. He told

236

me that he has been in Berlin for seven months. He already speaks German fluently. With shining eyes, he spoke of the opportunities given to each citizen in his country:

"I was a railroad worker. Very keenly interested in politics. I got the right backing and was sent to a school for diplomatic training. For two years, I was at our London embassy. There I learned to speak the English language. My appointment here will also last two years. Before I was sent abroad, I spent two months in one of the recreation homes at the Crimea. The government pays all expenses."

"Sounds like Strength-through-Joy," I said.

"Yes, that is another of Nazi Germany's borrowed institutions. But I understand that here the beneficiaries have to pay for their privileges by deductions from their wages."

I should think they have to! I have tried a sort of cross-section checking on this particular Nazi accomplishment. The answers were unanimously alike: My laundrywoman went on one of the Strength-through-Joy journeys:

"Certainly, it was nice to see Norway," she said, "but I did not feel rested. Not a moment of relaxation. Never left alone. There is always somebody controlling what one says or does. One can't talk to any foreigner, can't get hold of a newspaper. And they never stop blowing their propaganda horn. Also, the trip was very strenuous. We were squeezed together in a third-class compartment. No, I'd rather travel alone. Maybe I can't afford such a long distance, but at least I'd be my own master."

The grocer, the seamstress, the shoemaker—all of them answered in this vein. The Strength-through-Joy at home is just as much of an ordeal as these cattle-like excursions. Theater performances have to be attended. All sorts of mass celebrations are obligatory. The masses have to attend and listen to important broadcasts. Never a breathing spell for anybody. Never a quiet, individual moment of seclusion or relaxation. The Third Reich steers its sheep through the routine of work and holiday.

Is this preference of orders over free action really typically German?—or is it just that the Gestapo has complete possession of the German body and soul?

January 7, 1937:

The Bulgarians celebrate their Christmas holidays a week after our New Year's. I was invited to their ball.

Ex-Tsar Ferdinand, father of King Boris, held court, with his Adjutant, Peter Gantchew, as master of cermonies. Gantchew is a passionate Nazi and is the agent of German-Bulgarian trade and cultural relations. He enjoys every privilege the Third Reich can bestow on a foreigner.

"His Majesty wants to see you," he told me when I arrived.

I was not prepared for a court appearance. I hastily borrowed a pair of elbow-length white kid gloves, struggled into them, fished my "Ludwig's Cross" and "Red Cross Order" out of my pocketbook, pinned them to my evening gown, and went to execute my curtsy.

Ferdinand is one of my wine clients. "The burgandy is delicious," he greeted me. "Please send me another shipment." Glittering on his lapel was the Bulgarian swastika, encrusted with diamonds. I knew this wasn't going to be any place for me.

"Sit down, child," he said. "I'm bored with all these people."

We began a diplomatic third degree; at least, he began it. I hear a great deal of inside information, and the ex-Tsar knows it. He was trying to pump me for some reason I could not quite make out. My replies were cautious. Finally, I felt cornered.

"Your Majesty," I pleaded, "I really cannot be impartial about much of anything here. Most of the regulations affect me personally. All I can say is I am sorry to see my beloved Germany thrown back into medieval darkness." He persisted, nevertheless. "I am neither sufficiently erudite nor well informed. Your Majesty is no doubt able to get whatever information he wishes from his Adjutant."

Ferdinand was dejected. He shook his head. "The old boy has so many other things on his mind. Would you believe it, I red-pencil the newspapers and send them to him, instead of his doing that for me. It's those women! He's just been divorced again. His last wife was a charming creature. I was just getting used to her. By the way, what do you think about the Duke of Windsor... I mean, what do they think about the Duke of Windsor... I mean, what do they say in the embassy boudoirs?"

I was tactful. "Your majesty, I wouldn't dare pass judgment on a royal love."

He gave up then, and after saying a few gracious words about his friend, General von Seeckt, who had been buried the day before, dismissed me kindly. I don't trust him. He spent too many years with his cousin Duke Edward in Coburg for me to believe that his wearing of the swastika is nothing but a "diplomatic gesture."

January 12, 1937:

Lavish birthday celebration of the Third Reich's Number Two Man, at the Opera, which was cleared of seats for the occasion. A scene of Roman festival splendor that would have caused a revolution in almost any other country.

The tables were banked with enormous masses of carnations, lilacs, and exotic orchids. Dinner started with mountains of caviar. Champagne ran in a continual gushing stream all night long. The lavishness was on a scale almost bordering on insanity.

Rolf, who had induced his servant to get himself included in the crowd of hired footmen, told me what happened backstage, as related to him by his servant. It seems that, contrary to the usual custom at such banquets, there was no arrangement for the delivery trucks to return for the unused food and wine. It was just dumped down and paid for...by the German Reich. The waiters, dishwashers, footmen, hat-check girls...all of them staggered home under entire haunches of venison, lobsters by the score, cases of champagne.... As there was no paper with which to wrap anything, they carried their loot away in expensive linen napkins adorned with the Prussian crest.

Goering is a rather fictional character, in many ways, and some of the stories about him are not too easy to take. They say that he gave a dinner at his hunting lodge in the Schorfheide. During the course of the meal, he left the table and reappeared in the extraordinary costume of the acient German, rawhide shirt and bearskin. He had a spear in one of his pudgy fists. With the other, at the end of an iron chain, he dragged a pair of bisons down the center of the room. Here he treated his guests to the spectacle of two bisons mating, much to the stupefaction of everyone there. This was German "Blood and Soil."

February 2, 1937:

The new Chancellory of the Reich was inaugurated with a dinner of Babylonian splendor. Three companies of S.S. and S.A., disguised as footmen, watched over "Emperor Adolf's" personal security.

They say it cost a mere trifle of three hundred millions. In its oriental pomp, it contains a thousand rooms, a cinema, concert hall, costly murals with painted scenes from the operas of Wagner, and a hall longer than the Hall of Mirrors at Versailles. Also an air raid shelter with bedrooms, bathrooms, movie theater, kitchen, and hospital rooms.

At Goebbels' orders, there were articles in the papers about the "old" Chancellory. Actually, its venerability dated back to Bruening's time. It was reconstructed in 1930-1932.

Some of Berlin's most beautiful palaces are being torn down to satisfy Adolf's craving for more new and splendid buildings, including about a dozen palaces belonging to diplomats. "We get new houses, and a considerable compensation from the Third Reich," said the Danish Minister. "All because the Fuehrer wishes to cut streets across Berlin. Ludwig II at least created artistic treasures when he constructed his castles. Hitler replaces national treasures to build highroads for his troops even in the heart of Berlin!"

Ribbentrop is pulling every kind of wire in London in order to secure the recall of Sir Eric Phipps. The ends of most of these wires are hidden cleverly in the Clivedon set. Sir Eric is not pliable enough to suit the purposes of New Germany.

Apparently, Phipps, himself, has asked to be transferred. He is to be sent to Paris, which he loves almost as dearly as he does his own country.

Rolf tells me that Ribbentrop is trying to persuade Hitler and his generals that England is afraid of Germany. "She will not dare to protest anything we do."

February 5, 1937:

Luncheon with Nachat, at his request. After we had discussed the wine order, I perceived that there was something else on his mind. He expressed himself at last, in his unique mistreatment of the German tongue.

"You watch out, no? Don't being too decent with all people. Remember the newspaperman, Wilhelm Staar, whom you have introduced so kindly within my house? The impudent fellow came here one week ago and told me that the Ministry of Propaganda not like that diplomats invite so much Bella Fromm.

"I told him I invite in my house who I want and you get the hell out of here. I was so mad that I went immediately to the French Ambassador. This repulsive Staar had seen already François-Poncet and heard similar answer there."

"Do you advise me to turn down your invitations from now on?"
He shook his head vigorously. "Would be insult of great
magnitude. Now we shall all invite you even more often."

"What do you think I ought to do?" I asked.

He looked at me sadly. "Bella, I am very sorry, but advise you to
leave the country as soon as possible."

February 16, 1937:

Went with Rolf to a reception at the François-Poncets'. There
are many rumors and signs of trouble ahead, and Rolf was deeply
concerned over them.

"Hitler is trying hard to get on friendlier terms with Russia," he
said. "He wants his rear protected. The S. S. is being strongly
reinforced...in Munich, they have nearly six thousand S. S. men
in constant readiness for emergencies. It looks to me as if our
Leader is none too sure of the uncompromising loyalty of the
army. There have been lots of resentful murmurs about the
'shipments of human beings' to Spain."

Made endless futile efforts to obtain an extension of my
passport for my occasional trips to Switzerland and Paris. I was
summoned to police headquarters at *Alexanderplatz* to submit my
complete pedigree. The outlook does not seem promising. The
police sergeant in charge, a trustworthy anti-Nazi whom I have
known for a long time, studied my document carefully and said:

"Some pedigree! Seven generations traced back without a gap.
Unfortunately, I doubt whether it will do you any good. You see,
my pedigree isn't bad either, and it won't do me any more good
than yours does you. Thirty and more years in the service, and
now they're sending in Nazi lads to take our places, while we get
transferred to some hole in the provinces."

February 20, 1937:

Magda Goebbels appeared at the Turkish Ball. It has long ago
become evident that she is a most unhappy woman. Goebbels is a
conscientious libertine. He spends a great deal of his time in the
lowest dives in Berlin.

"Magda wants a divorce," Mammi told me. "She has a list of the
names of more than thirty women who were intimate with her
husband."

But there isn't a lawyer in Germany who would dare handle the

case. Hitler, too, has vetoed the idea of a divorce, not wishing to
cast a blemish on a party reputation!

March 9, 1937:

Gay party at the house of Dr. Keil, a nephew of Fritz Thyssen
and related to the Krupps. They had invited a cross section of
Nazi and anti-Nazi, Aryan and non-Aryan, prewar and postwar
society.

Met Marga Richter there, the assistant to Eva von Schroeder at
the Nazi People's Welfare. Marga's husband, a physician, has come
to sudden Nazi power. She is so anxious to show her loyalty to the
Nazis that she has even gone to the trouble to change her naturally
dark hair to an approved Nordic hue. She is everywhere, the
personified "lady" of the Third Reich. Minnie the cook in her
Sunday best. She accepts her new social standing boisterously,
running around madly everywhere, afraid she might be missing
something or somebody important. Likes to drink but can't take
it.

She was quite high, and suddenly remembered that she was
fond of me. She began to cry, blubbering in my lap, drenching me
with her salty grief. She swore me to secrecy, but what I got out of
her had its interest.

"Do you know why we haven't been able to buy onions here for
such a long time? We have been experimenting with a new kind of
poison gas."

"My husband left for Japan this morning, with a staff of
physicians and army officers. He is in charge of the commission to
check on the effect of the new poison gas which Germany sold to
Japan for her war in China. For God's sake, darling, don't tell
anybody!" The latest barbarism Nazi culture has adopted made
me shiver.

March 13, 1937:

"Well, Hanfstaengl has been kicked out," Louis P. Lochner told
me. So it is true! His secretary, Mrs. Gritz von Hausberger, an
American, told me some time ago that Putzi was in lots of trouble
and that Hitler will no longer receive him.

March 21, 1937:

The Minister of Iraq and his wife, Princess Zeid el-Hussein,
entertained at dinner. The table was loaded with purple orchids,

which are quite difficult to get hereabouts, and the Princess's fingers were loaded with gems so large they looked as though she had looted a crystal chandelier.

They like it here, the Prince and the Princess, who can both call the King of Iraq a close relative. She is decidedly Semitic looking, which belies her passionate Nazi bias. A few days ago, Rolf tells me, during a Nazi dinner, she denounced Fritz Grobba, German Minister to Bagdad, for fraternizing with Jews and helping them.

The Nazi government is exceedingly shrewd about the representatives of these small countries, putting itself out to show them honor out of all proportion to their importance. The result is that the flattered diplomats send back glowing reports about Germany.

There were numerous Italian guests. The Nazi bigwigs complimented them on their remarkable new highway through Libya. Rolf explained to me that a Germany military commission has already been sent out to inspect the "hard road" through the desert. "It's hardly even a pretext, this inspection tour. The road is to be used for a breakthrough to Egypt, when the occasion arises."

The Persians, too, are being made a target for Nazi affability. They refer to them as "Iranian" and pure Aryans. But I have found it difficult to locate a blond, blue-eyed one, as the Nazis claim "pure Aryans" to be.

Something of a scandal was caused by Prince Carolath, son of "Empress" Hermine, who brought his lovely blonde mistress to the Turkish Embassy Ball. It came out that she was a salesgirl, and there were lots of shocked complaints. The Prince was entirely unruffled.

"Why not?" he demanded with a charming arrogance. "Society is full of important Nazis who drag along, legally, ex-cooks, seamstresses, and shopgirls."

April 10, 1937:

Hans Dieckhoff, head of Section III (Great Britain, the Americas, Turkey, and the Middle East) at the Foreign Office, is going to succeed Luther in Washington. He's a Nazi but apparently only a lukewarm one. Because of his constant grin and his singular resemblance to the stone figures you find in rococo gardens, they call him the "pouting Cupid." His hair is kinky. Lucky for him it's blond. A relative of Ribbentrop's, but there is little love lost between them.

He's a "March casualty," and that's probably the reason Ribbentrop makes no particular effort to warm up to him.

Eva Dieckhoff is an *Auslandsdeutsche*, born in Turkey. Attractive in a way but cold and aloofly arrogant.

They live in Dahlem and entertain on a large scale.

April 15, 1937:

Sir Eric Phipps and his wife left for Paris. They were delighted to go to France. Now we are expectantly awaiting Sir Nevile Henderson. He is coming from Buenos Aires. Ribbentrop asserts that the new Ambassador understands the New Germany much better and will be more sympathetic to rightful German aspirations.

That's just what I fear.

May 22, 1937:

Headlines:

"Seduction of boys in catechism class"—"Silesian priest sentenced to three years of prison" because of "perverted fornication"—"Sexual transgressions of Catholic priests."

"All this is fiendishly invented to persecute the Catholic church," reported a priest in the Nuncio's office. They are also harassing the Protestant church. They want to put an end to Parson Martin Niemoeller's strong influence on his congregation. People flock by the thousands to the tiny church in Dahlem to listen to his sermons."

Mrs. Orme Wilson of the American Embassy told me once in 1934: "Many members of the corps go all the way to Dahlem to listen to Niemoeller. We make a point to be out there at least two hours ahead of the service, otherwise there is no chance to get inside. Hundreds attend his sermons outside. They all want to hear the inspired words of their gallant parson."

May 25, 1937:

At a dinner party in the French Embassy, I was introduced to the new English Ambassador. He looks extremely British, very elegant and sporty. He seems fascinated by the Nazis and speaks highly of Prime Minister Goering. He did not, however, mention anything about his presentation to Hitler. Apparently, that's where he draws the line. Or was it just an oversight?

I heard Sir Nevile's enthusiastic description of his visit to Goering's estate, "Karin Hall," and to his *Reichsjaegerhof* Rominten. The Englishman seems to see only the brilliantly entertaining side of this barbarian's game.

In order to keep up the medieval character of his place, Goering goes around in a sleeveless leather doublet, snow-white shirt-sleeves of homespun linen bulging around his arms, and medieval high boots to the middle of his thighs. Goering calls his estate "Karin Hall," in memory of his first wife. But it has been dubbed "Emmy's Lust" by the malicious Goebbels.

I was standing around with some of François-Poncet's guests, and near us was Chief of Protocol von Buelow-Schwante and his wife. Out of a clear sky, Af Wirsén asked, "Just what business has Lord Lothian had around here recently, anyway?

Buelow's wife darted in with an answer. "Oh, he was one of Goering's hunting guests." Buelow's face was a study; the question had come so suddenly. It's quite clear, nevertheless, that Lord Lothian hardly came for the hunting.

June 30, 1937:

Reception in honor of the Congress of the International Chamber of Commerce. Arrangements for the Congress were made by the I. G. Farben concern. I had been approached to assist as hostess to the delegates' ladies. Had refused, as I knew it was only a blind to lead foreigners to believe that there was no discrimination between Nazis and non-Nazis. Dr. Schacht and his wife, however, had sent me an invitation to the reception, and I attended the party.

There were thousands of guests—the affair was held at the *Stadt-Schloss*—and many of the foreigners seemed more impressed by the fact that they were being entertained where the last German Emperor was wont to sip his coffee than that the Nazis poured it for them. I was with my friends of the American Embassy.

Met Mr. Thomas E. Watson, president of the International Business Machines Corporation and chairman of the American section of the International Chamber of Commerce. We struck it off quite well together, and it appeared to please him when I said I hoped to be able to make my home in America some day. So pleased, in fact, that he promised then and there to make me his German secretary the day I arrived. I wonder whether he would remember if some casual wind blew me into his New York office one day?

I looked for Sir Nevile, but apparently he was not there. The gossips report that he has sobered up a bit from his recent brown intoxication and has remarked on the danger of holding out a friendly hand to a group that is quite capable of cutting it off.

"The arrangement would not have been too bad," he is reported to have said. "That is, to have Germany take the lead on the European continent while England and the United States continue to exercise control over the sea. But Hitler is such a fool!" he sighed.

The Nazis know how to put on a show when they wish to mislead foreign opinion. An old English friend of mine, with a party, was led through a concentration camp. "Unfortunately," he said, "I got the feeling that most of the 'prisoners' they showed us were spurious. The rest of my group said I was crazy."

I assured him that he was not crazy; that is, no more crazy than the average Englishman who, according to Noel Coward and tradition, goes out in the midday sun. The trick was an ordinary Nazi routine with which we were so familiar that it always seemed extraordinary to us that any human being with ordinary intelligence could possibly be taken in by it. The real prisoners were hidden away, and healthy, strapping Storm Troopers in prison clothes took their places.

July 2, 1937:

They've arrested Pastor Niemoeller, charging him with subversive activity! They dare anything, knowing there is no armed minority strong enough to oppose their most outrageous acts. It is true that Niemoeller was of the opposition, but it was not a political opposition. Merely an opposition to the encroachment of the state on the Christian faith.

Pastor Niemoeller was a submarine commander during the World War. He is a tall, slender, fair-haired man, gallant in his actions as he is sincere in his convictions. His war experience is described in his book, *From Submarine to Pulpit*.

He is a curious case, for he is antidemocratic and antirepublican. It is simply accidental that he does not belong to the National Socialist party. His brother, Wilhelm, is a party member, and he, himself, has been an admirer of Hitler since 1924. During the Weimar Republic, he opposed parliamentarianism, Pacifism, Marxism, and Judaism. On January 30, 1933, he welcomed Hitler's election. "I am confident that Hitler will support collaboration between church and state," he said.

The awakening came characteristically. The Nazis espoused the cause and the faith of the German Christians, a group which was pleasing to the party because it sought to fuse the Nazi racial dogmas with Christian faith. Niemoeller entered the fight as adjutant for Bodelschwingh, who had been made first German *Reichsbischof.* The party, however, insisted that Bodelschwingh soon be replaced by the navy chaplain, Ludwig Mueller, who suppressed the Confessional church.

Disillusioned, Niemoeller appealed to Hitler himself. "Just attend to your own affairs and leave all that to me," Hitler told him sharply.

Fearless, Niemoeller traveled everywhere, relating to overflow crowds in his crisp military way the facts of Nazi attacks on Christian doctrine and organization. He became enormously popular, and the party had good cause to hate and fear him.

Twice a month, on Mondays, the Dahlem church held "open evenings" for the study of the Bible and catechism. Crowds flocked to these in such numbers that they were transferred from the parsonage to the parish house, and then to the church auditorium. Extra subway cars and busses were put on to accommodate the traffic. Many came out of political interest. Niemoeller never attacked an action of the state unless a vital Christian issue was at stake.

An amusing incident caused Niemoeller to comment on the inadequacy of confirmation instruction. A young couple expressly requested him to refrain from using an Old Testament text for the customary remarks at the marriage ceremony. When asked for suggestions as to what he might appropriately quote, the couple quickly proposed: "As for me and my house, we will serve the Lord," or "Whither thou goest I will go."

Niemoeller, in a letter from confinement, wrote:

"How fine not to have to learn anew that the rock remains unshakeable in whatsoever may befall us."

A confession of confidence and faith from a sincere, though contradictory, character.

July 10, 1937:

Yesterday, I saw *Broadway Melody* at a small theater in the Olivaer Platz—under "well-guarded" circumstances which did not prevent me from enjoying it thoroughly. After I had parked "Mucki" and was scouting the street for the friends with whom I had an appointment, I suddenly felt that I had aroused the keen interest of two S. S. men. They jotted down my license number and scrutinized me surreptitiously. One of them raised his camera and took a quick snapshot. I always take an awful picture, so I was quite sure nobody would recognize me.

My friends turned up, and we bought our tickets. Seeing that I was a mere cinema fan obviously reassured the two men, but now my curiosity had been aroused, and I waited to see what would happen. The arrival of Heinrich Himmler, complete with his dirty-blonde, insipid, fat wife and grim bodyguard, confirmed my suspicions about the presence of the Black guards.

Just a Nazi leader sneaking into a tiny cinema to revel in outlandish glamour. The two uniformed detectives on duty had taken my searching glances for political plotting. Thank heaven, once again, the ever-looming threat of Gestapo "justice" was dissipated. With a sigh of relief, I plunged into the rhythmic tunes of *Broadway Melody.*

Frau Himmler has grown latitudinously since I last saw her. Of course, when you make whipped cream your favored dish, you can't expect anything else. The pleasures of the table are apparently about all the pleasures she gets, since Himmler keeps her at home, mostly with Gudrun, their only daughter, known as "Puppi."

July 12, 1937:

Had luncheon with Rolf at the Kaiserhof. In the lobby, we met Kannenberg, who is now employed in the Fuehrer's household. We are old patrons of Kannenberg's wine tavern at *Dorotheanstrasse.* That fat man's face beamed in recognition of old cash customers.

"Being in the Fuehrer's employ has improved your waistline," I remarked.

"He picked the winning side," said Rolf.

Kannenberg glanced around uneasily. "I had to close the joint," he said, "business was so lousy. You think it's easy what my wife and I have to go through now? Just you try to get up a daily menu under such circumstances! The Fuehrer, as you know, does not eat meat. Very little fish. And there are many vegetables he does not like. You have to be a magician!"

He looked around quickly again. "But I'm not supposed to talk about it. It's a criminal offense for us to talk about anything that is connected with his private life."

Rolf regarded his girth. "How much of the food do you have to eat before Hitler believes you won't poison him?"

Kannenberg colored. "That's not funny. You have no idea how careful we have to be. When my wife prepares his meals, no one is allowed to approach within ten yards of the pots." Then, *sotto voce*, "As though anybody would want to eat that insipid stuff."

July 15, 1937:

Professor Latz came to say good-bye. I asked him why he was leaving so abruptly. He said it was due to Emmy Goering. She had phoned him to meet her at an obscure little Grunewald cafe.

"Nobody must know I talked to you, Doctor," she told him. "But you and your wife have been so loyal in your friendship to me for so many years that I felt I had to warn you. It is time for you and your wife to leave the country. As soon as you possibly can. Things are getting bad here, and I can no longer protect my old friends."

I always had a feeling about Emmy Goering, a feeling that her character had its sound spots, in spite of the sincerity of her love for the rotund Hermann. Her first husband, a well-known Communist, was a man of fine attainments and culture. He undoubtedly had much influence in the development of Emmy Goering's character.

August 20, 1937:

Well, they finally threw out Norman Ebbutt, of the *London Times*, because of his frank reports on Nazi cruelty. As far as one could tell, the English Ambassador did not move a finger for him. I cannot help reflecting how different Ambassador Dodd's reaction was when they tried to expel Louis P. Lochner of the A. P.

My dear old friend, Frederick T. Bierchall, of *The New York Times*, again advised me to listen to Dodd. "Go to the United States while you can still get away. We'll all help you find a way of life for yourself over there, child."

I cannot go now. I still have influence enough in various places to help people. Only yesterday, I was able to provide one of these

Nazi victims with the papers that facilitated his departure. This
was a certain Dr. Hans Kraft, a World War veteran, who had a
flourishing practice. He was denounced by a Nazi doctor, who
wanted his practice, and disappeared one night. After a great deal
of effort, his family discovered that he was in the Buchenwald
concentration camp. They got hold of a friend in a South
American country who was willing to pay the bond for his
immigration to that country. Then for eight months they tried to
get the Gestapo to release the doctor, but they were unable to
prove that money was available for his emigration. A social worker
recommended the case to me, and I went to work. After two
weeks, I was able to get a visa for him through my diplomatic
friends. Getting him out of Buchenwald was far more difficult. I
got Rolf's friend, Hellmuth, who ranks high in the Gestapo, to
look into the matter.

Another two weeks went by, and Hellmuth called to say that the
man would be released the minute we had a visa for him. I told
him it was ready.

Yesterday, I got word from Hellmuth to be at the consulate at
11:00 A.M. There I finally saw Dr. Kraft, guarded by two plainclothesmen. A rather tall man, but sagging with weariness, blond
hair cropped very close, the familiar hunted look in his eyes. He
was very emaciated, trembled continuously, and could hardly rise
from his chair. I had to fight to keep the tears back when I saw this
poor wreck of a human being.

I had told his sister to accompany me with all the necessary
papers and proof. Finally, the Gestapo men were convinced by the
visa and the other documents, and left their prisoner in our
charge. Last night, he left for Paris, to wait until his boat sails from
Cherbourg.

It is this sort of work that makes me forget for a while the strain
I am living under.

August 21, 1937:

At a luncheon today, they were talking of the Fuehrer's odd
behavior at the Bayreuth Festival. It becomes increasingly difficult to fathom and predict the workings of that confused and
emotional mind. One of his staff said that race and creed mean
nothing to Hitler...or rather, not as much as good Wagnerian
interpretation.

Hitler does not object to the "race irregularity" in the baritone, Ludwig Hofmann, whom he receives in his "royal" box after every performance. "During the first *Meistersinger* intermission, he sat with Hofmann and other performers in the restaurant."

"It was really surprising," recalled one of the foreigners, "to see how he neglected that bloated Frau Winifred for a mysterious blonde. She turned out to be the wife of the *Kammersaenger*, Max Lorenz. He giggled and jabbered and slapped his thighs in hysterical glee, as he always does in private conversation. There was no trace of his professional grim and curt seriousness."

The mysterious blonde was formerly known as Lotte Appel, a soprano from Berlin. The Lorenz golden voice has hypnotized the Fuehrer into forgetting the "racial disgrace" of a Jewish wife, and it was not necessary for that marriage to be dissolved. Like all non-Aryans, she had been barred from dressing rooms and theatrical premises. But the Fuehrer, under the spell of her husband's Siegfried, opened them to her and invited her, especially, to accompany her husband to Bayreuth.

"If the slightest discrimination is made between my wife and myself," Lorenz is reputed to have said, "I am through."

There are stories of other similar cases going the rounds. Hitler's "artistic" vein induces an unaccustomed leniency in him on occasion. Heinz Tietgen, "General Intendant" of the *Staatsoper*, is a case in point. It has become obligatory to raise one's hand in salute when the two national anthems—the *Horst Wessel* song is the other, of course—are played. And they are played constantly and everywhere.

Tietgen was invited to Bayreuth by Hitler to act as temporary *Intendant* at the festival. Tietgen refused and handed in his resignation. Hitler sent for him and asked his reason.

Tietgen was frank. "I am one of those who are not permitted to raise their hands in salute to the national anthem. I wouldn't want to, anyway. So I had to quit."

"Who told you to raise your arm?" screamed Hitler. "I will not permit you to!" He turned to his Adjutant. "Give special instructions that Mr. Tietgen is not bound to salute."

Since the Nazis discovered Wagner and appropriated him, I have not been near Bayreuth. It's interesting, however, to notice how carefully they ignore the possibility of the non-Aryan taint in Richard Wagner. It has always been common gossip that he is really the son of the Jew, Ludwig Geyer, who was stage director at

Teplitz, in Bohemia, at the time Wagner's mother took the waters there.

I think a great deal of Hitler's musical enthusiasm is just acting. Other rulers patronized opera and the drama, which makes it obligatory for him to follow the great tradition. I've watched him sit through hours of serious music, and it bores the life out of him. Once I watched him during a performance of *The Merry Widow* in Munich. It was amusing to see how eagerly he listened—and looked. The full-bosomed and somewhat aging Valkyries of Bayreuth never seemed to strike the same artistic and aesthetic chords in the ascetic Fuehrer as the slender, seminude chorus maidens of Munich.

August 22, 1937:

There were many Nazis among the guests of Brazilian Ambassador Moniz de Aragao. They seemed particularly at ease in the beautiful villa, which had formerly belonged to the banker von Mendelssohn.

Gauleiter Ernst Wilhelm Bohle, the formidable head of the *Auslandsorganisation* of the party, was there. Photos flatter him considerably. He is small, ugly, and swarthy. Not a trace of the Nordic master race. In fact, you find very few of the legendary blue-eyed, fair-haired beautiful Nordics among the important party personages. Like Rosenberg, Darré, Hess, Lippert, and many of the others, he was born outside Germany—in Bradford, England—and grew up in South Africa.

The Nazis are magnificently ruthless in the way they try to cheat and deceive foreigners with their statements. Talking to the Brazilian army officers in whose honor the party was given, one said: "It's incredible the speed with which the whole outside world is rearming. France has a brand-new type of plane, and they are rolling off the assembly lines by the tens of thousand. What chance have we Germans to compete with that?" A typical Nazi tactic to hide their gigantic preparations.

Aragao has been a good friend to me for fifteen years. He has helped me save the skin of many of my persecuted friends. I smuggled another list into his hand tonight, people who will come to seek his assistance within the next few days.

He was sincerely regretful. "It's getting rather difficult for me to continue helping, Bella. We've had so much trouble with Germans lately that they're going to put up the bars on immigration in my country."

"I had feared that would happen one day," I said. "You've issued far too many visas to visiting Nazi agents."

Among the German guests was General Walter von Reichenau, who commands the Seventh Army Corps in Munich. Reichenau was one of the first officers to turn Nazi. Today, he introduced me to his wife, Countess Maltzahn, an extremely unpleasant personality. She must have been very wealthy.

A member of the embassy's younger set tells me that Reichenau is extremely anxious to be instrumental in cementing South American relations with the Third Reich. He is said to have been in Mexico last year.

September 8, 1937:

The Swedish Minister, Af Wirsén, came to tea. "The Nazis are delighted," he said, pointing to Henderson. "The English Ambassador is attending their Party Day. What is more, the American Chargé d'Affaires, Prentis Gilbert, and François-Poncet are going, too."

Dodd would never have done that. In fact, before he went off to the States to report, he left word for the Chargé d'Affaires, who at that time had not yet arrived, *not* to attend the Nuremberg meeting. "Dodd," said Wirsén, "considers Party Days as a domestic issue."

If he does, I must disagree with him, though I adore him. The Nazis have been shrewd enough to declare time and again, "State and Party are identical."

Finally got a six months' passport extension at police headquarters this morning. That means that for another little while I can continue to send the generously granted ten-mark money order to my child. It also means that I can travel beyond the German borders, if I wish. But you have to undergo such hostile inquiry, if you really attempt it, that it is hardly worthwhile.

September 13, 1937:

Until recently, I was a staff writer on the monthly publication of the *Norddeutscher Lloyd*. The Berlin director, Fritz Koethe, who always liked me very much, made a point of sending me on a vacation trip each year. This time he gave me a round-trip ticket for the new excursion boat cruising from Swinemünde to Finland.

It was an eight-day vacation. I stopped over in Danzig, rested a couple of days in Zoppot, and stayed for seven hours in Poland. A longer sojourn was "not obtainable," although I had a recommendation from the Polish Ambassador.

The ship was packed with "Hitler Youth," "Hitler Maidens," and "Strength-through-Joy" excursionists. So much *"heil-*ing" and *"Horst Wessel"* roaring went on that I kept to my cabin most of the time.

Zoppot, too, is filled with the unsavory Nazi noises. At least by the sea there was a silence and serene stillness. It was cool. The Nazis seem not too keen on bathing, thank heaven.

Danzig, with its lovely buildings and beautiful churches, was spoiled by swastika flags and Black and Brown Shirts. Here the sight is even more painful than in Berlin.

One morning, I took the bus to Poland. I was the only traveler. Frontier control on both sides was extremely thorough. I was astonished at the sight of the vast Gdynia Harbor dominated by four Polish warships riding at anchor.

The city itself is full of contrasts. Fifteen years ago, it was nothing but a fishermen's hamlet. It skipped the usual period of development with boomtown impatience. Skyscrapers still side by side with miserable little huts entered through the kitchen only. Behind the kitchen, two cubbyholes serve as bedrooms. Each little hut has a tiny plot of garden. None has a w.c. In one of the huts into which my curiosity had driven me, an old, gray, shriveled woman, one of the exceptions who spoke German, showed her hospitality by dragging the *chaise percée* from the fireplace side and offering it to me. It is customary to empty the contents of this useful piece of furniture in the tiny garden.

I could not find a trace of the much emphasized Polish-German friendship. I guess it is just a Goebbels fancy! Seven miles beyond the German frontier, hardly anybody understood German, or, at least, they pretended not to understand. Neither post office nor restaurant answered any of my German questions with other than a shrugging silence.

A little old Jew at the post office offered me his services as interpreter. He seemed to trust me and complained: "So many Nazi agents come from the other side. Of course, they are not in uniform. But we detect them by their behavior. That's why we are so extremely cautious. We don't want any business with them. They'll gobble us up one day."

Deeply worried, he added: "We Jews fear the Nazis even more than the Poles, although the Poles have for generations permitted pogroms against us. At present, they treat us more decently. Probably to secure our loyalty against the Nazis. The Nazis have their adherents among the great landowners here, and certain elements of the government. These Nazi-sponsors are the ones who will betray our country in case of a plebiscite. There is a constant flow of trucks from Germany, bringing the landowners every kind of material and quantities of gasoline."

September 16, 1937:

I got the usual news of the Nuremberg Party congress from Louis P. Lochner and the others. Unity Freeman-Mitford, in her usual ecstasy, dogged Hitler's heels, as last year and the year before, the party badge tossing stormily on her heaving sweater.

Unity is heartily unpopular with most Nazis. Ribbentrop dislikes her. Hess is jealous and suspicious. He repeats, where it will do the most good, the late Roehm's remark about her: "She pinches her lips so tightly because she has crooked teeth." But Hitler seems to like her, and that's all anyone needs around here. Evi Braun, former assistant to Hitler's "court photographer," Heinrich Hoffmann, has given Unity some rather bitter moments. She is terrified that Evi might make headway into the sanctified heart of Adolf.

There was even a delegation from Arabia, brought to Germany by special invitation. It may be a remote part of the world, but not too remote for the plots and counterplots of the Nazis. Agitation has started there in earnest, the Arabs and Jews set against each other. Anything to make trouble for England.

September 17, 1937:

Everybody who is anybody in Berlin likes to attend the parties in the home of the Californian, Olga Sutro Manson, who spends several months of every year here. At her tea today there was much talk of Hitler's outrageous attacks on Russia in his Party Day speech. Also that Mussolini is coming to Berlin, though the exact date is being kept secret.

One of the foreign ladies, speaking of the wife of the Italian Ambassador, said that Signora Attolico was a dangerous person and not to be trusted.

"A couple of weeks ago," asserted Madame de Courten, wife of the Naval Attaché of the Italian Embassy, "Signora Attolico told me flatly she would not ride in my car with the non-Aryan Signora Renzetti. Her motive was not merely jealousy of a beautiful rival in the Italian colony."

September 29, 1937:

Mussolini is here. He was received with Augustan pomp at the Heersstrasse Station—a little suburban railway stop. The reception was grandiose, including a complete upholstering of walls and ceilings in shining white silk, to soften the dreary impact of an ordinary railway station.

The remote station had been chosen to give the Roman conqueror an initial treat. He was to enjoy Berlin's finest boulevard rolling along through Charlottenburg, through the Tiergarten, the triumphant Brandenburger Tor, to the "Linden."

Friends of mine who have a house at the *Knie*, in the most convenient position to watch the road for miles ahead, had asked me to come to see with them the spectacle of the procession to an open-air play in honor of the Duce. They had sent me a permit without which no mortal could approach the vicinity of the boulevard or any house in the neighboring streets. The slip was issued by the superintendent of the building and marked "Be sure to be here not later than three o'clock." You couldn't enter or leave any building within a wide radius of the road for three solid hours before the actual procession was to pass by!

S. S. guards crouched on roofs, behind machine guns. Streets and side lanes were barred. All this in preparation for the two "most beloved" dictators' appearance before their enthusiastic worshippers!

I had parked miles away from the taboo section and pushed my way patiently through the roped-off neighborhood. Holding my pass in front of me, I followed instructions meekly, making a detour here, crossing through a side street there, having endless hands grab for my pass, and receiving clipped "O.K.'s."

There were very few voluntary onlookers. The German people have grown tired of waiting hours for a passing glimpse of important personages. They are tired out by the time they have to wave their flags and shout their welcome. Of course, shops and schools and factories were closed for the occasion. Order was given to attend in "spontaneous rapture." But the "volunteers" were small in number. The excuse of illness was largely used. The usual chains of S. S. and S. A. stood there, lining both sides of the road. I was amused to see that the "pushing crowd" consisted mainly of a mob of disguised Storm Troopers in mufti.

I heard a man cursing in Berlin slang: "Now we can wait here until our knees are way up in our bellies."

It was after six o'clock when the first cars began to roll by. Always a Nazi coupled with a Fascist. In front, a driver and footman. Then the "Roman Imperator" and the "German Imitator" passed. They sat in gloomy silence side by side. Tense and uneasy. Mussolini's bulging black eyes with the shimmering white of the eyeballs darted rapid glances left, right, front, back. His brutal chin stuck out in theatrical defiance. He was obviously displeased with the ride in the open Mercedes. His complexion is swarthy. There is nothing noble about his features. He seemed bored, even annoyed. Probably he is just fed up to find so many scenes in the Nazi picture-book borrowed from his own displays. I just had time to see that the Duce had donned no special uniform, as Goering would have done on such an occasion. He wore a dark uniform with the Fascist insignia and the ugly black headgear of the Fascist. The great men drove out of sight. We left the balcony and went inside for dinner.

Meanwhile, the show at the Sport Field had been drenched by torrents of rain. When, three hours later, the cars came rollng back, the whole show looked even drearier. The flags were soaked, the flowers wilted. The Nazis and Italians, in their drenched clothes, looked miserable and uncomfortable. Still, the Spartan Nazi tradition scoffs at closed cars! The "cheering crowd" stood shivering behind the S. S. and S. A. chains.

October 1, 1937:

The Japanese Ambassadress, Viscountess Mushakoji, entertained with a musicale. Mammi had a lot of gossip about the festival in honor of Mussolini. She had been at the Sport Field, where she got the sniffles in the pouring rain and her new hat was ruined.

Mussolini, it appears, was furious. During the banquet after the festival, he sneezed and shivered. Soon after dinner, he retired to bed with hot-water bottles and aspirin.

"In Italy," he is reported to have protested, "we have sense enough to put up our tops when it rains."

He fell hard for Emmy Goering. His passion is such that poor Emmy is afraid to remain alone with him in a room.

"I hear at the Foreign Office," said Rolf dryly, "that Mussolini sent a messenger to Goering this morning with a pair of solid gold antlers encrusted with diamonds."

October 14, 1937:

The Duke and Duchess of Windsor came to Berlin for a three-day visit. Labor Leader Robert Ley is their host, not Hitler or Goering. The English Ambassador ignored the visit. To inquiries at the office, Ribbentrop, during his yesterday's air visit in Berlin, replied: "I have no time for the Windsors, and anyhow, they're out of the picture."

Ribbentrop had been on good terms with Wally Simpson for years. According to the gossip here, the baskets of orchids he used to send her were the talk of London.

The official reception was staged at Ley's palace. The place is glamorous enough, complete with all modern luxuries including a swimming pool. It is situated, of course, in fashionable Grunewald.

Ley hired everything for the monster reception from a famous hotel, including butlers and waiters. *Reichsarbeitsfuehrer* Hierl, the leader of the "shovel brigade," told about it. Long before the Windsors showed up, the Nazi officials swarmed in, accompanied, as usual, by their roughneck chauffeur bodyguards. No pleading could stop them from assaulting the tables loaded with exquisite refreshments for the royal guests. In no time, the tables were swept bare.

It took some fast telephoning and some diplomatic stalling to get things ready again. A truck with fresh delicacies was rushed to the house. Platters and dishes were hastily refilled. The reception turned out to be almost as regal as Ley had planned it.

It had been a difficult time for him because he had remained sober for three days previous, afraid that, in his usual state of intoxication, he might misbehave. He is normally a cruel, violent man with thick lips, hooked nose, and a face eternally flushed with temper and liquor.

It's funny how men like that can get women so different from them that they almost seem to come from another world. His wife is slender, fair, and well-groomed. She is soft-voiced and dis-tinguished, as aristocratic-looking as he is vulgar.

October 20, 1937:

The Nazi press sings the praises of the Duke and Duchess. The papers tell the touching story of how Wally, at the frontier, emptied the entire contents of her purse into the hands of an S. A. man. "For the Strength-through-Joy funds," she was quoted as saying.

October 31, 1937:

The Dodds gave a farewell party for the American Consul General, Douglas Jenkins, who is happily leaving for London with his wife. The Ambassador was depressed. He told me that President Roosevelt had promised to replace him as soon as a suitable sucessor could be found.

"It would surprise you to learn how hard it is to get someone who is acceptable both here and at home."

Novermber 15, 1937:

The Japanese Military Attaché has a magnificent house. In fact, no other military attaché in Berlin can boast of anything half as elaborate. This afternoon, the Brown Shirts indulged themselves in getting drunk at Oshima's house bar. I saw with what disgust the Japanese watched their "German friends." The Japanese are most restrained in their consumption of drinks. One young officer, who came here to study German military strategy, was an exception, however. He became rather arduous in courting the ladies after several cocktails. He was immediately detected by the vigilant eye of the General, who sent one of his comrades to remove him from the scene.

Hiroshi Oshima is an excellent host. He saw to it that all his guests had a good time. I happened to see a small model of an airplane in Oshima's room. My discovery seemed to embarrass him. But he was smooth and composed enough to light up a polite smile. "This is a German plane model," he explained. "I'm sending it home to Japan."

Axel von Blomberg, who was also there, told me afterward that the Japs had placed a big order for planes with us.

"Emperor Wilhelm II used to call them the Yellow Peril," I said. "Has the color changed in recent years?"

He smiled, "They need our advice and assistance in rebuilding their army."

"I hope you won't regret that one day," I said. "They're nobody's friends. They're shrewd and reckless, and they don't mind dying." I've never felt that they could be trusted, especially the over-polite Oshima, with his noncommittal Asiatic smile. You never find out what's hidden behind that smile. He is a good friend of Joachim von Ribbentrop's. Between them, they worked out the anti-Comintern pact without consulting their Foreign Ministers. Hitler's Adjutant, Fritz Wiedemann, supports the plan for closer relations between the Reich and Japan.

November 25, 1937:

An American Thanksgiving Day dinner at the former Imperial Automobile Club. Mrs. Dodd and Consul Raymond H. Geist were the hosts, as the Ambassador was indisposed. After dinner, I got the news that the Ambassador has been recalled abruptly.

I think the suddenness of this too-hasty and premature granting of his request has shaken him. He has sacrificed his health and his nerves for four years here, trying to wake the United States, and the world in general, out of its unhealthy coma.

Brandenstein was around tonight. He said that Schacht has at last been thrown out of the Finance Ministry. He's probably served his purpose, and the party doesn't waste any sympathy over those whom it has squeezed dry.

He is still at the *Reichsbank.* Secretary of State Walther Funk will replace him as Minister, and Funk will be replaced by Otto Dietrich, former Reich chief of press, a revolting fellow with eyes so constantly red-rimmed as to make him appear to have some repulsive disease.

Ribbentrop, always generally disliked here, is becoming more and more unpopular, also in London. Goering's already high blood pressure rises alarmingly at the mere mention of the wine salesman's name. Although he collects all the jokes made at his expense in a huge leather book, he is particularly annoyed at one Ribbentrop concocted lately. He referred to the decoration-hungry Hermann as "that Christmas tree."

December 10, 1937:

At the *Bierabend* of the Russian Embassy, Louis P. Lochner of A.P. and Fred C. Ochsner of U.P. said that they had seen Carl von Ossietzky. After endless futile attempts, the Gestapo finally permitted them to call on the Nobel Peace Prize holder. He is kept in strict confinement at the Westend Hospital. "He was, of course, brought in by two male 'nurses' who looked like Gestapo men. They did not move out as long as we were there."

As far back as Emperor Wilhelm's time, Ossietzky had fought against war. He was one of the first men to warn against the Nazi danger, and he had also predicted a second war. In the early thirties, he was jailed for his writings against rearmament. By the end of 1932, he had been released. Foreign colleagues wanted him to take up residence outside Germany. He refused. After the *Reichstag* "fire," he was one of the first victims arrested and has been dragged from concentration camp to concentration camp since.

"Ossietzky could hardly stand on his feet," my colleagues said. "He seemed doped, too. Up to now, he had always refused to accept the Nobel award. He did not want the foreign exchange paid into the hands of the gangsters. This time he said, "I have made up my mind to accept the award. I will put the foreign exchange at the disposal of Germany." He spoke automatically and monotonously. Apparently he had instructions as to what answers he was to give. The quick glance he gave us, as he spoke, startled us. The guards got restless and insisted that the patient was too weak and had to be taken back to rest. We had to leave."

December 24, 1937:

The offensive has been resumed on a large scale in the embattled Goebbels ménage, this time because of a charming interlude the Don Juan had with Lydia Baarova, the wife of the operetta tenor, Gustav Froehlich.

Tenors, as everyone knows, are unpredictable, and Froehlich did the most unpredictable thing he could have done. He lay in ambush for Goebbels and gave him a thorough trouncing. Goebbels, somewhat annoyed, found a pretext to have Himmler take Froehlich into "custody." This irritated Foehlich's friends, who caught up with Goebbels and gave him another—worse—beating.

Goebbels claimed an automobile accident had spoiled his beauty. Magda, however, in an endeavor to find out what was happening inside Germany, had tuned in Radio Moscow, which gave her the full story about her gay Lothario.

1938

CONTEMPORARY EVENTS

February	4	Army Minister Werner von Blomberg and Chief of Staff Werner von Fritsch dismissed by Hitler. Hitler appoints himself Supreme War Lord. Wilhelm Keitel becomes Chief of the General Staff; Walther von Brauchitsch, Commander-in-Chief. Foreign Minister Neurath is replaced by Joachim von Ribbentrop, German Ambassador to London.
February	15	Austrian Chancellor Schuschnigg is summoned by Hitler to Berchtesgaden.
March	11	German army marches into Austria.
March	15	Hitler is in Vienna.
April	10	Nazi plebiscite in Austria
May	3-11	Hitler visits Mussolini. Foreign Jews, on order of the German Gestapo, are incarcerated during the visit.
June		A month of further Jew-baiting and persecution in Germany.
August	3	Lord Runciman goes to Prague to "mediate between the Sudeten Germans and the Czech government."
August	25	Hungarian Regent Admiral Horthy in Berlin. Monster army show.
September	14	British Prime Minister Chamberlain flies to Berchtesgaden to discuss the Czechoslovakian situation with Hitler. In Czechoslovakia,

	Sudeten Germans and Czechs are fighting each other.
September 22	Chamberlain's second visit to Hitler, at Godesberg.
September 24	Hitler demands Sudetenland on October first.
September 30	Hitler, Mussolini, Chamberlain and Daladier sign the Munich pact, giving Germany Sudetenland. Once again war is "avoided."
November 7-12	New wave of Jew-baiting. Thousands are taken to concentration camps. Synagogues are burned.
December 6	Joachim von Ribbentrop and George Bonnet sign good-neighbor declaration in Paris.

January 1, 1938:

Upon my return to Berlin from a trip to the Bavarian mountains, it did not surprise me that my apartment had been searched. They did a careful job, but it did not avail them much. Since I learned that I was being spied on, I have kept no secrets of any kind in the house. I had put such entries in my diary, as were still in this country, into the care of Louis P. Lochner.

January 8, 1938:

"Prince Louis Ferdinand is engaged to be married to the Russian heiress to the throne, Princess Kyra," gossiped Brandenstein. "A proper royal match! They still seem to think the Nazis are going to put them back."

That will be the end of the charming parties in the Prince's cozy little four-room apartment on the Matthaeikirch-Strasse. "My father simply loves my flat," said the Prince. "Recently, I was tactless enough to return from a little trip ahead of schedule. I must say that I found myself an intruder in my own apartment!"

January 12, 1938:

Louis P. Lochner slipped me a nice piece of gossip over the phone: "Your friend Blomberg is going to marry a 'foundling,'

Eva Gruhn." "Louis P." had heard two descriptions, one that she was a "girl of easy virtue from the *Friedrichstrasse*"; the other somewhat milder, "a typist at the Ministry."

When I saw Blomberg recently at the Italian Embassy, he told me that his daughter Sybille was studying in Hamburg this winter, and that he would not do much entertaining. Now it's clear why he was eager for splendid isolation.

Sybille apparently refused to approve her father's second marriage and now continues her studies out of town.

January 15, 1938:

The ring draws closer and closer. Now one must have a permit for the sale of wine. These permits are not issued to non-Aryans.

"Bella," said Rolf, "it's getting late. The time has come for you to leave."

It's going to be hard to start all over again. Sometimes I wonder how people get the will and the strength to face the struggle from the beginning once more! I understand why some people end their lives. It takes less courage than to start all over again.

My international friends are being awfully nice to me. They invite me to all their parties. At the American Consulate General, they told me I could have a visa whenever I asked for it, which gives me a comfortable feeling.

There are so many here who still need help that it's heartbreaking to go while they still have their eyes and their voices raised to the silent and unanswering heavens.

Last week was very grim. They decided to oust non-Aryan physicians. I ran around in circles, from Minister Frick and Secretary of State Stuckhardt, at the Home Office, to Professor Sauerbruch and Minister Seldte, doing all I could to plead for them.

January 26, 1938:

Spent one of my cherished Wednesday nights with the Beue Tann. The Chinese Councilor of Embassy seemed optimistic as to the final outcome of the hostilities: "China is boundless. China is willing to sacrifice. She will fight for thirty years. China will win." Tann is a gentleman of traditional culture. Tann's father was the first high Chinese dignitary of modern times to be honored by a state funeral.

February 3, 1938:

Tea at Mammi's. Some diplomats there. More than ever before, she is eager to be on good terms with the Nazis.

The conversation was animated. Papen has been rechristened. They call him "Judas the Traitor" and "Swing high—Swing low," after the new American movie. Just now he seems pretty low. He's been having a streak of bad luck. Today he was recalled from Vienna. Apparently he didn't do a good job with the *Anschluss* preparations, or, maybe, he sided with the German generals who are opposed to it. Hitler wants Austria at any price.

In Vienna society, they don't trust him, either. "He gets many refusals for his gala musicales, and his name is often missing from the list of those invited by the first-rank diplomats," said Tauschitz, the Austrian Minister.

I have my doubts about Tauschitz. His words vary according to the person he is talking with. Rolf agrees with me. Rolf has just returned from Switzerland, where, by chance, he saw Prince Starhemberg, who violently disagreed with Schnuschnigg's weak-kneed policy toward Hitler. The Prince fears that the Nazis are feverishly preparing for the invasion of Austria. He spoke of returning to Vienna in the near future. Rolf warned him against it and also against going to Berlin. Hitler is furious at Starhemberg's friendship with Mussolini.

I hear that the Prince has abandoned his anti-Semitism and expressed sympathy for the Jews in Germany. Rolf said Starhemberg considered Papen was playing a double-crossing game in Vienna and constituted a grave menace to Austria.

February 4, 1938:

Adolf is wild with rage. His army chiefs, Blomberg and Fritsch, and quite a few conservative officers are in disgrace.

Blomberg is reported to have fallen out of favor because of his new wife. Her background has suddenly turned out to be shocking. It's the same background she was known to have a few weeks ago, when both Hitler and Goering were witnesses at the wedding.

Neurath is dismissed. Ribbentrop has finally wormed his way into the Foreign Ministry. Wilhelm Keitel is Chief of the High Command. Walther von Brauschitsch is Commander-in-Chief, replacing Fritsch. Goering has moved up to the rank of Field Marshal. Hitler has raised himself to the post of Supreme War Lord, obviating the need for a Minister of War.

It looks as though they're getting ready for *Anschluss*, and it seems to be in the process of being engineered by the fat Hermann. They are sweeping aside everyone who refuses uncompromising approval.

The "Affair Fritsch" has annoyed the military clique, however, as they consider him unjustly treated. Blomberg, for his part, is in a difficult position. Owing to his doglike devotion to Hitler, he never had too firm a footing with the high army officers. The Nazis, on their side, were always suspicious of him, feeling that he was not basically one of them. In addition to this, Himmler and other important S. A. authorities never forgave him his refusal to rank S. S. and S. A. leaders with army officers.

February 14, 1938:

Another street-collecting Sunday! This time, beggars on horseback. Mounted S. S. and S. A. trot along the sidewalks, clattering their collection boxes. An S. S. man knocked down two children and did not even bother to dismount!

There is no one in this country to call them to account.

February 22, 1938:

Cocktail party at the American Military Attaché's, Major Percy Black, who seems to be an efficient officer. He is one more of the rare individuals who are not deceived. I am sure he reports according to the facts. He has collected a great deal of information about Germany's secret rearmament program and the location of underground airdromes.

March 5, 1938:

Pastor Niemoeller was acquitted two days ago. Yesterday, as he was about to be released, two Gestapo bailiffs appeared in the Moabit jail and dragged him to Sachsenhausen. Such proceedings are quite routine. When a regular court acquits, or when a sentence has been served, the Gestapo step in. "A term of education in a concentration camp to get acquainted with the doctrine of the Third Reich," they call it.

In Niemoeller's case, they found another of their shabby pretexts. They wanted him to sign a paper pledging full support of the Nazi ideology in his future sermons. His unfortunate wife waited outside the Moabit gates to take her husband home. She had to watch him taken away. God knows whether she and her children will ever see him again.

It is all so depressing. At Nachat's party, I heard that the Austrian Chancellor Schuschnigg has been summoned to Berchtesgaden.

I know Austria's fate is sealed.

March 12, 1938:

The blow against Austria, although expected, had a paralyzing effect on all of us. Hitler has hurried "to the support of the poor brother nation in its hour of internal difficulty." It was well-prepared. The Austrian Nazis fomented disorder. The Austrian Nazis appealed for help. The German Nazis marched in.

Dr. Schacht was in Vienna last week to rescue his sister and his non-Aryan brother-in-law from the predatory arm of the Nazis. He smuggled them *and* their money across the Dutch border.

March 19, 1938:

Guenther, one of Rolf's friends who had been ordered to Vienna with the economists' commission "to coordinate the Viennese economy" with the shortest possible delay, returned to Berlin yesterday.

"I am not going back to Vienna," he said, "though the job isn't finished. I guess I just can't take it. What they forced upon us here, piecemeal, during these five ghastly years, they have crowded down the throats of the unfortunate Austrians in a single day. A cold brutality that is more than the human nervous system can stand. If I could only get away!" he lamented.

Rolf, too, was feeling very low. "The cabinet sessions with Hitler are really unbearable. Adolf talks for hours on end, soaring hysterically to the clouds as he chases his divine inspiration. You have to bring him back to reality, step by step. Austria is just the beginning. He longs for Czechoslovakia. Everything points to our occupation of that country by October at the latest. There will be no resistance. Then the Corridor and Poland."

"We have a pact with Poland," I pointed out. "And a naval agreement with England."

When we were children together and I could not keep pace with him in our games or at climbing trees, he used to look at me contemptuously. Now he looked at me again just that way.

"You are too stupid," he said, just as he used to say in our childhood days.

March 20, 1938:

Horcher has opened a restaurant in London. The Horcher restaurant in Berlin is, of course, internationally known. Even before 1933, it was largely patronized by the Nazi leaders. Horcher-London has the same *raison d'être* as had the Pavillon Horcher at the Paris Exposition last year.

Horcher's espionage expenses are covered by the Third Reich. Microphones are built into the tables, and waiters report to the Ministry of Propaganda.

This is not new or particularly secret. The secret of Nazism in practice, as *Mein Kampf* states time and again, is to do the most outrageously secret things quite openly. The Nazi success with this practice has been so great that there is nothing they will not dare.

March 25, 1938:

Shigenori Togo, once Councilor of Embassy to Berlin and up to now Ambassador in Moscow, has come here to succeed the elegant Viscount Mushakoji. Togo, it appears, is annoyed with his Military Attaché, General Oshima, whom he calls a Nazi. I wonder whether his annoyance doesn't sometimes strike closer to his home. His German wife, a typical Nazi upstart, deserves rather close attention, I should imagine.

Dr. Alexander Nagai, who, up to last year, had served twelve years in Berlin as Japanese Commercial Attaché, has come back on a visit. He is accompanying Admiral Godo. They are here to extract a good-sized load from Germany, it is understood.

At the Japanese Embassy reception, I talked to Nagai for a while. "What do you think Ribbentrop is going to do?" he asked me. "Into whose back does he sink the knife, Russia's or Japan's?"

"Into the back of the greater fool," I said. "One of you is going to have to pick the chestnuts out of the fire for the Third Reich."

April 7, 1938:

Musicale given by a Foreign Office official. *Kammersaenger* Watzke was star of the evening.

The last song on the program was Handel's beautiful psalm, "Oh, give thanks unto Jehovah."

The last verse ends, "Oh, give thanks unto Jehovah, to Him that divided the Red Sea in sunder, and made Israel to pass through the midst of it...."

The startled guests gasped when they heard the words Watzke was singing:

"Oh, give thanks unto Jehovah. He that reunited the German people in one mighty Reich!"

The last verse was absolutely drowned out in the hilarious laughter of the foreigners. The Germans were furious.

Watzke occasionally had given recitals at my charity teas. In response to my question, he said: "I couldn't very well sing the original text."

"A *musician*," I snapped angrily, "would have omitted the beautiful psalm entirely. An *artist* would not have gone out of his way to defame it."

April 14, 1938:

The new American Ambassador was guest of honor at the annual banquet of the American Chamber of Commerce.

Hugh Robert Wilson, the typically correct diplomat, had been looked forward to eagerly in Berlin. His wife, beautiful and elegant, is very much the great lady.

I hope brilliant Hugh Wilson will be able to see through the transparent Nazi infamy with the perspicacity of my friend Dodd.

May 25, 1938:

Inauguration of Major and Gertrud von Duering's new villa. Trudchen is not a bad sort and has always been very nice to me. Today, she was daring enough to introduce me, as her friend, to Hitler's Adjutant, Fritz Wiedemann. He is well-mannered and extremely polite. But his facial expression is evil and sinister.

Captain Wiedemann has just come from London where he apparently succeeded in beguiling a few English statesmen. "They all protested about our attitudes on church and race," he said. "It's really too bad, but Hitler is unyielding."

Wiedemann, who is slated to be the successor of Manfred von Killinger as German Consul General in San Francisco before long, has already had a career in the States. He was Hitler's superior officer in a Bavarian regiment, during the World War. Nothing much was heard of him prior to 1933. Then Hitler sent him to the Chicago World's Fair. Unofficially, he was active in the Nazi movement over there.

Subsequently, he made other trips to the United States in order to direct the "Friends of New Germany," a Nazi organization which later changed its name to "German-American Bund." Through conferences with Bund leaders from everywhere in the United States, Captain Wiedemann directed the promulgation of Nazi propaganda.

In 1934, he was in Germany and took part in the June purge. After the purge, Hitler walked in constant fear of his life. He made Captain Wiedemann his private Adjutant. Wiedemann's diplomatic career began at this point. He helped Ribbentrop negotiate the anti-Comintern pact with the Japanese. A few weeks ago, he was sent to the Balkans on a mission to bring them closer within the German economic and political sphere.

It is common knowledge in Berlin that the real purpose of his appointment to San Francisco is to spread Nazi propaganda in America. Also, from the West Coast he will be able to direct German and Japanese espionage activities, for which his previous Japanese contacts adequately fit him.

May 26, 1938:

I'm going as soon as I can. I have applied for emigration, but it will take weeks before all the papers and permits can come through. Cybe Follmer, my old friend at the American Consulate, has set August 18 as the date for issuing my visa. "By then," he said, "I hope everything will be straightened out in regard to your papers."

I hope so, too. I feel that I must manage to get out before it is too late. War seems inevitable, and I think it's going to engulf all Europe, if not all the world.

"Now that Blum has let Spain down," said Rolf, "France is in a divided and weakened state. Hitler will certainly try to take advantage of his moment. The point is, whom does he hook up with? With England against Russia, or with Russia against England?"

"You don't really think the people of Germany would stand for an alliance with Russia, after the hatred they have been taught to have of Communism?"

He laughed. "How can you be so naïve!" he said pityingly. "The Germans don't like to think for themselves; that's part of Hitler's success."

May 28, 1938:

Hans Thomsen, Councilor of Embassy at Washington, called on me today. He was ordered back to Germany to accompany Hitler on his trip to Italy. We conversed rather evasively, unable to find the key to our old cordiality. After all, he is in the service of Hitler. Just the same, I spoke of suffering, of injustice. He listened gravely.

"Don't think we have an easy time of it over there," he said. "Hatreds and rebuffs all the time."

I felt he had something on his mind. Suddenly, without committing himself, he said sincerely:

"Gonny, I am sure, needs her mother in America. You ought to try and leave Germany." And in that one sentence he found the genuine old friendly warmth. I understood what he really wanted to convey to me, and I was grateful.

June 1, 1938:

Unless the ideas on which the Third Reich is based are completely exterminated from the poisoned minds of our youth, I see little hope for a better Germany ever to arise. Driving out to Potsdam, I came across a group of youngsters, dressed in the Hitler Youth outfit, beating up a skinny, undersized, fair-haired boy. I stopped!

"Aren't you ashamed, eight big strong fellows like you, jumping on a six-year-old kid?"

The oldest of the gang explained: "We discovered that this dirty swine was nothing but a Jewish bastard. He refused to answer the *Heil* Hitler salute and said he was Jewish. So we took his pants off to find out whether he is circumcized."

I took the trembling child home to his parents.

June 3, 1938:

Through newspaper extras and radio broadcasts, the news is spread of the birth of a baby girl to Hermann Goering and his wife. The child, born at 1:40 this morning, was welcomed by a crowd that had gathered for days outside the gates of the hospital, where they had been ordered to wait "spontaneously" for the event.

Since the news went around that Emmy, "the First Lady of the Reich," was to have a baby, there have been all sorts of rumors making the rounds. Serious doubts were cast on Hermann's ability. Many guesses were ventured as to the name—and nationality—of the father. It was remembered that Mussolini had enjoyed himself keenly at Karin Hall. The child is to be named Edda, for Mussolini's favorite daughter.

June 8, 1938:

Chief of Protocol Buelow-Schwante is on the way out. "Ribbensnob" is mad at him. It seems the "court etiquette" for Emperor Adolf's Italian trip, which, strangely enough, had been arranged in Berlin instead of Rome, was bungled, and the Chief of Protocol had to take the blame. There was a violent and embarrassing scene in Rome between Buelow-Schwante and Ribbentrop, because of inadequate placements at one of the banquets.

Buelow is said to have quoted the words used by the King of Saxonia when he was forced to abdicate in 1918: *Macht euren Dreck alleene.*—"Do your own dirty work!"—and gone off to Berlin.

June 15, 1938:

"General von Fritsch has been recalled from banishment," said Loerzer, at the Italian Embassy. "They only gave him a regiment in Hanover, however. All the army officers stuck loyally to Fritsch. They were quite indifferent about Blomberg."

Farewell luncheon with my dear friends, the Comnens. He has been appointed Rumanian Envoy to the Holy See.

The boudoir of the lovely hostess was a sea of flowers. As we chatted together, I was struck once more by her beauty. Tall and slender, with ravishing blonde hair framing a cameo-like face of alabaster whiteness in which a pair of large blue eyes twinkled incessantly with fun and gaiety, Antoinette is one of the most popular women in the diplomatic set. She is the diplomat's dream—a perfect wife, an excellent hostess, a charming dinner companion. She says the right thing to everybody and, even more important, the wrong thing to nobody.

My eye was caught by an enormous bunch of orchids. Antoinette selected two ravishing flowers and pinned them to my white dress. I asked for the name of the chivalrous donor.

"Never mind," she said with a charming smile. A little card dropped from the blossoms: "Your obedient servant, von Ribbentrop."

I unfastened the flowers and put them on a little table.

June 18, 1938:

Helped free another twenty-one people from Buchenwald, that awful concentration camp near Weimar. I feel guilty about leaving so long as there is any chance to help.

I sent a young physician to the *Amerika Institut.* He wanted letters of introduction for the United States. But Goebbels has given orders that there is to be no help or advice for non-Aryans. The chief of this so-called "Mediating Institute" is a Nazi, Dr. Carl Bertling. He uses the office as a platform for party propaganda. He recently returned from a propaganda tour through the States where he lectured on German *Lebensraum* in that country, under the sponsorship of the *Amerika Institut,* which was founded long ago by the American bankers Schiff and Speyer.

June 23, 1938:

Probably my last trip through Germany. Even Weimar, the city of the Muses, has become drab and dreary. Soldiers' barracks are everywhere. An airport is being built in the forest.

In Frankfurt, they have changed the *Paul Ehrlich Strasse* into *Heinrich Himmler Strasse.* The man who saved humanity with his cure for syphilis has been replaced by a sadistic butcher.

"Germany is bristling with arms." "Germany is invisible," "The Austrian corporal is plunging us into another world war." "What is the use of having sons? I had hoped the boy would take over the business and I could rest in my old days. Now he has to go and do two years' military service." These were some of the comments at the numerous gasoline pumps I stopped at.

June 28, 1938:

Another wave of Jew-baiting. Scenes of ferocity and misery are carved in my mind. My friend Mia, a member of the diplomatic corps, had warned me about it in one of our cryptic telephone conversations. We met and covered the town from end to end in my car. Mia had a cleverly camouflaged camera for obtaining evidence to be smuggled out of Germany.

The renowned old linen house of Gruenfeld was the first place we saw surrounded by a howling mob of S. A. men. Mia took a picture of them "working" on an old gentlemen who had insisted on entering the shop.

We proceeded, finding the same thing going on everywhere. Varying only in violence and ignominy. The entire *Kurfuersten-*

damm was plastered with scrawls and cartoons. "Jew" was smeared all over the doors, windows, and walls in waterproof colors. It grew worse as we came to the part of town where poor little Jewish retail shops were to be found. The S. A. had created havoc. Everywhere were revolting and bloodthirsty pictures of Jews beheaded, hanged, tortured, and maimed, accompanied by obscene inscriptions. Windows were smashed, and loot from the miserable little shops was strewn over the sidewalk and floating in the gutter.

We were just about to enter a tiny jewelry shop when a gang of ten youngsters in Hitler Youth uniforms smashed the shop window and stormed into the shop, brandishing butcher knives and yelling: "To hell with the Jewish rabble! Room for the Sudeten-Germans!"

The smallest boy of the mob climbed inside the window and started his work of destruction by flinging everything he could grab right into the streets. Inside, the other boys broke glass shelves and counters, hurling alarm clocks, cheap silverware, and trifles to their accomplices outside. A tiny shrimp of a boy crouched in a corner of the window, putting dozens of rings on his fingers and stuffing his pockets with wristwatches and bracelets. His uniform bulging with loot, he turned around, spat squarely into the shopkeeper's face, and dashed off.

The little old Jew kept his poise and tried to reassure *us*. "I am only glad that my wife died ten days ago. God spared her this ordeal. We have been starving for a long time. Business was dead. The law prevents us from getting out of a lease or dismissing an employee as long as a penny can be squeezed out."

I was worried about two old protégés of mine whom I had helped with little sums of money and food during the last two years. They had lost their two sons during the World War. Killed for Germany! We went to find out whether they had suffered.

Their shop was in ruins. Their goods, paper and stationery trampled into the gutter. Three S. A. men, roaring with obscene laughter, forced the trembling old man to pick up the broken glass with hands that were covered with blood. We stood there, choking with rage, trembling in horror, impotent and helpless.

Next day, when we returned to bring them food and see what else we could do to help them, we found two coffins surrounded by silent neighbors. The faces of the old couple seemed peaceful and serene amid the broken glass and destruction. As we put down our basket and stood there wretchedly, a young woman spoke to me. "It is better for them. They took poison last night."

A big department store nearby had also been despoiled. It happened to belong to English Jews. Consequently, the municipal authorities were forced to remove the paint from the huge stone building. The less fortunate Jewish shop owners, of course, were left to scratch the filth off their walls as best they could. Whenever a boycott was "called off," they got just a couple of hours, respite "to return their shops to the original state."

I deemed it wiser last week to stay away from home for a while and went to spend some time with Aryan friends, the key to whose house I have carried in my pocket for the last two years. My foreign friends informed me that non-Aryan drivers were dragged from their cars. They were taken to police stations and released after a day or two. Their cars were kept. People who had the slightest driving fine in their records, even years back, were kept under arrest. Some of the trials, I learned, surpassed the most vivid imagination. One of the most dreaded police sergeants opened each inquisition by barking: "Jewish swine, step back five meters from my desk, you stink foully."

After about a week, I returned to my house. To exchange the experiences of the last few days, I met with a couple of friends in a small bar on the *Kurfuerstendamm*. There had been a silent agreement among Jews to frequent this restaurant, which had not so far put up the "prohibited to Jews" sign. Whispering to each other in a remote corner, we kept an eye on the renowned Dobrin Café across the street. It is patronized by Jews, especially bachelors who have had to manage without servants since the "Nuremberg regulations."

Suddenly, we saw a Gestapo truck drive up. It stopped outside the café. Ten armed S.S. men went in, while ten took posts outside. The guests inside were arrested and driven out like cattle. The sentries outside amused themselves by molesting non-Aryan-looking passersby and loading them on the truck. We watched, horrified, and decided to leave. The proprietor refused to let us pay our check before he got permission to let us go. He was scared, too. After an hour, we were dismissed. Too upset and worried to go home, we spent hours on a bench in the Tiergarten. Passing the little bar around 2:00 A.M., we saw the sign, "Prohibited," neatly displayed in every window. That night, every place known to admit Jews was raided.

July 4, 1938:

What a contrast! Garden party at the American Embassy, in the tradition of Sackett's time. The Wilsons are fine hosts. One of the French diplomats said tartly: "The beautiful Ambassadress will undoubtedly be the next objective of Ribbentrop's efforts to worm himself into the good graces of the Americans." We were in a group with Otto Tolischus, Sigrid Schultz, and the Lochners.

"Have you been in the North of Berlin lately?" whispered Rolf. "There's something going on. The concentration camps are being enlarged. Better get out, Bella. We're all with you. Here you can't help much any more. Nobody can. If we don't stop interfering for your "public enemies," we'll all land in concentration camps ourselves. Outside Germany, you may be of greater help than within these walls."

I am waiting for my papers.

July 20, 1938:

So far I have gathered a collection of twenty-three of the necessary documents. I have made a thorough study of the employees and furniture in fifteen official bureaus, down to the most humble clerk and the smallest inkwell, during the hours I have waited for another of my precious scraps of paper.

Today, I had to see an important official at the Home Office. He received me with a lusty "*Heil* Hitler!" His parting words, however, were illuminating.

"I hope I get the hell out of here before the war breaks out," he said. "I'll call on you in New York."

Maybe he can be trusted. It's doubtful. I've heard too much from him about the careful supervision the Third Reich gives to German citizens in foreign countries.

"They are presented with gifts, such as shortwave receivers with which they can listen to broadcasts from their homeland, the poisonous propaganda that prepares them to become Nazi stooges. Magazines, published in every language, are shipped over the seven seas and distributed freely. International news agencies are furnished with false reports from Germany. German citizens all over the world read and hear of the great achievements of their Fatherland. If only these people realized how lucky they really are to be under the protection of democratic countries!"

July 28, 1938:

Badly shaken by the sudden death of young Paul von Schwabach. He was deeply in love with Carmen von Wedell, from Potsdam. They couldn't marry because he was only half-Aryan. For two years, we all tried to pull every possible wire to obtain the necessary special permit from Hitler. Yesterday, the final veto came. He took his life.

The Schwabachs do not dare announce the truth. "He died of pneumonia," Mammi said.

Carmen tried the same escape. Poison. She is desperately ill in the hospital, but her life may be saved. For what?

Old von Schwabach is a very sick man. He refuses to admit anyone, even the family physician. His relatives fear that he, too, may take the same way out.

August 10, 1938:

Rolf has found devious shortcuts and sent me to comparatively decent officials. I simply can't imagine how other emigrants, without any wires to pull, ever manage to overcome the abyss of deliberate difficulties. One of the things I had to do was to pay all taxes for one year ahead, that is, for a period when I would not be in Germany at all.

Only a few days are left before the final date given me at the American Consulate, and I haven't yet gathered all the papers and permissions I need. Luckily, I remembered Schacht's promise to Ambassador Dodd. I sent him an S.O.S. Today, I got the reply. Schacht has ordered my case to be rushed at the Foreign Exchange Office:

Most honored Lady:

I am charged by *Reichsbankpräsident* Dr. Schacht, who last Friday departed on a short vacation, to confirm with thanks your communication of August 5. The application which you enclosed has, in accordance with your wishes, been sent to the Foreign Exchange Office with a recommendation of the President. In addition, I have explained the matter to the Referent over the telephone, and I trust that you will have no more dificulty.

Heil Hitler,
Yours very obediently,
Von Koppenfels.

August 11, 1938:

Went with Schacht's letter to the Foreign Exchange Office yesterday. Today everything was settled. Tomorrow I am to receive the final confirmation.

From the Foreign Exchange Office I went to a luncheon at the new Bolivian Minister's. He grew up here and is fully devoted to Germany. He and others like him are the type that spread the doctrines of the Third Reich in South America. Maybe the game is not without its profits for those who play it understandingly.

August 18, 1938:

The doors at the American Consulate General are opened at 9:00 A.M. This I know because I stood in line from seven o'clock on. My turn came at about ten minutes to one.

I was ushered in to my good friends, DeWitt Warner and Cybe Follmer, who regarded me in astonishment. "For heaven's sake, Bella! Why didn't you have someone announce you?"

"Two reasons," I said. "I didn't want any special privileges, and I enjoyed waiting in anticipation of the moment when I was at last to see you sign the visa."

There was a whirlwind of good wishes, hugs, farewell kisses, and backslapping. When I found myself outside, the American visa in my hand, I had to sit down on the stone steps and cry in my grateful happiness. Again and again I looked at the document. I caressed the red silk cord that secured the pages. I actually kissed the golden seal. I mentally pledged my true and loyal adherence to my future homeland.

Does this seem maudlin? I'm sure it will not seem so to anyone who, having lived in the present Germany, finally has the door opened for escape into a democratic world.

I got up, brimful of new energy. Furniture had to be packed. Boat passage had to be secured. I hurried toward my car but could not get through a living wall of S. S. troops. I climbed a little fence to see what was going on. A number of open Nazi cars swished down Bellevue Strasse.

In the middle car, General Erhard Milch sat with the French Aviation General, Victor Vuillemin. He has come with some officers to pay a visit to the German air force. What will they show him? He won't learn enough to do the French army any good.

August 23, 1938:

There are many new policemen in Berlin. They are all from the ranks of the S.A. and are especially inconsiderate and rude. Probably picked for their special qualifications to identify and assault non-Aryan cars. A decree has been issued directing non-Aryan automoblies to change their license plates. The new numbers are "Jew numbers." From 355,000 upward. I did not drive to the Motor Traffic Office right away. Instead, I drove to a car rental firm. "Do you want this car for five hundred marks?" I asked. The salesman was speechless. My current "Mucki" was a 1938 model of far greater value. It did not take long before we came to terms.

"Only one condition," I added. "You will rent the car to me, free of charge, until September 5, 1938. Insured by me, of course."

I informed the Motor Traffic Office that "Car number 1 A 1266 is no longer my property."

August 25, 1938:

Admiral Horthy, Regent of Hungary, is here. A handy pretext for displaying German might. Field guns mounted on motor trucks, tanks, a motorized Big Bertha. Marching, mounted, driving, flying troops. The foreigners were excited.

This parade was intended to support the Runciman action in Prague. It will obtain the desired results as soon as Mastny, the Czech Minister, informs his Foreign Office. England and France will get their reports about Hitler's bellicose "peace" army.

"The Sudetenland will slip into Hitler's hands without a single shot being fired" had been Rolf's prediction in March.

Rolf says now, "Chamberlain has had his chance to make a deal with Stalin. He won't, though. He's scared. More scared of Communism than he is of brown uniforms. His skin will be drying on Hitler's wall before long."

August 27, 1938:

The people at the Czech Legation are frightened and discouraged. How far will Hitler go to get his Sudeten Germans? Most of Europe is in suspense.

"Lord Runciman is ready to trade a slice of our country for peace," said the Czech Councilor. Rolf later said to me:

"Peace for another year! Another priceless year of preparation for Hitler, so that he can strike his mightiest blow at Europe."

August 28, 1938:

François-Poncet seems hypnotized by Hitler and, at the same time, scared and impressed. I went to Wannsee to say good-bye to the François-Poncets. He wished me a clipped good luck and disappeared.

Jacqueline was apologetic. She started to unburden herself: "I am frightened. Everything is so obscure. André is jittery about politics. He's nervous. Don't blame him. He's afraid he might be accused of conspiring with Jews. Please don't tell anyone that our courier took your trunks and furs to Paris. We want to help you...you know that. But we had better keep out of trouble, if we can."

I did not stay long. It was not the good-bye that I had expected. I am very fond of Jacqueline François-Poncet. But these times do strange things to people and to friendships.

September 1, 1938:

The president of police, Count Helldorff, has an enormously profitable racket. He seizes the passports of such emigrants as are still well off and sells the passports back to them for whatever sum he can get. In some instances as much as two hundred and fifty thousand marks.

They pay it. No price is too much if it's liberty one is buying.

Bribery in Germany has become highly organized and seems almost legal now. Secretary of State Erhard Milch needs a large sum in foreign currency to arrange for the emigration of his purely Jewish first cousin, a doctor. He demanded the money from the *Reichsbank* and got it. A necessary transaction that enabled him to get rid of the last remaining evidence of his "irregular" origin.

September 2, 1938:

An enormous shipping van which I bought drove up to the front of the house. It is like a big room without windows. It is hauled on a truck, driven directly to the harbor, and put on the boat. Besides costing me twenty-five hundred marks, and because of lumber shortage in Germany, it was very difficult to get...until I found the right person to bribe.

Three officials of the Foreign Exchange Office are checking and rechecking every item that goes in, down to the last pot and the smallest and most trivial ashtray. Everything I had bought during the last six months had to be paid for with a two-hundred-percent ransom to the Third Reich, which lovingly showers a terrific mess of red tape on the harassed emigrant as a farewell present.

For nearly three days, this packing, checking, and rechecking has gone on. Officials from offices and departments I never heard of, departments that must have been invented only for their nuisance value, come pestering me every hour of the day. I am continually being cross-examined.

September 4, 1938:

The van is downstairs, sealed and fastened. They will come and take it any minute now. "Berlin-New York" is painted in big letters on its sides. It makes me feel blue and happy at the same time.

God knows how things will look when I start unpacking this huge red case. Will I ever have a chance to unpack it? Won't they drag me away at the very last minute? For five years I have managed to slip by with many a narrow escape. I hope my nerves won't give way during these last two days. I told almost nobody exactly when I am to leave. Rolf told me not to.

"Very often they turn up with some fiendish trick, just when you think you are free and on your way."

This morning, I received a farewell letter from Rolf. Handwritten, but unsigned.

I know you despise the German Aryans. You are right. But, believe me, there are some among us who suffer under the curse of being German. We are deeply ashamed of the reversion to the Middle Ages that our country has undergone. Today, I understand that we are once more called *Boches*. It has its justice. Don't forget me. I hope to be sent directly to the front when war comes. I am going to shoot backward. I swear it. I don't care about the consequences.

September 6, 1938—Paris:

The last two days were a nightmare. At the last minute, I discovered that I needed a Belgian visa, because of the one-hour ride at night through that country. I could not get it without photographs. It took a great deal of scurrying around, but it was all finally arranged. At nine o'clock, the night express came thundering into the station. Farewells and tears. At the far end of the platform, in civilian clothes, was Rolf. We had agreed that he was not to run the risk of being seen with me at the train. My eyes were so blurred by tears that I could hardly see his face. The train had already started. Good-bye, Rolf...God bless you....

Four and a half years ago, my child had left on the same train, from the same station, on her adventure in search of freedom and a new life. And now, I, too, was going on the same quest.

The heavy luggage was booked, sealed, and stamped. My few suitcases were in the rack above me. The passport was in order. I traveled luxuriously in a Pullman sleeper. Perhaps for the last time. I had not spared money, because I had to leave the rest in Germany anyway. Exhausted, I went to bed.

About 2:00 A.M., I was badly frightened by the sudden apparition of two uniformed figures. Drugged by my first sound sleep in weeks, my senses momentarily reeled with terror.

"Frontier pass control," one of them announced gruffly.

I asked them to let me put on some clothes, but they made me leave the door open while I dressed.

"Emigrant's passport!" announced one. "Jewish bitch! Trying to smuggle out her valuables, I suppose."

I kept my mouth shut. They turned everything inside out. They took the soles from my bedroom slippers. They squeezed the toothpaste from the tube."

"Have you anything that should not be taken out of the country?" demanded one.

"You've seen for yourself everything I have," I said.

"You Jewish whore!" one shouted at me. "Trying to smuggle out all that jewelry." He pointed to the little heap that had been emptied out on the bed.

"I am not trying to smuggle anything out," I said. "All that has been the property of my family for generations. Here is the permit issued by the Foreign Exchange Office."

"We'll have to check on that with Berlin," said he. "We reach the frontier in half an hour. You'll have to get off the train."

My protests were futile. I said I would miss the boat.

"Then take the next one."

They seemed to be deliberately unaware of how hard it was to obtain passage. Cancellation, or even delay, was impossible, with so many hundreds eagerly awaiting their turn. I had a vision of being sent back to Germany and having to go through the business of laboriously collecting my exit papers all over again. My heart almost stopped.

The two went outside for a whispered consultation. When they returned, they submitted a statement for me to sign:

"I am a Jewish thief and have tried to rob Germany by taking German wealth out of the country. I hereby confess that the jewels found on me do not belong to me and that in trying to take them out I was eager to inflict injury on Germany. Furthermore, I promise never to try to reenter Germany."

I signed. I had to get out of this country. This was a country to get out of if you had to do it naked.

Half an hour later, the train crossed the border. I was in safety. My heart was pounding, and I began to cry. Tears of liberation. I was uneasy up until the time the train stopped at the Gare du Nord.

The statement, together with my jewels, had gone into the pockets of my tormentors. I am sure they will go no further up the line. If they reappear, it will be in the shop of a pawnbroker.

I was glad that I had been wearing the ruby pin and ring that my mother had worn. Before going to sleep, I had slipped them into my pocketbook, and they had been overlooked. This morning I found them, along with the platinum watch Hassan Nachat Pasha had once given me. These three pieces I dearly love.

September 9, 1938—"S. S. Normandie":

Safe aboard this gorgeous boat! It is almost too much for me to believe. Then, when I do become acutely aware of my good fortune, I feel almost guilty, remembering the unfortunate ones who wait, trembling, desperately hoping for their chance to get out. There *must* be a way to help.

On the sixth, I arrived in Paris. It was always grand, arriving in that lovely city where I have passed unforgettable hours. This time it was a sad visit, for I was sure I would never see it again. The atmosphere there is changed almost beyond recognition. The Parisians are gloomy, fretful.

"No war, for God's sake!" they are saying.

I collected all the trunks, suitcases, handbags, and parcels that I had managed to send to Paris during the last months through the help of diplomatic friends. And, most important of all, the stacks of loose-leaf notes from my dairy which I had been sending to a dear friend for years, whenever the opportunity presented itself.

In the Champs Elysées, somebody touched my shoulder. I almost fainted.

"Be at peace, Bellachen, there is no Gestapo here." It was just an old South American diplomatic friend, smiling his pleasure at meeting me there. He is very pessimistic about the future.

"I give Hitler a year," he said. "He will be ready then, and all hell will break loose."

"Oh, shut up!" I said. "Nice thing to say to someone who has just escaped."

I found a forgotten hundred-mark note in one of my pockets. If the two creatures at the frontier had come across it, they would never have believed I had not hidden it purposely. I would have gone back to Germany and a concentration camp.

There wasn't a bank in Paris that would give me a sou in exchange for it. It was refused also at the American Express Office. Somehow, this pleased me.

The magnificent ship glides through the waters to the new land. I cannot get myself to join in the gay cheerfulness on board. There is an atmosphere of luxury and freedom from care, but I am not yet in a mood to breathe this air. I find I cannot yet stand fun and laughter. A paperhanger from Austria did that to me.

Epilogue

My Last Encounter with the Nazis

The sight of the New York skyline revealed depths of feeling in me hitherto unplumbed. I experienced an *awareness* of freedom that only people who have lost their freedom can know. The joy of being safe in a country where liberty is a matter of course swept over me in a wave of emotion that left me dazed.

But this was a personal reaction, for I soon learned that opinion here had changed little since my visit in 1935. It was almost shocking to see that, except intellectually, the Nazi danger was still not realized in the United States. Actual realization of danger comes only through emotional perception, and there were few here whose senses had been aroused to its imminence. That accounted for the puzzling unpreparedness I found all around me, an unpreparedness for something that lay upon us so heavily and so actually in Europe.

Most people were completely ignorant of the new psychology in Germany, that of a mind gone berserk, a nation shouting too loudly and too insanely to hear the voice of reason. Even statesmen and politicians, I found, were mostly blind. My warnings were listened to because I had just come from Germany and everybody was interested in my firsthand point of view and experiences. But this interest was academic, not concerned with something that touched anyone here personally.

Giving up my attempts to stir people from their complacency, I turned to the business of living and saw at once that I was in for a difficult struggle. For the first time, I had to fight for my daily bread; for the first time, I did not know where to find the rent for my quarters, which consisted of a depressing little furnished room.

285

For a week, I worked in a factory, making cotton gloves. For years, it had been my hobby to make gloves for myself and as gifts to my friends. Madame François-Poncet even asserted that she had never worn more beautiful or better-fitting gloves. Now, alas, instead of working with fine leather, I was only embroidering little flowers on cotton gloves. I had to stitch them just where the ribs usually are. After all, everything has to be learned, and I was not too handy. But the other girls were wonderful to me. Especially a colored girl of delicate bone structure. She helped me a lot.

This readiness to help encouraged me tremendously and increased to eight dollars the five dollars a week I would probably have made without assistance. But after one week at this "profitable" job, something better turned up.

An employment agency, apparently with only my name left in its files, asked me to report as quickly as possible to replace a sick cook. Thus I found my second job in the United States. I cooked, washed pots, dishes, and glasses, and on the housemaid's day off, had to take care of the silver, too. It was a distinguished house in the East Seventies. The address alone might have been worth money to some people. There was a very aristocratic housemaid and a snobbish governess. The governess had gorgeous legs, but she waddled like a duck. Funny that anybody could waddle on such perfect legs!

I enjoyed taking care of all the beautiful things. Polishing the heavy silver platters brought recollections of my own beautiful belongings. Those trays and cups and chandeliers and platters my grandmother and my mother had been so proud of. In the lift van at the New York free port, they waited for me to make enough money to claim them and unpack them in some little apartment.

One day, my employers gave a big party. Would I set the table? Did I know how to serve at table? For the housemaid had gone on her vacation, and the cook had come back to work.

Did I know how to serve at table! "For fifteen years, I did nothing else on the other side!" I lied convincingly.

Then I went through some nerve-racking moments. Dinner here is not served the European way. Let's see, how was the table set at the Sacketts' and the Messersmiths'? Where does one put the butter knife. This suddenly became a question of national importance. From which side did the servants remove the plates? I began to get scared and a bit wobbly.

However, everything went smoothly enough. I got excellent

references. From the substituting job, I climbed to the position of waitress "for special work." I remembered François-Poncet's prophecy: "Maybe one day you will be ambassador for special work." I progressed from eight dollars a week to eighteen! I could have gone further. Soon, I could have served both lunch and dinner. But my feet were on strike. Often, after midnight, I would stand on a street corner waiting for my bus and crying because my feet hurt so. But I was happy. Grateful. Content. I was doing all right; doing much better, even, than I had thought I would.

When I stood there in my black uniform trimmed with lace collar and lace cuffs, with a little apron to match, I could feel like patting myself on the back. I could not help smiling when I thought what Johann and Lisbeth, my Berlin servants, would have had to say: whether they would have approved of their *gnädige Frau*. When I opened the door, helping guests off with overcoats and wraps, I often wondered whether Johann would have approved of my technique in putting the essential yard between the guest and myself and racking my arms to assist. I could see him helping General von Schleicher into his officer's coat, and lovingly smoothing the wrinkles in back, before he handed him his cap. Then again, I remembered how Johann used to brush Rolf's overcoat, remarking apologetically: "It's a shame the way Wilhelm neglects the Count's things."

I would fall into luxurious reveries. What if the people I knew in Berlin should see me! I would listen to the talk at the table and find it most illuminating. Then I decided that some time I would write a story: "I Was a Hired Waitress." I would write about the twenty-five-pound turkey which, one night, I had to drag around a table of twenty-six people before I was allowed to put it down for the host to carve. I was out of breath, but you'd never have known it. People who wait on you at table must never get out of breath.

Or perhaps I would write about the little housewife who instructed me to come at six o'clock when dinner was at seven-thirty, saying that she would lay the table herself. She forgot about it, and even the canapés were not ready. And the host did not know how to mix the cocktails. Still, I managed to have everything ready by seven-thirty.

Then there was the thrifty housewife who always put the money on the kitchen table at eleven o'clock, even if there were dishes to be washed till one o'clock. Fat Mary, of 65th Street, will hold a place of honor in my memories. She always put food for the next day into my suitcase. When I objected, she reassured me: "You must have a boyfriend, honey. What will he think of you if you don't bring him something you can't afford?"

I wonder whether Mizzi, my housekeeper on the other side, also used to wrap up some food for the old hired woman, Frida. I hope she did. One should have been much more considerate in these matters. I felt remorseful. Poor old thing! For many years, she had come to my house every Tuesday to help with my weekly dinners. Would she be proud to know that we were colleagues? Does she serve the Nazi houses now? I am sure she would scold me. "But, *gnae Frau*, the soup spoon has to be across the top of the cover plate."

"Yes, Frida," I could say now, "but *we* in the United States place the soup spoon to the right of the cover. And each plate is carried off separately. That's to avoid the clatter."

She would shake her head. Also, she would be shocked to see me wearing a low-cut blouse when serving at table. "That is most inappropriate." Under the rosy hue of her sixty-five-year-old cheeks, she would blush a deeper red. She would hurry back to the kitchen and grumble about it to Mizzerl.

There are also acidulous housewives. One was mean enough to say to me, when she asked me to come to her house again: "But only if you have learned to turn out smoother and rounder butter balls." Good gracious, weren't there more important things in the world to worry about than butter balls lacking perfect roundness?

But all careers end sometime, and this one was no exception. A young diplomat whom I had known in Berlin was invited to a fine house in Gramercy Park. When I opened the front door, there he was! My reflexes worked perfectly. Before he could utter a cry of surprise at my "fancy dress," I clapped my hand over his mouth. It was a rather intimate gesture for a housemaid to put her hand over the mouth of a guest, but I had no alternate. But later on, he told the hostess. After dinner, she came to the kitchen and led me to her bedroom. "What can I do for you? I was so embarrassed to have you serve at table after I learned who you were."

I protested in vain. She refused to have me wash dishes and serve at table any more, not understanding that no job at all was a worse predicament for me than serving. That I did not consider it a loss of dignity, since dignity is an innate quality. Instead, she slipped ten dollars into my pocketbook. That *would* have been a loss of dignity. Before I left, I put it back on her dresser. Then I took my uniform off for the last time.

Next morning, a letter from Washington was in the mail. A friend had intervened for me. I was to return to the Refugee Committee, which I had unsuccessfully asked for employment on my arrival. My letter of introduction had gained me access to the inner sanctuaries. But that seemed to be about all. There were no paid positions, I was told. They needed volunteers only, and they could not use my experience. It seemed they could make use of my experience now.

But this proved again to be a vain and disappointing hope. Nobody asked about my experience, only whether I could type-write. I certainly could. On my way home I felt shocked at my own exaggeration. Was I to start this career, too, by fibbing?

In the old country, I had had a secretary. I had never succeeded in getting beyond a brief letter. When little Kraus saw my work, she would say: "Ach, I'd better type it again. It will look nicer." Undoubtedly, she was right. It always did look nicer after she had retyped it.

For three days and three nights I practiced on a rented typewriter. Then I was thrown out of the rooming house when the people next to my room got angry and threatened to choke me.

For two and a half years I was a typist. From seventy-five dollars a month, my salary rose to ninety dollars. Not efficiency. Through the union.

I was seated in one room with sixty-five girls and as many typewriters. Numerous telephones rang incessantly. Here again I found very nice co-workers, and one of the girls became my loyal friend. Her name was Gladys, and life should be wonderful to her if God ever rewards people for the good they do. She was a great help to me in this work to which I was unaccustomed. It was hard, cruel work. I am convinced that it is easier to crush rocks than to write copies and cut stencils at top speed all day long. I suppose that there are people everywhere who tyrannize their subordinates, and this place was no exception.

But whenever I began to feel my altered mode of living too strongly, my thoughts went back to Germany and what I had gone through there. No material hardships, however painful they are, can be compared to the horrors of a life under the Gestapo regime, even if one is living in comfort.

These recollections were enough to restore me to a feeling of safety and contentment, and I went on living the life of an average American typist. I did not dream that the Gestapo would get on my trail in America, and that my most exciting experiences with the Nazis would take place here in this free city of New York.

Before I left Germany, Rolf and I had worked out a code. He had promised to write regularly and tell me about everything that went on in Germany. Since my arrival in the United States, I had been receiving letters from him on almost every boat, and sometimes more detailed ones through various diplomatic pouches. The code letters sounded innocent enough, but they conveyed to me everything that was transpiring in the inner circles of the German government.

I had felt it my duty to place this information as well as an account of my experiences in Germany at the disposal of the government authorities in Washington, and consequently, I had paid several visits to the capital, where the news I received was found extremely interesting.

I had been passing this information along to Washington for almost a year, when, a few days after the outbreak of the war in September, 1939, a phone call burst upon me like a thunderbolt while I was sitting in my office. "Police headquarters speaking. Are you Mrs. Bella Fromm?" a deep pleasant voice was asking. "When can I see you?" I had a funny feeling in the pit of my stomach when I heard the word "police." In a fraction of a minute, hundreds of memories flashed through my mind, concerning the horrors of the Gestapo. It is an ugly and unfortunate word to use to a German. It took me over a minute before I managed to ask what crime they wanted me for. The reply was another shock.

"No crime," said the pleasant voice. "We want to protect you." Protect me? Why? Against what?

I did not do any efficient typing the rest of that working day. Finally, I dashed home and waited in fear and trembling for their visit. It was not long before two men arrived, one a very tall and slender, handsome man about fifty years old. Large, honest blue eyes dominated his clean-cut face. His assistant, also in civilian clothes, who was by no means a small man, looked almost insignificant beside him. They showed me their authority: colored enamel badges in light leather cases.

But even that did not reassure me. I sensed persecution and horror. Then, a memo which the captain showed me knocked me out completely. Hot and cold shudders ran down my spine when I read what the commissioner of Police had written to the chief of the Anti-Sabotage Squad.

First, there was my exact personal description. Then, an account of my activities in Berlin; my connections with many well-known statesmen from all over the world; my friendship with American diplomats. American officials in a neighboring state had discovered that the Gestapo was on my track. Four German agents were said to be on their way to New York "to murder this woman."

I read my sentence of death in this memorandum, and I began to tremble. Then I cried a little. I could not be sure that these two men were not trying to lure me into a trap. I had never seen the signature of the New York Commissioner of Police, and it might have been forged, I considered. The name of the captain might have been invented, or perhaps an officer of that name really existed and my visitor had merely borrowed it. I was bewildered by the numerous questions the captain asked. He inquired about my friends in Germany, about my friends here. He asked about various things in the Third Reich. Perhaps these questions were essential, or perhaps they were just a ruse to find out who my friends were and discover to whom I gave information. With regard to Germany, my bill of health was none too clean. Rolf had hinted in his last letter that the Nazis regretted their consent to my departure.

I played dumb. The captain and I talked around in circles. Finally, he gave up and advised me to phone him as soon as I had made up my mind. Then he gave me a telephone number and left me to my own devices.

I checked on the telephone number. It turned out to be the connection of the Police Athletic Club. Although the captain had told me that this was a temporary number, I felt increasingly suspicious.

I did not get much sleep that night. Next morning at the office, I asked for two hours' leave. An important appointment at the Custom House was accepted as a valid excuse. By now I had come to the conclusion that the whole affair was a lie or a frame-up. They'll probably ridicule me when I show up in Centre Street, I thought. Still, I was determined to go. At police headquarters, I aroused respectful interest when I asked for Captain George Mitchell.

Thank God, at least the name existed. Now it only remained to be seen whether he was my visitor, I thought. After a great deal of checking and several little detours, I succeeded in establishing the legitimacy of my business with him. I was accompanied to another building, taken upstairs in an elevator, and directed to a room straight ahead. When the door was opened, I found myself in a vast, light room. Inside, quite a few distinguished-looking gentlemen stood around. All of them had energetic faces, and all wore well-cut suits. In the midst of these gentlemen, whom I had apparently disturbed in conference, stood my captain. I practically heard the bump of the stone falling off my chest! Careless of the gentlemen in the well-cut suits, gaping in amazement, I ran up to my captain, flung my arms around his neck, and burst into tears.

First, I stammered my suspicions and then my apologies. It was all right, he said. He even thought it better that I was not credulous; it would simplify the job. The captain had felt at once that I did not trust him. Now everything was fine. I was to meet the two detectives immediately who were going to protect me in shifts from now on. We made up for everything I had left unanswered the previous day. For more than an hour, I gave them all the information I could. I was an interesting case.

"After all, one does not often come across people who have known and watched Himmler, Heydrich, and other killers," I learned.

I was pleased that the captain accepted my offer to help him in various investigations.

And thus the days of my bodyguard started. For more than a year, Eddie and Jimmy shadowed me. They never left me alone. They were loyal and reliable. They convoyed me to the movies, to parties, when I went swimming, and, of course, on my daily way to and from work. Unfailingly, I would see Eddie's or Jimmy's honest face beaming at me from the door of my office several times a week at noon. Pretending surprise, they would murmur a "Pardon me" and vanish. This would happen when I sometimes used my lunch hour to catch up on my typing, and they, meanwhile, had waited for me downstairs.

I felt sincere gratitude for the two young men whose zeal and unselfishness I shall never forget. Once, I wanted to go to Radio City. At the box office, Eddie said: "I'll take you to the entrance and then wait outside."

Eddie waiting outside? That sounded strange, but, of course, I agreed. I had hardly sat down when I heard Eddie's familiar cough. I turned my head and looked into my protector's beaming face. He did not want me to pay for his ticket and was now immensely pleased that I had fallen for his ruse. Another time, he gave me the full life story of a newly employed elevator man in the building where I was living, whose presence I had not even noticed.

During the first days of my protection, nothing much happened. I wrote and suggested the Commissioner of Police Valentine might use my bodyguards for more important tasks. The commissioner was a wise man. He gave an evasive answer, and the bodyguard remained. Soon I was to find out that everything was not as peaceful as it had appeared to be. The lull before the storm was caused by the fact that the German agents were still on their way to the United States.

By the middle of September, 1939, it became evident that the Gestapo agents had arrived in New York. They started with an immediate telephone offensive, and they continued to keep the wires humming. The New Order boys were certainly not miserly with their nickels.

They opened fire at eight o'clock in the morning. "Your bodyguard is waiting downstairs with the car, but we'll catch you in spite of it." Also, they reported daily at the office. "Well, Bella Fromm, when are you coming down for lunch?" As soon as I was home from work, the phone would start ringing: "Just to find out if you arrived home all right." And unpleasant little remarks like "Let's see whose nerves are tougher."

After a while, I would get pretty upset, but my bodyguards laughed: "Now, take it easy." This seemed a real war of nerves; but soon I got used to it and managed to give the agents some quick repartee.

All of a sudden their methods changed. It seemed they wanted to find out about my friends in Germany before they tossed me into my grave.

It was up to me to frustrate their former aim; Eddie and Jimmy took excellent care to thwart the latter. After I had been under the care of my bodyguards for six solid weeks, a man phoned one day. He pretended to have arrived recently, a refugee from Germany who would not give me his name before meeting me, as he had assumed a false name on this side of the water and grown a beard.

He had run away from the Nazis, who, he was convinced, were after him seeking his death.

I could not help asking where I came into the picture. Why, yes, in his confusion, he had forgotten to give me Hellmut von Krueger's regards. My blood curdled. Hellmut is Rolf's intimate friend, and also anti-Nazi.

I did some rapid-fire thinking and said that I knew no such man, not even by name. The voice on the other end of the wire became hesitant. But its owner seemed to be well equipped with a series of names, all from a certain section. I would surely know Dettmar Wedige, he trusted, one of Krueger's friends? I had met Dettmar in diplomatic circles. Although he was a full-fledged Nazi, I knew he had to deal with Rolf in official matters. In a flash, I realized that a denial might harm Rolf. In Nazi Germany, I had learned to grasp a situation and fling a retort over the phone without hesitation. Consequently, I displayed the most vivid interest in Dettmar.

Commonplace answers confirmed my suspicion that he did not know the persons he mentioned but acted under orders, using names given to him. Anyway, I continued to probe carefully. The unknown caller told me that he had met Dettmar for luncheon every so often, in fact, the last time just before leaving Germany.

Now, I happened to know that this same Dettmar lived with his mother outside the city, and that his sister was a physician in Berlin. To see each other as often as possible, brother and sister had made it a habit to meet almost daily for luncheon in a restaurant which I occasionally frequented. The "refugee" was at a loss when I asked about Dettmar's sister. He did not even know about her existence, nor was he informed that Dettmar had a mother with whom he lived.

I pretended an unsuspecting interest, and the Nazi fell for my ruse. Yes, he would come to have tea in my house tomorrow. I pictured him rubbing his hands and slapping his thighs with glee, the way his Fuehrer does when he feels he has put over a good one.

Maybe, I thought, he intends to bring along a henchman with whom he is already discussing whether to shoot or to stab me. Stabbing is better: it causes less noise. Surely, they'll bring along huge and appropriate knives. How curiously detached one becomes in the face of danger, I thought before I fell asleep.

The next day being Saturday, I did not go to work. In defiance of all strategic regulations, I looked out of the window for my guest. I was reassured by Eddie's presence behind me in the room.

The Nazi showed up on the dot. A scrawny-looking, darkish little shrimp, no model representative of the Teutonic master race, climbed out of a taxi, paid the driver, and started for the house. Here a turn of events changed all that I, and presumably Herr Himmler's agent, had expected. Two well-dressed gentlemen accosted the Nazi. I had never seen them before. Apparently they had been waiting for the visitor. For a moment, the three of them stood talking. Then the two gentlemen displayed the familiar enamel badges in their leather cases, whereupon the three of them climbed into a black limousine. A week later, I was told: "He was just one of those Nazi agents we had wanted for a long time." Later on, I read in the papers about the trial. I got incidental credit for "having helped to make such a good catch." That was all. The American police do not like to discuss these things.

My bodyguards had checked up on every occupant of the building in which I was living and in the surrounding houses. In searching one of the buildings opposite my apartment, they discovered two German agents who were in possession of weapons, shortwave transmitters, and a considerable amount of American currency. The agents, who could easily observe my apartment from their windows, were also in possession of several snapshots of me, the address of my office, and a list of addresses of several of my American friends. They also had in their possession airplane schedules to Mexico, and the detectives found addresses of various people who played important roles in this strange case, particularly a German woman physician about whom I learned a great deal later on.

Most important was the fact that the two young men were supplied with Mexican and German passports in spite of their persistent assertions that they were American citizens. It was beyond doubt that these two young men were German agents and that they were connected with the suspected intention to kidnap me.

Their arrest was the first result, and my guards said that even if nothing else happened, this catch was a good enough justification for the precautionary measures.

Eddie or Jimmy used to fetch me every morning with their car and escort me to my office. They waited faithfully for me at five o'clock to bring me home. They had always insisted that I sit in the front beside them. One afternoon in the seventh month of my police protection, Eddie was driving as usual. We had hardly entered Central Park when he suddenly turned into a road which we had never taken before.

"Eddie, you are taking the wrong road," I reminded him.

"Oh, no," he replied. "I just want to try out another one."

Next morning, Jimmy drove, and he chose an even more unusual road, avoiding the park altogether. To my questions, they always gave evasive answers. I noticed that they were constantly looking in the mirror and watching what was going on behind us. I got suspicious, and, looking back, I discovered a car. But in the streets of New York, cars are always following each other.

For days, each morning and evening we took a different road. A few days later, it became clear to me that we were being followed by the same car. From the second week on, I also became aware that behind the car following us there was a third car, and we crossed the streets of New York in this procession.

It was plain to me what was happening. So I did not bother Jimmy and Eddie any more with unnecessary questions. After the third week, Eddie again drove through Central Park, taking the usual road.

"Well, Eddie," I asked, "did you catch them?"

He replied with another question: "Do you think I would drive through the park if we hadn't?"

Apparently, my bodyguards had been guarded just as I was being guarded. Thus, the gang was hunted down which had been ordered from Mexico to kill me. The police found traces leading to a German physician, a woman who had taken over the practice of Dr. Ignatz Griebl, the physician who had escaped to Germany.

Dr. Ignatz Griebl was a naturalized American citizen and practiced medicine in an office on East 86th Street in Yorkville. Griebl was one of the founders of the German-American bund, and was obviously one of the heads of the German spy organization in the United States. He was involved in the famous espionage case which led to the arrest of several employees of the German liner *Bremen*. However, he was able to escape to Germany, in 1938, before his arrest.

His office was taken over by a woman physician who became his successor in other things besides the medical profession.

This woman used her M.D. as a cover-up. Actually—I found out some time later—she was the head of the gang. She gave them their orders and kept them supplied with money. Her orders to liquidate the Bella Fromm case, because the first "special emissary" had failed, was only incidental to the main part of her work.

In the tenth month of this exciting life, a new episode began for me. One morning, the telephone rang. A strange voice, giving an English-sounding name, said:

"I heard from your friends that you want to take English lessons. I am a professional teacher and would like to see you."

My first reaction was: "No, this must be a mistake; I do not want to take English lessons."

Suddenly, I realized that this might be another agent. I fell into the spirit of the game and was eager to lead another Nazi agent into the hands of my guardians. So I said:

"Well, I did not want to take English lessons, but you give me the idea. I might take some if you have good references."

We made an appointment for the next day. "Will you give me your phone number, in case I should not be able to keep my appointment?" I asked.

He did. I hung up and immediately called the number he gave me. It was nonexistent. So I was sure that this was the next act in the play.

Apparently, the "teacher" had not given a minute's thought to the possibility of my not receiving him alone. That was his big mistake. He was perturbed to find one of my bodyguards at the coffee table. There was no doubt in his eyes that this man who sat there comfortably in his shirt sleeves, a huge revolver bulging from his belt, was a detective. The "teacher" got that peculiar pinched look around his nose.

When he began to feel uncomfortable, Eddie took charge of him. "You cannot give English lessons to anybody. You had better come with me and give me some German lessons; I need them now." And they left.

When I asked Eddie what had happened to my "English teacher," his reply as usual was evasive. "I don't know. What else do you want me to do? It is enough for me to know that he is in safe hands. Isn't it enough for you?"

Some weeks had gone by when Eddie put a newspaper clipping on my table, a long article with the sensational headline: NAZI SPY RING UNCOVERED HERE. WOMAN PHYSICIAN SOUGHT AS LEADER OF BAND INTENT ON SABOTAGE. It was an article about the arrest of that mysterious woman physician, the successor to Dr. Ignatz

Briebl, whose name I was never able to find out, but who was obviously the head of the gang of Nazi agents who had arrived from Mexico.

After thirteen months, my police protection was terminated in the fall of 1940. I said good-bye to my two bodyguards with mixed feelings. They had guarded me devotedly. Now the emergency seemed to have passed. I was relieved that once more I could look out of the window and walk through the streets without danger leering at me from around the corner. I looked at the world with new eyes. I felt as I did when after fracturing my ankles I was able for the first time to walk on the streets again.

I was naturally curious about what happened to those Nazi agents, who would certainly have succeeded in dispatching me to the other world had it not been for the intelligence and vigilance of the American police.

But the replies I got from my friends didn't change: "They have been taken care of. You should not worry any more. Everything is O. K. You have done a swell job, and we are very grateful for your help. We could not have gotten all of them without your assistance."

I felt mighty proud.

But I certainly don't feel proud that the first case in which I failed as a newspaper reporter was my own.

Dramatis Personae and Index

Adlon, Louis. Owner and director of the most famous Berlin hotel. *Page 87*.

Adolf Friedrich, Duke of Mecklenburg. Former Governor of Togo, brother-in-law of the Queen of the Netherlands. He voted for Hitler because he was afraid of Bolshevism. Devoted himself to the Nazi cause and used his international connections to travel abroad selling Nazi ideas and doing espionage, especially in economic affairs. He was dubbed *Der Grossherzogliche Nazi Agent* and acted on the special advice of Hjalmar Schacht. *Pages 48, 67, 216, 224*.

Agramonte y Cortiyo. Ambassador from Spain to Germany, 1935-1936. Falangist and, of course, pro-Nazi. The German Nazis protected him during the start of the Spanish Civil War when he refused to leave the Spanish Embassy in Berlin. Was recalled in July, 1936, but did not leave Germany. *Pages 206-07, 222-23*.

Albert, Dr. Heinrich. German Finance Minister, 1922-1923; lawyer in partnership with Alois Westrick, German commercial attaché at Washington, who was expelled by the United States in 1940. Albert was also involved in sabotage activities in the United States in 1916-17. *Page 44*.

Alexander, King of Yugoslavia. Slain October 9, 1934, at Marseilles, together with French Foreign Minister Barthou, when he arrived to sign a pact between his country and France. The assassins were Fascist agents. He was a brilliant and courageous man, a Francophile and an anti-Fascist. *Pages 146, 184*.

Alfonso, King. Formerly King of Spain. Now in exile in Italy. *Pages 30, 31*.

Alpar, Gitta. Famous singer, now in Hollywood. *Page 68*.

Alvear, Marcelo Torcuato de. Former President of Argentina, 1922–1928. *Page 51*.

Amann, Max. Old friend of Hitler. Owner of the Eher-Verlag, which publishes the Nazi mouthpiece, the *Voelkische Beobachter*, and issued Hitler's *Mein Kampf*. Amann is also head of the *Reichspresse-Kammer* and obtained control of many former anti-Nazi German newspapers and publishing houses, including the Ullstein house, now the *Deutsche-Verlag*. Adolf Hitler is the silent partner in all of Amann's enterprises.

Aman-Ullah, King of Afghanistan. Dethroned in 1928; in exile in Italy. *Page 32.*

Andreae, Frau Edith. Wife of a well-known banker and sister of late Foreign Minister Walther Rathenau. *Page 116.*

Antinori, Francesco, Marchese. For many years press and protocol attaché at the Italian Embassy in Berlin. *Pages 60, 109.*

Aragao, Moniz de. Brazilian Ambassador to Berlin. *Page 252.*

Araquistain, Louis. Spanish Ambassador to Berlin in 1932. *Page 31.*

Arco, Count George. Engineer, famous for invention of television. *Page 175.*

Arco-Valley, Count Anton. Member of old Bavarian nobility. He was chosen by conservative officers to murder the Bavarian Premier, Kurt Eisner, February 21, 1919, in Munich. Was in prison at Landsberg when Hitler was a prisoner there, and refused to stay under the same roof with 'that gangster.' Hitler did not forget the insult, and it was on his orders that Arco-Valley was killed in the June, 1934, purge. *Page 175.*

Arnal, Pierre. Councilor at the French Embassy in Berlin, 1932-1938. *Pages 44, 215.*

Aschmann, Dr. Gottfried. German pre-Hitler diplomat who turned Nazi, fearing that his Jewish grandmother would be discovered. Chief of Press of the German Foreign Office until 1940, when he was transferred as Councilor of the German embassy in Brussels. *Page 216.*

Astor, Viscountess. Conservative M. P. First woman to sit in British Parliament. Her country place, Clivedon (Taplow, Bucks), gave its name to her social-political group. *Page 201.*

Attolico, Bernardo. Italian Ambassador to Berlin, 1935-1939. Like his wife, née Countess Pietromarchi, an opportunist who strung along with the Fascists. In Moscow before 1935, where they were said to have been on intimate terms with Russian officials, as later on they were in Berlin with the Nazis. *Pages 221, 231, 255.*

August Wilhelm von Hohenzollern, Prince. Fourth son of Wilhelm II, known as Prince 'Auwi.' Early Nazi. *Pages 45, 60, 64, 95, 109, 138, 157, 226.*

Austin, Bunny. English tennis champion. *Page 20.*

Bade, Wilfried. One of Goebbel's first functionaries. A fanatical and ambitious Nazi. He had to deal with the foreign correspondents. *Page 180.*

Baillet-Latour. President of the International Olympic Committee. *Page 223.*

Balugdzic, Zivojin, Yugoslav Minister to Berlin, 1927-1935. Anti-Nazi, pro-French. Famous writer. *Pages 47, 184, 197.*

Barthou, Louis. French Foreign Minister, assassinated with King Alexander of Yugoslavia at Marseilles, October 9, 1934. Strongly anti-Fascist and favored the French alliance with the Balkans and the East Locarno with Russia. The murderer confessed to having been in the pay of Mussolini. *Pages 146, 168, 169, 184.*

Bassewitz, Rudolf von. Chief of Protocol at the German Foreign Office, 1933-1935. Conservative at heart, he tried to serve the Nazis to keep his position. Dismissed in 1935. *Pages 78, 85, 139, 146, 216.*

Baumbach. Norbert von. Naval Officer. Member of an old *Junker* family. Close to the circle around his aunt, Viktoria von Dirksen. *Page 59.*

Beck, Josef. Polish Foreign Minister up to 1939. Signed the Polish-German friendship pact. Was pro-Nazi and anti-democratic. *Page 201.*

Beecham, Sir Thomas. English conductor of the London Philharmonic Symphony Orchestra. *Page 233.*

Behrenberg, von. Wealthy noble family; strongly conservative and anti-Nazi. *Page 104.*

Behrendt, Augusta. Mother of Mrs. Magda Goebbels. *Page 66.*

Bentheim, Prince. An unpleasant nobleman who had early turned Nazi and with his wife did salon espionage work in Berlin's diplomatic set. *Page 170.*

Bernhard, George. German political writer. For years, editor-in-chief of the *Vossische Zeitung.* Now in New York. *Pages 24, 139.*

Bertling, Dr. Carl. Early Nazi who used his position as director of the American Institute in Berlin to spread Nazi propaganda in the United States. *Page 273.*

Binchy, Dr. Irish Minister to Berlin, 1931.

Birchall, Frederick T. Famous English-born European chief correspondent of *The New York Times,* 1932-1939. Managing editor for *The New York Times,* 1927-1932. *Pages 44, 109–10, 249.*

Black, Percy. Assistant to the American military attaché in Berlin. An efficient officer with brilliant manners and smart appearance. Excellent sportsman. He was suspect to the Nazis. *Page 266.*

Chintschuk, Maria. Wife of Russian Ambassador. *Pages 37, 77, 104, 105.*

Cholmondeley, Lord. Son-in-law of the famous English banker and philanthropist, Philip Sassoon. *Page 32.*

Ciano, Galezzo, Count. Son-in-law of Mussolini and therefore qualified as Italian Foreign Minister. Very inefficient and also very arrogant. Edda married him because of his good looks and nobility, but since his family's nobility is very recent, the old nobility in Italy does not recognize him as genuine. *Pages 221, 230-231.*

Clemt, Herma. Actress. Friend of Emmy Sonnemann-Goering. *Page 197.*

Coler, Edit von. Was married to a Jew but dropped that wealthy husband to become a Nazi and a member of Himmler's salon spy set in Berlin. To worm herself into the social set of Berlin, she was appointed second dramatic director of the State Theater in Berlin. She continued her underground activities in the Balkans after Hitler's armies had occupied that region. *Pages 117-118, 196.*

Colijn, Hendricus. Dutch economist and statesman. Premier in 1933-1935 and again in 1939. *Page 116.*

Comnen, Jan Petrescu. Rumanian Minister to Berlin, February, 1928-April, 1930, and again September, 1932-April, 1938. The Comnens tried hard to keep in contact with both the old and the new German society. From 1930 to 1932, he was envoy to the Holy See and became Rumanian Foreign Minister in 1938. *Pages 82–83, 100, 272.*

Comnen, Maria Antoinette. Wife of Rumanian Foreign Minister. *Pages 82–83, 272.*

Coty, Francis. Perfume maker, newspaper owner. Wealthy, anti-Semitic. *Page 116.*

Curtius, Dr. Julius. Foreign Minister, 1929-1932. Member of German Peoples party (conservative). *Page 35.*

Dagnino-Penny, Dr. Eduardo de. Venezuelan Minister to Berlin, 1927-1937. Before that, Minister to Rome. Thoroughly anti-Fascist and anti-Nazi. Predicted another world war as early as 1930. *Pages 49, 80, 101, 135, 172–73, 181, 184.*

Daladier, Edouard. French statesman. *Pages 156, 263.*

Daluege, Kurt. General of the *Verkehrspolizei*—traffic police forces. Old 'party member' who cooperated in lining up Berlin after Hitler came to power. Close cooperation with the Gestapo. Daluege is an S.S. upper group leader, brutal and ruthless, a criminal and corrupt schemer who was one of the founders of the Free Corps. Provided the lists of persons to be rounded up after the *Reichstag* fire and of those to be slaughtered in the June, 1934, purge. Leading figure in installing the concentration camp near Berlin (Oranienburg, Sachsenhausen). Was sent to soften up the anti-Nazis in Austria, Czechoslovakia, Poland, and Norway, and since June, 1942, successor of Reinhold Heydrich in Prague, as *Reichsprotector. Page 138.*

Eckener refused to do election propaganda for Hitler after the occupation of the Rhineland. On Goebbel's demand, therefore, Eckener's name ceased to be mentioned in German newspapers. Eckener could not, however, prevent Captain Lehmann—a willing soldier of fortune—from dropping leaflets about the election from the new 'Hindenburg.' Eckener was very much opposed to the Nazi regime and never hid his feelings. *Page 219.*

Eddy, Sherwood. Practicing evangelist, socialist and humanitarian. An American lecturer and writer, and a very courageous man. *Pages 123–24.*

Eden, Robert Anthony. Conservative M.P. since 1923. Parliamentary private secretary to Sir Austen Chamberlain. Undersecretary of State at the English Foreign Office, 1930-1931. Lord Privy Seal in 1935. Secretary of State for Foreign Affairs until 1938, when he resigned in protest against Chamberlain's weak policy toward the dictators. Returned in 1939 as Secretary for the Dominions, later Secretary of War. Since 1941, Foreign Minister in Churchill's Cabinet. *Pages 186, 191, 194.*

Einstein, Albert. No introduction needed anywhere outside of Nazi circles. *Pages 37, 61.*

Eisner, Kurt. Bavarian Premier after the revolution in 1919; murdered that year by Count Arco-Valley. *Page 153.*

Emineh, Princess. Wife of Kemalettin, Sami Pasha, Turkish Ambassador to Berlin. *Page 134.*

Epp, Franz Ritter von. Before 1914, commander of the exclusive *Leibinfanterie* Regiment and Colonial Minister. Friend of the Bavarian Crown Prince Rupprecht. In the early twenties, he gave money to the Nazi Party out of funds of the Bavarian *Reichswehr*. He changed from monarchist to Nazi and became Governor of Bavaria in 1933. Rupprecht severed ties with him. *Pages 45, 57, 89.*

Ernst, Karl. S.A. group leader and adjutant to Ernst Roehm. A homosexual who, before Roehm discovered him, was a bellboy in a big Berlin department store. Shot in the June, 1934, purge. *Page 135.*

Erzberger, Mathias. Head of the Catholic Center party. During the First World War, made trips abroad for the purpose of preparing possible peace negotiations. He was very critical of the imperial government. After the German collapse, he was sent to negotiate the armistice terms with Marshal Foch and to sign the treaty dictated by the Allies. The Nationalists accused Erzberger of having sold out Germany to the Allies. Ebert appointed him his Minister of Finance. In 1921, radicals belonging to one of the Free

Corps shot him to death while he was on a holiday in South Germany. *Page 153.*

Faktor, Emil. Editor of the *Berlin Börsenkurier. Page 215.*

Fanck, Arnold. Moving-picture producer and director. *Page 130.*

Fattah-Yehia Abdal, Pasha. Egyptian Foreign Minister, 1931. *Pages 29, 159.*

Faupel, Heinrich. Retired German general. Educator of the Argentinean army until 1933. In 1934, became president of the Ibero-American Institute in Berlin, which was one of the camouflaged hotbeds for Nazism. On recognition of General Franco in Spain in November, 1936, Hitler appointed Faupel his Ambassador to Madrid, but soon recalled him and sent von Stohrer to Spain. *Pages 162, 234.*

Feder, Gottfried. One of the oldest and leading members of the Nazi party. He drew up the twenty-five-point program on which the party was re-founded in 1922. He invented the idea of smashing the department stores. In 1933, Hitler appointed him Secretary of State of the Reich Ministry of Economics. He fell into disgrace in December, 1934, and died in 1941 in retirement in Munich. *Page 125.*

Ferdinand, King. (See King Boris.)

Flack, Joseph. First Secretary of American Embassy in Berlin, 1933-1936. Recalled to European Department in Washington; assigned to Venezuela and back in Washington in 1942. *Page 156.*

Florescu, Radu. Councilor at Rumanian Legation in Berlin till 1933, later in Washington. Now a leading figure in the 'Free Rumanian Government' in London. *Pages 200–201.*

Focke, Karin von. Goering's first wife. *Pages 196, 245.*

Follmer, Cyrus B. For many years Vice-Consul at the American Consulate at Berlin, now in Washington. *Pages 270, 278.*

Franco, Francisco. Spanish dictator who stired up trouble long before his revolt in Morocco in July, 1936. With the help of Germany and Italy, he overpowered the Spanish regular government. After starting his war, Hitler tried to induce Franco to play along with the Nazis, but until now, Franco has succeeded in keeping out, as he is unable to set up a new army and to get support from impoverished Spain. *Pages 214, 223.*

François-Poncet, André. French Ambassador to Berlin, September, 1931-September, 1938. Art professor and member of the *Comité des Forges,* the organization of French heavy industry. Was torn between pro- and anti-Nazi sentiments, but now seemingly has decided to yield and has become active in Laval's Ministry of Propaganda in Vichy. *Pages 30, 33, 34–35, 36, 66, 68, 77, 80–81, 82, 87, 89, 91, 151, 154, 167, 173, 193, 195, 201, 205, 217, 230, 240, 241, 245, 253, 280, 287.*

Funk, Walther. Newspaperman before 1933. Belonged to Roehm group and also to industrialist circles. Close friend of many Jews. In 1933, became Secretary of State at the Ministry of Propaganda and Enlightenment; in 1937, Minister of Economics; in 1938, president of the *Reichsbank,* ousting Dr. Hjalmar Schacht from both latter positions. Very treacherous and slippery character. Asthmatic little man with a tendency toward overdrinking, like his wife, Sofie. *Pages 106, 155, 204, 215, 260.*

Furtwaengler, Wilhelm, German conductor. After his gallant but unsuccessful attempt to break a lance for his oppressed Jewish colleagues, he gave up the fight. His wife was very ambitious and pro-Nazi. She used to act as a volunteer actress for the *Winterhilfe.* The money collected was used for rearmament, not for charity. *Page 158.*

Fuad, King. King of Egypt. *Pages 31, 59, 83.*

Gantchew, Peter. Bulgarian general and Nazi leader who lived in Berlin. *Page 238.*

Geist, Raymond Herman. Versatile American foreign service officer who spent more than nine years in Germany. He had the most trying test as Consul, First Secretary of the Embassy, and Chargé d'Affaires in Berlin during the period when Germany occupied Czechoslovakia. He came back to the United States in 1939, and was appointed chief director of the Department of Commercial Affairs at the State Department in Washington. *Page 260.*

George, Hereditary Prince of Sachsen Meiningen. *Page 97.*

Gessler, Otto. Conservative. War Minister, 1920-1928. *Pages 9, 14.*

Gevers, de. Netherlands Minister to Berlin, 1906-1923. After 1918, his house was a meeting place for the old aristocracy. *Pages 15, 16.*

Gigli, Beniamino. Italian tenor. *Page 143.*

Gilbert, Prentis. Councilor at the American Embassy, 1937-1938. During the absence of Ambassador Dodd, he was Chargé d'Affaires and, against the advice of the Ambassador, accepted the invitation to the party meeting at Nuremberg. When Mussolini visited Berlin, he committed his second *faux pas* in hoisting the American flag in honor of the Italian dictator, an action which drew much amused comment in Berlin domestic and foreign circles. He died in Germany in 1938. Malicious Goebbels said: "God took revenge on Gilbert for being favorable to the Third Reich." *Page 253.*

Glaser, Dr. Max. A director of the Krupp Works. Wealthy former monarchist. *Pages 10–11.*

Nazis before they came to power. He is not a convinced Nazi but one of Hitler's soldiers of fortune. *Pages 150–51.*

Jung, Edgar. One of von Papen's secretaries, murdered June 30, 1934. Jung had to compose von Papen's speeches. *Page 168.*

Kannenberg, Gustav. Former wine tavern owner. Opportunist. Turned Nazi and became Hitler's major-domo. *Pages 99, 248–49.*

Kanya, Koloman von. Hungarian Minister to Berlin until May, 1933, then Hungarian Minister of Foreign Affairs. *Page 63.*

Kapp, Dr. Wolfgang. Director General of the Agricultural Mortgage Bank in Koenigsberg, East Prussia. Extreme nationalist, conspired with nationalistic groups. Led so-called Kapp *Putsch* in March, 1920, and fled to Sweden upon its failure. *Pages 9, 10.*

Karpf, Admiral von. One of the tutors of the German imperial Princes, and after the war connected with a Hamburg bank. *Page 10.*

Kaya, Prince and Princess. Brother and sister-in-law of Japanese Emperor. *Page 171.*

Keil, Dr. Adalbert. A soldier of fortune who does not have to worry about money. He is related to the Krupps and the Thyssens, and his law offices do very well. Ambitious and swashbuckling. *Page 243.*

Keiner, Dr. Elisabeth. Well-known interior decorator. Nazi. *Page 113.*

Keitel, General Wilhelm. Chief of the German High Command, appointed February, 1938, to succeed Werner von Blomberg. When Hitler came to the forest of Compiégne to sign the armistice with the French, General Keitel was Hitler's spokesman. When Hitler met Mussolini at the Brenner, October, 1940, again, Keitel was at his side. Hitler likes to have him as a link between the party and the generals. *Page 265.*

Kemalettin, Sami, Pasha. General of the Turkish army during the First World War. Ambassador to Germany from June, 1925, till April, 1934, when he died. *Pages 104, 134.*

Keppler, Captain Chester H. J. American Naval Attaché, 1934–1935. Now in active war service. *Page 192.*

Kerchove de Denterghem, Count. Belgian Minister to Germany, February, 1932, to September, 1935. Then Ambassador to France. *Pages 82, 95, 165.*

Kerrl, Hans. Nazi Minister for the churches, and Prussian Minister for Justice. Died in December, 1941. *Page 149.*

Khan, Ghulam Siddiq. Minister of Afghanistan to Germany. Brother-in-law of Aman-Ullah. *Pages 31–32, 59.*

Kiepura, Jan. Polish opera singer. *Page 188.*

Killinger, Manfred von. Sadistic early Nazi. Belonged to the group of former German officers who formed the various Free Corps. He was an accomplice in the slaying of Catholic German minister Mathias Erzberger, Foreign Minister Walther Rathenau and others. Hitler had sent him to the west coast as his Consul General, then as Minister to Slovakia and, in 1941, to Rumania. He is called 'Hitler's assassination expert.' *Page 269.*

Kircher, Rudolf. Editor-in-chief of the *Frankfurter Zeitung*. *Page 205.*

Kirdorf, Emil. *Geheimrat* head of the Rhenish coal syndicate. Supported Hitler from the early twenties. Half-Jewish. *Page 42.*

Klausener, Erich Josef Gustav. Chief of the Catholic Action. Prussian *Ministerialdirektor*. Head of the police force at the Home Office until 1933. Murdered in the June purge of 1934. Catholic leader and anti-Nazi. *Pages 25, 51, 168.*

Klemperer, Otto. One of the younger set of famous German conductors who had to leave Germany after Hitler seized power. He is now in the United States. *Page 157.*

Kloeckner, Florian. Wealthy industrialist, in steel and railroads. Member Catholic Center party. Contributed early to National Socialists. *Page 42.*

Knickerbocker, H. R. American journalist and lecturer. *Page 46.*

Koburg, Duke Edward. Leader of Motorized S. A. and chairman of the German Red Cross since 1934. Early Nazi and one of the so-called 'princely Nazi agents.' Made use of his international connections and traveled as a salesman of Nazi doctrines. Was especially successful in raising money for the German Red Cross in the German-American circles of the United States during 1939-1940. The money he collected was used for rearmament. *Page 138.*

Koerner, Paul. Secretary of State to Goering, with whom he flew in the First World War. Early party member. *Pages 15, 141.*

Koethe, Fritz. North German Lloyd Line official in Berlin. *Page 253.*

Kotze, Ulrich von. Aide to von Neurath. Conservative who turned Nazi. Minister to Latvia, 1939. *Page 216.*

Kraft, Dr. Hans. Psychologist. *Page 250.*

Krestinsky, Nicolai. U.S.S.R. Ambassador to Berlin, 1922-1930. Then Assistant Secretary in Russian Foreign Office. Killed in Russian purge of 1936-1937. *Pages 21–22.*

Kriegner, Dr. Egon. Journalist. Nazi. *Page 117.*

Krone, Walther, Captain of North German Lloyd liner *Berlin*. *Page 203.*

Krupp von Bohlen-Halbach, Gustav. Head of the famous German ironworks. Married the heiress of the famous Friedrich Krupp Works at the suggestion of Wilhelm II. Former nationalist turned

MacDonald, Ramsay. Co-founder of the English Labour party, and its leader. Three times Prime Minister of England. *Page 115.*

Mackensen, August von. Last surviving Field Marshal of the old German army. Nazi. *Pages 7, 54.*

Mackensen, Georg. Son of Field Marshal von Mackensen. Ambassador to Rome. Secretary of State at the Foreign Office, 1936-1938. Married to daughter of Neurath. *Page 230.*

Mahler, Gustav. Musician and composer. *Page 25.*

Manzel, Professor Ludwig. Father of Mrs. Edit von Coler. *Page 118.*

'Mammi.' See Carnap, von.

Maretsky, Oskar. Old party member. Retired into private industry in 1937. *Page 133.*

Margerie, Pierre de. French Ambassador to Berlin, October, 1922, to August, 1931. Brought about friendly relations between Germany and France, recognized early the looming danger of the radical circles in Germany and warned his government. Handed over a note of the French government to the German Foreign Office complaining about that fact in 1928. He died in June, 1942, in Paris. *Pages 17, 20, 24, 33, 35.*

Margerie, Roland de. Son of French Ambassador to Berlin, and Secretary at the French Embassy until 1933; then Councilor of Embassy in London. Paul Reynaud's Chef de Cabinet during his premiership. At present, French Consul in Shanghai. *Page 34.*

Marrados, A. Member of the Spanish Embassy in Berlin. *Page 223.*

Mastny, Dr. Frantisec. Czech Envoy to Berlin, September, 1932-1938. An intelligent and convinced Czech who had to report the decisions made at Munich in September, 1938. *Pages 82, 85, 87, 170, 193.*

Maurigi de Castelmaurigi, Marchese. Major of Palermo; close friend of Mussolini. *Pages 83, 103.*

Maurois, André. Noted French author. *Page 26.*

Mayer, Lathrop. Councilor at the American Embassy, 1936-1937. Later Minister to Haiti. Resigned in 1940.

Mayr. Councilor of Legation in the Personnel Division in the German Foreign Office. Old party member. *Page 160.*

Meissner, Dr. Otto. Chief of the *Präsidial-Kanzlei.* The asthmatic political chameleon who survived every change of government. Quisling number two in Hindenburg's office. *Pages 25, 35, 43, 50, 56, 59, 63, 68, 74, 75, 76, 85, 97, 160, 177, 180.*

Messersmith, George S. American Consul General in Berlin until 1934. Minister to Vienna, 1934-1937. Assistant Secretary of State, 1939. Ambassador to Cuba, 1941. Now Ambassador to Mexico. Acute observer of events in Europe before Hitler. Saw the approach of danger. Fought against injustice and helped many

secret feud between Frau Scholz and the wife of the Ambassador, Mrs. Eva Dieckhoff. Both ladies were extremely ambitious and vied with each other. *Pages 149, 200, 201, 202.*

Schroeder, Eva von. Old party member. A leader in the National Socialist Peoples' Welfare Organization. *Pages 73, 110, 141, 242.*

Schubring, Eva. Editor for the Ullstein newspapers. *Page 113.*

Schulenburg, Count von der. Early Nazi. Member of the German Tennis Guild and assistant to Tschammer-Osten, Reich sport leader. *Page 20.*

Schulenburg, Werner von der. Minister to Teheran and Bucharest. German Ambassador to Moscow from 1934 to 1939. *Pages 180, 231.*

Schultz, Sigrid. Berlin correspondent of the *Chicago Tribune*. A vivacious, courageous and efficient little person, who sacrificed much for her friends. She had known and loved pre-Hitler Germany. She was often summoned before the Gestapo for her critical reports. Her small parties were famous in Berlin society. *Pages 137, 276.*

Schulze-Pfaelzer. Former nationalist. Early Nazi. *Page 46.*

Schuschnigg, Kurt. After Dollfuss' assassination, Austrian Chancellor. Minister of Defense and Foreign Affairs until 1938. Arrested after the Nazi occupation of Austria in March, 1938; first held in Belvedere Palace, Vienna; later a prisoner in various German places, including concentration camps. *Pages 176, 262, 265, 267.*

Schwabach, von. Wealthy Jewish banking family. *Pages 189, 277.*

Seeckt, General Hans von. Founder of the *Reichswehr*. Chief of Staff of the German Army, 1920-1926. Pro-Nazi. Member of the conservative German Peoples' party. *Pages 21, 29, 135, 238.*

Seldte, Franz. Labor Minister since 1933. Founder of the *Stahlhelm*. Badly wounded in First World War. Weak nationalist who surrendered his group to the Nazi party in the summer of 1933. *Pages 63, 74, 109, 165, 264.*

Severing, Carl. Social Democrat. Started as a journalist. Served three times as Minister of the Interior in Prussia and in the Reich, from 1920 to 1932. *Page 55.*

Shirer, William L. Berlin correspondent of the Columbia Broadcasting System; author of *A Berlin Diary*. *Page 185.*

Sieburg, Friedrich. German correspondent and Nazi agent in Paris. Took up a diplomatic career at the behest of Hitler. Councilor of Embassy in Brussels and in Paris. Now in Lisbon. *Page 205.*

Siemens, Werner von. Foremost figure in the German Electrical Industry. Head of the Siemens-Schukert and Siemens and Halske Electrical Works. Snobbish music sponsor. *Page 156.*

Simon, Sir John. British statesman. As Foreign Secretary, he brought about the naval agreement with Germany in 1935. *Pages 187, 191, 194, 234.*

Skirpa, Kazys. For many years, military attaché at the Lithuanian Legation in Berlin. He had early conspired with the Nazis and when they forced Minister Saulys to be recalled, Skirpa, on the suggestion of Ribbentrop, became his successor in Germany. When the Nazis took over Lithuania, Skirpa was imprisoned because the Nazis did not trust him. *Page 95.*

Skoropadski, Pavel. Born a Cossack. In 1917, was installed by the Germans as *hetman* to coordinate the Ukraine. White Russian Nazi. Helped the Germans again in their last conquest of the Ukraine in 1941. Friend of Rosenberg. Has lived mostly in Germany since 1919. *Page 59.*

Smuts, General Jan Christian. South African Prime Minister. Leader of the Dominion in both world wars. *Page 116.*

Sokal, Franz. Motion picture director. *Pages 61, 131.*

Sommerfeldt, H. M. Chief of press to Goering until 1934. An early Nazi. Recognizing his error, he got out in June, 1934, and became a publisher. *Page 150.*

Soong, T. V. Former Chinese businessman and Minister of Finance. Since 1941, Foreign Minister. Brother of Mme. Chiang Kai-shek. *Page 125.*

Spanknoebel, Heinz. Detroit friend of Fritz Kuhn and co-founder of Friends of New Germany, since 1936 known as the Bund. *Page 203.*

Staar, Wilhelm. Former German officer. A shabby character who was delighted to trample on those who had helped him to make his living. Salon spy, especially appointed to watch South American diplomats. Poses as a monarchist and anti-Nazi. *Pages 61, 240.*

Stahl, Maria. Wife of Josef Terboven. *Page 170.*

Stalin, Joseph. Soviet Russia's Man of Steel. *Pages 231, 279.*

Stang, Ulrich. Since November, 1934, Councilor at the Norwegian Legation in Berlin. He was considered in diplomatic circles as a '150 percent Nazi.' Was on intimate terms with Wally von Richthofen, one of the Gestapo social informers of the Potsdam set. Mrs. Stang was not often seen in her husband's company; their daughter was engaged to an S.S. officer. *Page 220.*

Starhemberg, Prince Ernst Rudiger. Austrian who after the first World War joined the German radicals and served in a Free Corps. In 1930, he became leader of the Austrian *Heimwehr*, Minister of the Interior, Deputy Leader of the Patriotic Front, Vice-Chancellor in Dollfuss' cabinet in 1934, and in Schuschnigg's cabinet 1934-1936. Since 1939, in active service with the Free

Tann, Beue. Chinese Councilor to Berlin and Chargé d'Affairs at Stockholm. *Pages 125, 264.*

Tardieu, André. French statesman and historian. One of the authors of the Versailles Treaty. Several times Prime Minister. *Page 33.*

Tattenbach, Count Franz. Chief of Protocol at the German Foreign Office up to 1932, then Minister to Venezuela. *Page 33.*

Tauber, Richard. Famous tenor, now in London. *Page 55.*

Tauschitz, Stefan. Austrian Minister to Berlin until the *Anschluss.* A weak opportunist. *Pages 118, 165, 175, 177, 265.*

Terboven, Josef. A bank clerk in Essen before 1933. Now in control of Norway. He was known as the gigolo of a rich elderly woman, who was eager to get him in a good position. Through her connections with the industrialists of the Rhine and the Ruhr, Terboven was able to bring Hitler and his gang into contact with his future 'bankers.' Married one of Goebbels' mistresses on June 29, 1934. *Page 170.*

Thaelman, Ernst. Leader of the German Communist party. A defendant in the *Reichstag* fire trial. *Pages 14, 47, 94.*

Thomsen, Hans. Was a conservative at the German Foreign Office and became coordinating officer in Hitler's Chancellery. One of the best linguists at the Foreign Office. Accompanied Hitler to Italy. Until 1941, German Chargé d'Affaires in Washington. Handed the State Department the German declaration of war on the United States, December 12, 1941. *Pages 97, 98, 157, 228, 271.*

Thompson, Dorothy. American journalist. *Pages 170, 180.*

Thyssen, Fritz. Steel magnate. Catholic. Early supporter of Nazis (1923). In his book, *I Paid Hitler,* he tried to prove that he was a fool, not an opportunist. *Pages 40, 41, 42, 46, 49, 81, 98, 106, 107, 158, 164, 242.*

Tietgen, Heinz. General Intendant (supervisor) of German State theaters. *Page 251.*

Tilden, William. American tennis champion. *Page 20.*

Todt, Fritz. An old party member. Engineer who built the German highways and Rhine fortifications. Became Inspector General for Water and Power with the rank of Minister in 1941. Responsible for transportation and roads. *Page 119.*

Togo, Shigenori. Councilor of Japanese Embassy, then Ambassador to Moscow. Ambassador to Berlin in 1937. At that time disliked Nazis. His military attaché, General Oshima, concluded the Japanese-German pact with Ribbentrop, then Ambassador to London, without Togo's knowledge, whereupon the Ambassador asked to be recalled. Oshima succeeded him in Berlin, and Togo became Foreign Minister in Japan. Retired in September, 1942. *Pages 39, 117, 268.*

Watzke, Rudolf. German tenor. *Pages 268–69.*

Wecke, Colonel. Lent his name to a famous Berlin police regiment, which furnished the personal guard for Goering and became known as the General Goering Battalion. *Page 89.*

Wedell, Carmen von. Member of old *Junker* family. Betrothed to half-Jewish banker, von Schwabach. *Page 277.*

Weiss, Bernhard. Vice-president of police in Berlin until July, 1932. *Pages 38, 55.*

Wels, Otto. Former President of the Social Democratic party in Germany. Lived in England until he died in October, 1939. *Page 94.*

Welter, Dr. Erich. Editor of the *Vossiche Zeitung* and now with the *Frankfurter Zeitung. Pages 147, 162.*

Werthauer, Dr. Johannes. Famous Berlin lawyer. Died as an exile in Paris in 1937. *Pages 11–12.*

Wertheim, George. Owner of a big Berlin department store. Non-Aryan. Was forced to retire in 1936. *Page 10.*

Wessel, Horst. A cheap pimp. The brother of the man who really wrote the *Horst Wessel Lied* and who conveniently died in 1932. Horst found the song, signed his name to it. Hitler discovered and liked it so much that he took it as the party anthem. Horst was killed by the friend of a girl for whom he was acting as pimp. *Page 110.*

Westrick, Alois Gerhard. Berlin lawyer and intriguer. Made frequent trips to America, the last one early in 1940. When it became apparent that he was sent to do economic transfers and economic espionage, he registered with Washington as commercial attaché to become exterritorial. He had various residences and aliases during his stay in the United States until he was asked to leave in 1941. He transferred raw material and fuel to Germany via South America. To effect better relations with the United States, he wormed his way into the American colony in Berlin years ago. He had a female co-worker, Baroness Wangenheim, who also succeeded in establishing friendly relations with American diplomats long before she arrived in the United States as secretary and co-agent to Dr. Westrick. *Page 44.*

White, John Campbell. Councilor at the American Embassy in Berlin, 1933-1935. Then American Consul General in Calcutta, India. Distinguished diplomat of the old school and anti-Nazi. *Page 156.*

Wiedemann, Fritz. Colonel in the First World War. Later Hitler's Adjutant. From 1938 to 1941, Consul General in San Francisco,

became coordinator between army and *Reichsbank*. In 1937, became director of the Foreign Exchange Department of the *Reichsbank* and export comptroller. His job was to 'Aryanize' German trade. In 1940, was appointed director of the Netherlands finances, and later on held the same position in Rumania (economic coordinator). He is now Hitler's economic commissar in Tokyo. *Page 91.*

Wolff, Otto. Prominent Rhenish iron and steel baron with excellent connections in foreign countries. He had especially good connections in the Far East. Wolff was a close friend of General Kurt von Schleicher and moved in conservative circles. He died in 1940. *Page 49.*

Woodbridge, Frederick. American guest professor in Germany. *Page 44.*

Wronsky. Director of the *Lufthansa*. Early Nazi. Friend of Goering, Loerzer, and Milch. A dangerous Nazi functionary and a cruel egoist. Came to the United States on several occasions—the last time, after Hitler started his invasion of Poland, to obtain supplies for Germany's *Luftwaffe*. *Page 61.*

Zahle, Herluf. Danish Minister to Berlin, 1924-1940, where he died. Fine and distinguished gentleman of Danish court society. *Pages 9, 95.*

Zarden, Arthur. Secretary of State at the German Ministry of Finance until 1936. Schacht depended on his advice. Although he was not a so-called Aryan and was married to a purely non-Aryan, he was kept on as long as possible because of his ability. *Page 62.*

Zechlin, Dr. Walter. Press chief at Foreign Office until 1932. Then Minister to Mexico until 1935. Witty, capable official of the old school. *Pages 18, 49.*

Zeid el-Hussein, Prince. Minister of Iraq to Berlin, November, 1935, to end of 1937. He and his wife were sympathetic to Nazi ideas. *Pages 242-243.*

Zuckschwerdt, Wilhelm. Captain in the imperial navy. Pro-Nazi. Owned a silver fox farm on the American-Canadian border. *Page 198.*

Zulueta, Luis de. Spanish diplomat and politician. Ambassador to Berlin in 1933. *Page 125.*